T0328394

Praise for *Consulting Start-Up and Management*

"I recommend this book because it's a hands-on, application-based book that would make an excellent supplement to a course or as a reference book. I would readily use it in my daily business transactions."—Michelle Baron, *The Evaluation Baron, LLC*

"Every new consultant (and those considering independent consultancy) will benefit greatly from this book in many ways."—Vinita Channahsorah, *independent management and evaluation consultant*

"This book addresses a big and important gap in the evaluation literature. This book provides a clear and concise account of what evaluators and applied researchers need to know in order to succeed in independent consulting practice."—Stewart Donaldson, *Claremont Graduate University*

"This book is relevant for both new consultants and those with some experience for the wealth of examples and information included. It covers the breadth of the experience of having your own business while being a researcher, and a full person with a social life too."—Rita S. Fierro, *independent research consultant*

"I would highly recommend it to anyone starting a consulting career. The author has truly singled out the most important lessons to be passed on, both of the practical type and of those related to consultancy in a meaningful and balanced life."—George Grob, *Center for Public Program Evaluation*

"This book is practical and addresses the gap between what is learned in classrooms and what is learned in practice. Its user-friendly format is pitched for consultants and other practitioners, and it will also be very useful for students."—Jim McDavid, *University of Victoria*

"I am often asked by younger colleagues for advice about working as a full-time consultant. This book is an excellent resource to recommend."—Rosalie Torres, *Torres Consulting Group*

For my mother

CONSULTING
START-UP *and*
MANAGEMENT

A GUIDE FOR EVALUATORS
AND APPLIED RESEARCHERS

GAIL V. BARRINGTON
Barrington Research Group, Inc.

Los Angeles | London | New Delhi
Singapore | Washington DC

Los Angeles | London | New Delhi
Singapore | Washington DC

FOR INFORMATION:

SAGE Publications, Inc.
2455 Teller Road
Thousand Oaks, California 91320
E-mail: order@sagepub.com

SAGE Publications Ltd.
1 Oliver's Yard
55 City Road
London, EC1Y 1SP
United Kingdom

SAGE Publications India Pvt. Ltd.
B 1/I 1 Mohan Cooperative Industrial Area
Mathura Road, New Delhi 110 044
India

SAGE Publications Asia-Pacific Pte. Ltd.
33 Pekin Street #02-01
Far East Square
Singapore 048763

Executive Editor: Diane McDaniel
Editorial Assistant: Theresa Accomazzo
Production Editor: Libby Larson
Copy Editor: Cate Huisman
Typesetter: Hurix Systems Pvt. Ltd.
Proofreader: Sally Jaskold
Indexer: Jean Casalegno
Cover Designer: Gail Buschman
Marketing Manager: Helen Salmon
Permissions Editor: Adele Hutchinson

Printed in the United States of America

Library of Congress Cataloging-in-Publication Data

Barrington, Gail V.
Consulting start-up and management : a guide
for evaluators and applied researchers / Gail
V. Barrington.

p. cm.
Includes bibliographical references and index.

ISBN 978-1-4129-8709-7 (pbk.)
1. Consulting firms--Management.
2. Business consultants. 3. Entrepreneurship.
4. New business enterprises--Management.
5. Research-- Evaluation. I. Title.

HD69.C6B367 2012

001--dc23

2011021354

This book is printed on acid-free paper.

11 12 13 14 15   10 9 8 7 6 5 4 3 2 1

Brief Contents

Detailed Contents

Preface

At social gatherings I am often asked what I do. I explain that I am an independent research consultant. That's where the confusion begins. People understand research, although they think that it usually happens in a lab. They get the context of my work and see the value of helping the target populations I describe, like high-risk pregnant women, scientist innovators, and oil field workers. They see that my work is for a good cause, like providing evidence, evaluating the use of funding, influencing policy, or helping decision makers. Invariably, they ask, "How can you be a researcher and a consultant at the same time?" And their next question is, "How can you do all this by yourself?"

The first answer is that the intersection between business and research provides enough challenge, satisfaction, and income to keep me asking for more. After 25 years, my project-based research practice still involves the daily issues of running a small business and yet at the same time brings me the intellectual rewards that only research can provide. The second answer, of course, is that I get a lot of help doing this work. I rely on partnerships with clients; alliances with colleagues; and subcontracts with experts, statisticians, and research assistants whom I hire as needed. I am proud of what I have accomplished, and I love my independence, but I know that around the next corner a new project, problem, or issue is waiting for me. I am excited just thinking about it.

❖ THE BOOK AND ITS AUDIENCE

So why do you need this book? Your background is probably in education, health, psychology, evaluation, economics, political science, agriculture, human services, or any one of a whole host of other disciplines.

You have an inquiring mind and an independent streak. You gravitate to the scientific or technical side of things and ground your research in your disciplinary knowledge. Because you want to take your expertise "on the road," you are already well versed in the philosophy, theories, and methods in your field, but I bet that you never thought you would be managing a small business. Here's the thing—to be an independent consultant, you need to become an entrepreneur. It is my hope that this book will help you make that shift.

❖ ORGANIZATION OF THE BOOK

You need lots of different skills to be successful as an independent consultant, and these can be grouped into three important areas that correspond to the three main parts of this book.

Part I takes a look at who consultants are and what they do. It provides an overview of the consulting landscape and outlines current trends. You will see where independent evaluators and applied researchers fit in the big scheme of things. You will be encouraged to consider if consulting is the right career choice for you and if you have the personal attributes to be an independent consultant. Do you have the essential characteristics and values that will stand you in good stead? What about political skills? Do you understand the policy environment and political dimensions of the organizations in which you work? Do you have the strength and endurance to work and thrive on your own?

Once you determine that consulting is a career choice for you, it is time to get started. Part II explores the entrepreneurial skills required to run your own business. This practical section provides lots of suggestions and ideas related to your critical start-up activities. There are so many decisions to make. How will you decide where to work? Should you write a business plan? If so, what should it contain? How much should you charge? In order to bill clients, you need to figure out how to set your fees. To do that you need to determine how much it will cost to run your business. You will also need to track your time, because, as you may have guessed, in our business, time is money.

As all consultants know, marketing is our lifeblood, so once all these basics have been nailed down, we turn our attention to the most pressing question of all. How do you get work? First we take an in-depth look at ways of getting work. There are a lot more ways than you might expect, and in fact, your colleagues get most of their work through informal approaches. We will explore your competitive advantage, and you will see how to network, build referrals, develop strategic alliances, and foster repeat business. To follow up on requests for your services, we look at budgeting and writing proposals. Both informal letter proposals and responses to formal requests for proposals (RFPs) are reviewed. While you are probably familiar with writing an academic research proposal, preparing a proposal for a consulting engagement requires a different lens, and we will look at some of the key things you should consider. Samples are provided.

After you have acquired some contracts, you will need ways to manage your business. As your confidence grows, you will find yourself working on more interesting and more complex projects. A smoothly running business will free up your time to do what you love most, namely your research, so you have to set up systems to let this happen. Part III explores a number of pragmatic business management topics. We look at how to manage your money and where to find resources when you need them. You need to consider various ownership structures and decide which one is best for you. Should you stay as a sole proprietor, create an incorporated company, go into partnership with a colleague, or start a nonprofit company? We look at pros and cons and hear from some consultants about the choices they made. One thing we tend to do is avoid thinking about catastrophes and worst case scenarios, but risk management is critical when you run your own business. You need to protect your income. We discuss ways to manage risk and consider different types of insurance.

Every project comes with some kind of a contract, whether implied, verbal, or written. How can you protect your interests? We will review different kinds of contracts and contract clauses to help you know what to look for. Eventually a day will come when you are looking at a project that is too big for you to handle on your own. How will you find people to help you? Should they be employees or subcontractors? How can you manage them effectively? Then finally, we look at an important topic that is often ignored. How can you organize your documents and files, enhance the security of your materials and your clients' data, and manage the goldmine of information produced by your firm? How can you use this knowledge to improve your practice? How can you share these hard-won lessons with others?

Whether you have already struck out on your own and need to retool your business skills, or you are standing on the consulting shore testing the chilly waters, I hope you will find some useful information and advice in this book to help make your dream come true. Come with me and explore the business side of consulting. You may never look back!

Acknowledgments

There are so many people to thank. Let me start at the beginning by thanking Cynthia Phillips for encouraging me to make the connection. Thanks to all my colleagues at the American Evaluation Association, the Canadian Evaluation Society, and Claremont Graduate University who participated in my workshops and encouraged me to take up this challenge. Thanks to my panel members; while we may not be drinking coffee within these pages, the value of your conversation and contribution cannot be overestimated: Michelle Baron, Michelle Burd, Erin Burr, Shirah Hecht, Thomas Kinsey, Robert Richard, Raegan Tuff, and Susan Wolfe.

Thanks to my wonderful clients at Bow Valley College; no one has clients like you—your support and patience are unprecedented. Thanks to all former staff members at BRG—this book would not have been possible had we not learned so much together. Thanks for the technical help provided by Erin Burr, Lisa Thompson-Dobo, Monetta Bailey, and Zora Jelencic; you each played a critical role. This book rests on the incredible love and encouragement provided by my husband, my son, and my sister; even in the darkest days, there was never a question about reaching the end of this journey. And finally thanks to Diane McDaniel, Terri Accomazzo, Cate Huisman, Megan Koraly, and Libby Larson at SAGE Publications, for making my dream a reality.

PART I

Consulting and You

Although, as people often sagely comment, "Not everyone can be a consultant," few of the many books available on consulting actually explore personal suitability. In this section we get a bird's eye view of the consulting landscape and where program evaluators and applied researchers have a niche. Then we take a closer look at the personal attributes and essential values you need in the field. Based on my own experience and a lot of research on the topic, I offer my choice for the top five personal attributes and the top five personal values you need to be successful.

Political skills are important if you are doing research in any applied setting, but they are even more critical if you want to return at some point in the future and work for this client again. You need to know the players, the policy environment, the political dimension, the power of communication, and the importance of timing. Your awareness of these and other organizational topics can help you get up to speed quickly as well as leave with the organization asking for more.

Part I concludes with a chapter about maintaining work-life balance. It looks at some key survival strategies as well as ways to avoid burnout. You will have to actively manage your mental and physical health if you plan to be in consulting for the long haul.

1

The Consulting Landscape

Highlights:

- Explore the independent consultant's niche in the world of business.

- Discover why management consulting is one of America's best careers.

- Consider typical consultant roles and profiles.

- Examine trends and growth drivers as well as reasons for consulting business failure.

❖ MANAGEMENT CONSULTING

To start with, let's take a 10,000-foot view of consulting and look at the overall landscape. It is important to know our niche in the world of business. According to the North American Industry Classification System (NAICS), which is consistent across the three North American

Free Trade Agreement partners—Canada, Mexico, and the United States—we belong to Sector #54, Professional, Scientific, and Technical Services. Our human capital is the main resource we use to sell our knowledge, skills, and expertise (Industry Canada, 2010a). There are over three million firms offering these services in the United States alone (U.S. Census Bureau, 2006).

This industry has consistently grown over the past few decades, and according to the U.S. Bureau of Labor Statistics (2009a), it is projected to be the fastest growing industry between 2008 and 2018, with employment increasing 83%. Business and government have found that hiring consultants is beneficial, because the consultants are experienced and well trained, and they keep current with the latest technologies, regulations, and management and production techniques. They are also cost effective, because they can be hired temporarily, and they leave when the job is done. They are also free of the influence of internal politics and can perform their duties objectively.

About 40% of consulting firms focus on administrative or general management consulting. An additional third specialize in scientific, technical, or other management consulting. The rest offer a grab bag of services such as marketing, logistics, human resources, executive search, and environmental consulting (Bureau of Labor Statistics, 2009b).

Management consulting is serious big business. It is worth over $100 billion worldwide with 118 distinct types of consulting providing services to nearly 100 different client-industries (*US Industry Profile*, n.d.).

Consulting firms come in four sizes. The largest players are global in scope and have thousands of employees. Originally, eight big firms started in public accounting, auditing, and taxation and later developed consulting divisions. Due to various scandals and real or perceived conflicts of interest, they went through a dizzying series of changes, and only four remain (Independent Consulting Bootcamp, n.d.). These firms tend to be hierarchical in nature, and they rely on a few very effective marketers, or *rainmakers* as they are called, to generate sales. Their projects are often huge in scope and provide work for large numbers of analysts and managers. Because they have well-established methods and processes, relatively inexperienced consultants at lower levels of the firm can tackle complex problems in consistent ways (Bodegraven & Ackerman, 2009). Although large firms with over 500 employees dominate the industry, they account for only 0.1% of the sector (Industry Canada, 2010b).

Firms in the second tier have 50 employees or more. They tend to specialize in such areas as strategy, operations, or human resources. About 40% of all consulting jobs are found in firms such as these (Bureau of Labor Statistics, 2009a).

The third group is composed of small to mid-sized firms that are generally built on narrow but deep functional experience. They often rely on trends in the marketplace for their bread and butter. Sometimes they use a franchise model or affiliate with other firms to broaden their geographic market.

At the far end of the spectrum we find the largest proportion of consulting firms—75% in all. These firms employ fewer than five workers. Known as *boutique* firms, they are often run by a sole practitioner and provide specialized services, focus on a specific industry or practice area, operate in a single geographic region, or serve a single client. When needed, they can gear up for a particular engagement by subcontracting with specialists. Many long-standing firms have excellent reputations. They are often led by former executives, consultants who have left larger firms, individuals who do specialty consulting on the side while continuing their full-time jobs, or university professors who consult in their particular disciplines. About 26% of management consultants are self-employed; this is three times the national average for all occupations (Bureau of Labor Statistics, 2009b).

We should not forget one additional group, the internal consultants who work within large corporations or government departments and who act in a consulting role within their organizations. For example, in the Canadian federal government, many departments have their own program evaluation shops, and the use of internal consultants is seen as a cost-effective way to address their ongoing research needs. These individuals may conduct evaluations themselves or, more typically, may manage teams of contracted evaluators. Their role as middlemen is a challenging one, but their particular value lies in their understanding of the organization's culture and requirements. While external expertise may have greater credibility, these internal experts are often essential to shepherd the research to a successful conclusion in these complex bureaucracies.

In 2009, management consulting was singled out as one of America's best careers because of its staying power (U.S. News Staff,

2009). It has an excellent outlook despite a recessionary economy, has a high pay range, and reportedly has high job satisfaction. Not surprisingly, job competition is keen, and those consultants who have the most education and experience have the best job prospects (Bureau of Labor Statistics, 2009a). In particular, those who have a graduate degree, specialized expertise, and a talent for salesmanship and public relations will have the most opportunities.

The same website identified program evaluator as one of the 11 best-kept-secret careers. In fact both program evaluation and applied research have a distinct advantage. While academic researchers tend to focus on a single discipline, applied researchers can move from one discipline or program area to another, addressing a range of research questions and using a variety of methods. As Scriven (1991) so wisely stated, evaluation is a trans-discipline. Thus our skills appeal to a broad range of clients.

❖ TRAINING AND CERTIFICATION

There is a general lack of university-based training for management consultants, apart from a few subspecialties in some business schools. Many consultants already have graduate degrees, and many have a number of years of experience in management, human resources, or information technology. Others enter the field with a bachelor's degree, work as research assistants or research analysts, and work their way up from there (Bureau of Labor Statistics, 2009b).

Limited availability of formal training has resulted in reliance on either firm-based training, which is prevalent in the larger firms, or on professional development opportunities that are frequently offered by professional organizations.

There is no central licensing or registration for a management consultant as there is, say, for a registered nurse or a lawyer. A nurse cannot obtain work without a current registration; a lawyer must be an active, dues-paying member of the local bar association in order to practice law. The worst case scenario for these professionals is to be deregistered or disbarred. Unfortunately, there is no standard way to regulate consultants. Any individuals that offer advice in exchange for compensation can call themselves consultants. As one of my colleagues quipped recently, "All you need is ten bucks to get some business cards, and you too can hang out your shingle. Heck, you can even print your own cards!"

There are some alternatives to that dismal prospect, however. The most well-known consulting designation is that of certified management consultant (CMC) which is administered by national management consulting institutes that are members of a global association, The International Council of Management Consulting Institutes (ICMCI). There are affiliated organizations in both Canada and the United States: CMC-Canada and the Institute of Management Consultants USA, respectively. They certify those consultants who meet a minimum level of education, have a required amount of consulting experience, and pass required exams. In the United States, an interview is also required. Consultants must be recertified regularly and are required to complete a certain amount of professional development each year. These institutes provide a code of ethics and foster excellence and integrity in the management consulting profession. In the event of a serious breach or violation, some disciplinary action is possible, and a member's certification can be revoked. Unfortunately, only a small proportion of the management consulting population has this designation, but for those who do, it provides a competitive advantage.

There are also many discipline-related groups and professional organizations that provide practice guidelines and professional development activities. As a program evaluator, for example, I am an active member of both the Canadian Evaluation Society (CES) and the American Evaluation Association (AEA). In Canada, the CES recently initiated a professional designations program and now offers the credentialed evaluator (CE) designation to define, recognize, and promote the practice of ethical, high-quality, competent evaluation in Canada. Individuals who obtain the designation have provided evidence of their education and experience and have been judged to be competent by a panel of senior evaluators. In addition, through its maintenance and renewal requirements, the program promotes continuous learning. This innovative program is being watched closely by evaluation organizations around the world (Canadian Evaluation Society, 2010).

❖ THE CONSULTING ROLE

While the work of management consultants is as unique as their many clients and engagements, their overall role is straightforward. They study problems; collect, review, analyze, and synthesize information; and recommend solutions to managers based on their findings (Bureau of Labor Statistics, 2009b). More specifically, the role of evaluation consultants can be described as follows (Barrington, 2005):

> Consultants provide independent, objective information and advice to clients in a variety of organizational settings to assist them in achieving their objectives. In an evaluation context, consultants conduct research studies to assess program effectiveness and efficiency, collect and synthesize information, identify problems, and recommend solutions to improve organizational performance and implement change. Consultants provide their professional expertise on a temporary basis and have no authority to implement the changes they recommend. They have both academic and practical experience and have strong communication and instructional skills. In their independent capacity, it is critical that they model ethical business and research practice. (pp. 81–82)

Typically, consultants work with minimal supervision, and so they need to be self-motivated and disciplined, although the ability to work in teams is also becoming increasingly important. Other desirable qualities include analytical skills, the ability to get along with a wide range of people, strong oral and written communication skills, good judgment, time-management skills, and creativity.

❖ TRENDS AND GROWTH DRIVERS

Economic and business trends continue to be volatile, but while the future is hard to predict, there are a number of industrywide trends that you should consider while charting your consulting career path. Employment may be driven by the overall health of the economy, but management consulting is a good option, regardless of whether organizations are expanding or downsizing, because outside expertise is flexible and cost effective.

Growth drivers for management consulting have been identified in the following areas (Bureau of Labor Statistics, 2009b):

- Globalization—a knowledge of international contexts, emerging markets, and various cultures and languages will be advantageous to take expertise abroad or to work at home with agencies that are expanding globally.

- Regulatory changes due to the recent credit and housing crises will result in the need to hire advisors for the recovery process and policy development.
- Improved efficiency and the desire to be more competitive will result in a desire to streamline operations and strategy in business as well as in the public sector.
- Continued volatility in the information technology and e-commerce sectors will provide consulting opportunities.
- "Green" technologies and environmental initiatives as well as issues associated with global warming and carbon reduction will continue to grow.

For applied researchers and program evaluators, there is even a broader context for our work. Some other growth drivers I see include the following:

- Demographics, particularly related to the aging population and immigration, will continue to have an impact on policy in housing, skill development, and job training. As noted demographer David Foot contends, demographics explains two thirds of everything (Footwork Consulting Inc., n.d.).
- The scope and influence of the social economy—including the traditional voluntary and nonprofit sector, grassroots and religious associations, social enterprises, and philanthropic foundations—will continue to expand. For example, in 2006, independent grant-making foundations in the United States had assets of $509 billion. The Bill & Melinda Foundation is just one example of the global impact of philanthropy today.
- Health trends will continue to dominate our lives. Problems associated with weight and obesity, physical inactivity, dietary intake, substance abuse, chronic conditions, and aging will absorb more and more of our tax dollars. Research will be required to study both medical innovations and potential pandemics. Health policy, health care management, and health outcomes will require continued study.
- At home and abroad, social issues associated with poverty, famine, natural disasters, war, violence, and terrorism will continue to rock our world; emergency preparedness, management, and recovery will also benefit from effective research; and developing countries will increasingly rely on consultants for advice.

- Knowledge has become its own industry. Knowledge management and translation will become more challenging as social media continue to change the way we work. How can we share what we have learned and put our research findings to effective use?

It seems we will not be running out of work any time soon.

❖ CONSULTANT PROFILES

Finally, let's take a closer look at management consultants. The 2002 U.S. Survey of Business Owners provided a profile of the owners of over three million firms. Two thirds were owned by men, and 93% of owners were white while 4.6% were Asian, 3.8% were Hispanic, 2.7% were black or African American, and 0.7% were American Indian or Alaska Native (U.S. Census Bureau, 2006). As a group, consultants are more mature than the overall average. In 2008, 50% of U.S. consultants were at least 45 years old; in all industries, 42% of individuals had reached this age (Bureau of Labor Statistics, 2009b).

Management consultants are concentrated in large urban centers, although I know a number of sole practitioners who work successfully from remote locations, and some never meet their clients in person. Still, travel is usually a requirement of the job, and work-life balance is often a concern. Stress levels are high and deadlines tight. Most consultants work more than 40 hours a week and are not compensated for overtime.

By now you are probably dying to ask about income. Salaries vary depending on years of experience, education, geographic location, specific expertise, and size of firm. Not surprisingly, consultants in large firms in metropolitan areas have the highest wages. The overall sector average salary in 2008 was $81,670 (Bureau of Labor Statistics, 2009b). Those employed by a firm usually receive benefits such as health and life insurance, a retirement plan, vacation, and sick leave, and sometimes other benefits such as profit sharing and bonuses for outstanding work. Self-employed consultants have to provide their own benefits.

Thanks to a 2004 survey of members of the AEA's Topical Interest Group (TIG) on Independent Consulting, we have a profile of evaluation consultants. Of the 713 individuals who belonged to the TIG at that time, 261 (37%) completed the survey (Jarosewich, Essenmacher, Lynch, Williams, & Doino-Ingersoll, 2006).

When compared to the broader management consulting sector, their demographics provide some interesting differences. Far more were women (71%), and somewhat fewer were white (81%), while 7% were black or African American and 5% were Hispanic or Latino. Nearly two thirds were between the ages of 40 and 59, although there was a wide range of ages, from under 30 to over 70. They were well trained, as 55% had doctoral degrees, and 41% had master's degrees. Their main areas of study were education, psychology, and evaluation, although other, less well represented, disciplines included sociology, statistics, anthropology, economics, public health, and public administration.

Almost half were self-employed and worked full time; nearly all the rest worked part time. A few worked for consulting firms or were faculty members. Their experience as self-employed consultants was 8.2 years on average and ranged from 1 to 27 years, and only one third had prior consulting experience. More than three quarters of them worked from home.

For those who were self-employed and operated their businesses for a full year during 2003, the median gross business revenue was $120,000, and their median 2003 personal income was $75,000 (in 2003 U.S. dollars). Jarosewich and her colleagues concluded that the consultants with the largest personal incomes tended to have larger business revenues, more billable hours, and fewer employees.

❖   A WORD OF CAUTION

While some of this information is encouraging indeed, a word of caution is needed here. Many management consultants are self-employed because business start-up and overhead costs are low in this field, but many also fail each year due to a lack of managerial expertise or an insufficient number of clients (Bureau of Labor Statistics, 2009b). To succeed, you need to have excellent organizational skills, great marketing skills, and a high degree of motivation. Those in the United States must also be able to cover their health care benefits.

The challenges facing start-up consultants often remind me of Mickey Mouse swinging precariously on a vine over a group of hungry, grinning alligators, but remember, he made it to the other side of the swamp, and so can you. Potential threats are best kept at bay by vigilance, agility, and knowledge, and that's what this book is about. Let me guide you to firm ground with the skills and tools you need for your journey to independence.

❖ USEFUL RESOURCES

- Explore NAICS Sector 54 on *Management, Scientific, and Technical Consulting Services,* including the nature of the industry, working conditions, employment, occupations in the industry, training and advancement, outlook, and earnings:

  In the United States: http://www.bls.gov/oco/cg/cgs037.htm

  In Canada: http://www.ic.gc.ca/cis-sic/cis-sic.nsf/IDE/cis-sic54defe.html

- Find out more about the Certified Management Consulting designation:

  In the United States: http://www.imcusa.org

  In Canada: http://www.cmc-canada.ca

  International: http://www.icmci.org/home

❖ DISCUSSION QUESTIONS AND ACTIVITIES

1. Do you think that applied researchers and program evaluators fit in the NAICS Sector #54, Professional, Scientific, and Technical Services? How are they similar to and different from other management consultants?

2. Compare your demographic profile to the owner profile summarized from the 2002 U.S. Survey of Business Owners and to the profile of the independent program evaluators who

completed the 2004 AEA survey. What similarities and differences did you find?

3. The chapter describes some growth drivers that will fuel the need for applied research and evaluation in the future. Which of these drivers are still influential? Are there additional drivers not mentioned in the text? How can you prepare your skills for consulting work in these domains?

❖ REFERENCES

Barrington, G. V. (2005). Consultant, definition. In S. Matheson (Ed.). *Encyclopedia of evaluation* (pp. 81–82). Thousand Oaks, CA: Sage.

Bodegraven, A. van, & Ackerman, K. B. (2009, May 1). We're consultants, and we've come to help. . . . *DC VELOCITY*. Retrieved from http://www.dcvelocity.com/articles/20090501basictraining/

Bureau of Labor Statistics. (2009a). *Career guide to industries, 2010–11 edition: Management, scientific, and technical consulting services.* Retrieved from http://www.bls.gov/oco/cg/cgs037.htm

Bureau of Labor Statistics. (2009b). *Occupational outlook handbook, 2010–11 edition: Management analysts.* Retrieved from http://www.bls.gov/oco/ocos019.htm

Canadian Evaluation Society. (2010, April 4). *Professional designations program.* Retrieved from http://evaluationcanada.ca/site.cgi?en:5:6

Footwork Consulting Inc. (n.d.). *David Foot: Profile.* Retrieved from http://www.footwork.com/profile.asp

Independent Consulting Bootcamp. (n.d.). *Big 5 consulting firm: Setting the standard in the global consulting industry.* Retrieved from http://www.independent-consulting-bootcamp.com/Big-5-consulting-firm.html

Industry Canada. (2010a). *Canadian industry statistics (CIS): Definition—professional, scientific and technical services (NAICS 54).* Retrieved from http://www.ic.gc.ca/cis-sic/cis-sic.nsf/IDE/cis-sic54defe.html

Industry Canada. (2010b). *Canadian industry statistics (CIS): SME benchmarking: professional, scientific and technical services (NAICS 54).* Retrieved from http://www.ic.gc.ca/cis-sic/cis-sic.nsf/IDE/cis-sic54bece.html

Jarosewich, T., Essenmacher, V. L., Lynch, C. O., Williams, J. E., & Doino-Ingersoll, J. (2006). Independent consulting topical interest group: 2004 industry survey. *New Directions for Evaluation, 111,* 9–21. doi: 10.1002/ev.192

Scriven, M. (1991). *Evaluation thesaurus* (4th ed.). Newbury Park, CA: Sage.

U.S. Census Bureau. (2006). *Characteristics of business owners: 2002. 2002—economic census, survey of business owners, company statistics series* (SB0200CS-CBO). Retrieved from http://www.census.gov/prod/ec02/sb0200cscbo.pdf

US Industry Profile: Management consulting services. (SIC 8742). (n.d.). Retrieved December 31, 2009, from http://www.answers.com/topic/management-consulting-services

U.S. News Staff. (2009, August 28). America's best careers 2009. *U.S. News & World Report.* Retrieved from http://usnews.com/money/careers/articles/2009/08/28/americas-best-careers-2009.html

2

Personal Characteristics

Highlights:

- Examine some of the benefits and risks associated with an independent consulting career.

- Consider the five important characteristics of successful independent consultants.

- See if you have the endurance you need to take on this career's challenge.

[Ann] earns more than $100,000 a year and works anywhere between 10 and 50 hours a week. Her home-based office overlooking Lions Gate Bridge has an easy chair and a fireplace. When she needs to take a break, she heads out for an energizing run or swim. She'll need all the energy she can get, because U.S. clients are calling her. . . . She is living the dream of every fledgling consultant. More important, she's fulfilling her career-long dream of creating better-managed companies. . . . "My level of job satisfaction and pure happiness has escalated beyond my wildest hopes."[1]

While this is certainly the dream that many people hold, they often wonder, "Is consulting right for me?" There are some real benefits to this career choice, as Harris (2001) points out:

- Freedom—the ability to choose when, where, and how you work
- Variety—a range of projects with variation in features such as length, topic, level of detail, and client
- Independence—not having to account to others for your activities
- Home-based work—the convenience of working on your own premises if you so choose

The reality, though, is that a career as an independent consultant is not for everyone. Greiner and Metzger (1983), the management gurus that I consulted when I started out, also described consulting as "the most damnable profession in the world." Based on that observation, there are obviously some risks involved. Harris cites several:

- Loneliness—there is nobody in the next office with whom to discuss your work projects.
- Peaks and valleys—you may not know if you will be earning any money next month or how much it might be.
- Pressure—you never have an hour that is really free, because your business is always on your mind.
- Marketability—it may be difficult to reenter the job market afterward if consulting does not work out for you.

It is important to know from the outset if you have what it takes to survive in this tough field. Most books on consulting launch directly into how to set up your business, how to get contracts, or how to work with clients. They leave personal competencies until much later, if they include them at all. By then it is way too late, because, in your own mind at least, you are already moving down the consulting road.

One of my associates used to joke that to be a successful consultant you needed to be a middle child. She meant that this birth order forced you to become a negotiator and a peacemaker. As was once said on the *Early Show*, "A firstborn is a company's CEO, [but] the middle child is the entrepreneur" (CBS News, 2002).

Understanding your strengths will help you make your career decision. After researching the personality traits of independent consultants and discussing them with colleagues, students, friends, and family, I have identified five important characteristics.

❖ 1. INTELLECTUAL CAPACITY

It seems obvious, but you have to be smart, well trained, and experienced to sell your research skills. Let's assume that you already have specialized in a professional area such as education, health, social work, or public administration, or that you have honed your skills in a discipline such as psychology, sociology, anthropology, or statistics. This knowledge is the foundation of your expertise, and you are already able to assimilate, analyze, interpret, and synthesize information. You have strong research skills and good critical thinking skills, and you can exercise your professional judgment as needed. Problem solving is second nature.

This competency profile for evaluation professionals in the federal public service sums it up:

> Evaluation professionals plan, design and implement sound evaluation methodologies to assess and inform organizational programs, polices, and initiatives. They quickly comprehend the objectives of new programs, policies, and initiatives to which they are exposed and the context in which they operate. They are adept at systematically collecting and assimilating substantial quantities and types of information. Evaluation professionals use their strong cognitive skills in critically evaluating and interpreting research findings and in identifying gaps in, and limitations of, the evidence. They formulate plausible hypotheses, consider alternatives, and draw appropriate conclusions from research findings. (The Centre of Excellence for Evaluation, Treasury Board of Canada, 2002, Cognitive Capacity, para. 1.)

While this is where you may begin, even more is required. "Do I need an advanced degree?" you wonder. In my view, the answer these days is, "Yes." Not only do you need the intellectual capacity, you need to demonstrate to clients that the world has recognized you for it. As early as 1980, Cronbach and his colleagues (1980) were suggesting that a doctoral degree in a social science was a minimum academic requirement. There are several reasons why this idea is even more critical today.

One reason is the upward migration of credentials. Nursing is a good example of this phenomenon. Twenty years ago, there was a rush for registered nurses to get bachelor's degrees. Ten years ago, obtaining a master's in nursing or health sciences was considered a good career move. Today, programs offering a PhD in nursing are increasing in number and, in addition, an advanced professional degree has emerged. The doctorate of nursing practice (DNP) in the United States and the doctorate in healthcare (DHC) in the United Kingdom are becoming desirable credentials. In October 2004, the American Association of Colleges of Nursing membership voted that the DNP would be required as the entry-level degree for all new advanced practice nurses by 2015 (Dreher, Donnely, & Naremore, 2005). At that time, there was only one such training program in the country, but many master's programs have been positioning themselves to offer this degree before the deadline. If you are considering becoming a consultant in the health sector, a doctorate will soon be essential.

Another good reason for an advanced degree is market demand. As we learned in Chapter 1, competition for management consultants is likely to remain keen, and those with the most education and experience will have the best prospects (Bureau of Labor Statistics, 2009). In the competitive process that is often used to select a consultant, brownie points are always awarded for educational background. An advanced degree will let you out of the gate with an advantage.

A third reason is credibility. Postdoctoral studies or joint advanced degrees are becoming more common in a number of fields, and many research programs are moving toward interdisciplinary or translational research. If you plan to sit across the table from clients with a research background, you will need to speak their language if you want your advice to be accepted.

In some cases, however, specialized training or other accreditation may be more appropriate. Perhaps your area of expertise is too new to have a doctoral preparation program. In other cases, an MBA may seem more relevant. Some consultants have suggested that a project management designation is useful. As well as formal training, field experience is essential. A deep portfolio allows you to relate to different clients in different contexts. This lived experience provides a strong connection upon which to build your relationship and provides a greater understanding of the situational complexities so hard to put in words. As one client commented to me recently, "You get it! We don't have to explain so much." This speaks to the value of maturity, so if you are coming to consulting a little later in life, you have much to offer. On the other hand, if you have youth on your side, plan to expand your portfolio through as many varied experiences as possible.

❖ 2. SELF-CONFIDENCE

They say that consultants should have low ego needs. This is patently absurd. How can you have low ego needs and be self-confident at the same time? What people probably mean is that you can't be a "high-maintenance" individual, nor can you expect to take center stage. So how are you going to do this? Katz and Kahn (1978) looked at self-determination as the basis for job satisfaction. They explained as follows:

> The reward is not so much a matter of social recognition or monetary advantage as of establishing one's self-identity, confirming one's notion of the sort of person one sees oneself to be, and expressing the values appropriate to this self-concept. (p. 407)

By internalizing your professional goal, namely to be a good evaluator or applied researcher, your self-gratification comes from doing your job well. You can then convey that belief even when faced with criticism or opposition.

Self-confidence flows seamlessly into leadership. While a consultant is often seen as a "hired hand," you must still be cooperative and inclusive in your approach. This modern management style is well suited to environments filled with change and uncertainty (Rosener, 1990). Your job is to motivate those around you to take on the challenges associated with the research enterprise. Through collaboration you will need to move your clients toward solutions that they might never reach on their own. When you leave the organization for your next project, you will take a sense of satisfaction with you, and don't be surprised at the positive feedback you receive; you deserve it.

❖ 3. MOXIE

Moxie is a wonderful word that originated as the name of the first mass-produced carbonated beverage in the United States. It was said to be an invigorating drink that gave the drinker "spunk" (Moxie, 2010).

Moxie has moved into the public lexicon to mean such things as courage, energy, and vision. It is something you will need a lot of if you want to be a successful consultant.

When you think of courage and daring, you might think of the three musketeers heading off into battle against all odds, but moxie is actually a lot more subtle than that. It is the capacity to go against the common view, to walk into a room of fractious stakeholders who don't support the evaluation and don't want to hear about the findings. It is the ability to land in a strange town at midnight, scrape the snow and ice off your rental car, and locate your motel without the benefit of a map. It is being able to get up the day after you have lost the best proposal you have ever written and start all over again. You need to be resourceful, take risks, and persevere despite setbacks. Despite all this drama, you also need to thrive on solitude. Your life, your week, and your work day are blank canvases. It is up to you to fill them.

Does this prospect excite you or fill you with dread? Energy and enthusiasm for this challenging work gives independent consultants their edge. Their vitality comes from being out there on their own. David Maister, the management consultant's consultant, sees passion as a key ingredient (Church, 2000). Doing work to which you feel connected makes your job more rewarding and in the end will bring you better financial results. He says, "The people who are winning out there are not smarter than the others. They are winning because they have the passion to do what others know they should do, but don't" (p. M1).

The final component of moxie is that vision or that big-picture thinking that allows you to see patterns and develop innovative ways to win stakeholder commitment and do your research. Von Oech (2008) has written extensively about creative thinking. He sees it as a self-fulfilling prophecy. Creative people give themselves the license to pay attention to even their smallest ideas. They know that one of them will lead to a breakthrough. Patton (2008) has suggested using metaphor to develop new understanding and better communications. Creative comparisons appeal to a wide range of stakeholders, deepening their understanding in unexpected ways and offering new perspectives for problem solving. Although you still need that killer logic best utilized by Sherlock Holmes, even that famous detective used his intuition to frame it. As Jakob-Hoff and Coggan (2003) commented, evaluators need to combine their more tangible competencies with their intuition, "to sniff the air and smell a rat" (p. 137). Unfortunately for us, that important little voice was never nurtured by our schooling, and we need to find ways to incorporate it into our problem solving.

❖ 4. ADAPTABILITY

Our work is defined by rigid parameters set out by proposals and contracts, yet the whole world is in a state of flux. How can you conduct useful research with such uncertainty all around you? The answer, of course, is that you have to be adaptable, able to take any situation and make it work. For example, you find that your proposed telephone interviews won't work, because the target group is transient. What about coffee shop intercepts? Your client wants to observe your focus group despite your protestations. What about offering follow-up interviews for participants with something confidential to share? You can't use financial incentives, because participants are likely to spend it on drugs. What about giving them coupons to the local grocery store instead? With experience, your research designs will become more and more open-ended to account for the unexpected issues you can be sure you will encounter in the field.

I was recently invited to a jazz concert at a local community center. The pianist soon discovered that the piano had not been tuned. A couple of critical base notes were markedly off key. She was really frustrated by this impediment but kept on playing and soon figured out some alternatives. She even incorporated some humorous lyrics about problem keys into her next song. At the end of the evening, she received an extra round of applause for her grace under fire. Being light on your feet will allow you to respond to change, ensuring that your business survives and your research stays relevant. The trick is to keep playing and make it look effortless.

❖ 5. ENDURANCE

It is important to decide as soon as possible if consulting is a stopgap measure or a long-term commitment, because being an independent consultant can change you in ways that may be irreversible. While some people choose self-employment, others fall into it through chance or circumstance, by virtue of their age, skills, employment options, or location. Barbara Moses, who is a well-known career consultant and national columnist, commented, "Even those forced into self-employment as a temporary measure often discover that they thrive on it, to the point where they can no longer imagine going back to work for an organization" (2002).

Still, from time to time, it is quite common for independent consultants to be tempted by the security, wages, or status of regular, paying jobs.

However, as employees they often chafe under the constraints imposed by organizations. Sometimes they go to work for former clients, but they may find the environment is quite different and much less appealing when seen from the inside. Based on my observation, these individuals will not stay and will move on again. They may return to consulting, but it can be an uphill struggle if their networks are out of date. Moving in and out of consulting suggests a lack of direction and does not look good on your résumé, so it is better to decide soon if you have the endurance required not only to get into consulting but to stay there.

The biggest factor in your decision will be your financial sustainability. Can you afford to support yourself for up to six months while you look for contracts? Do you have enough savings to tide you over, or a partner who is willing to take the load while you get on your feet? Do you have childcare or elder care costs to consider? These critical questions will help you make your decision.

Many people decide to ease into consulting by working part time in a paying job as they develop their consulting practice on the side. This approach has the advantage of more security, but there are a couple of drawbacks. Because you are not so hungry for work, you may not try as hard to find it. You may also get stuck with one foot on either side of the great divide between the employed and self-employed. While some people stay in this dual role permanently, it may be difficult to self-actualize in either one career or the other.

Before you set your sites on independent consulting, think about the key questions in the list below (Maynard, 1992). (For the full checklist, see Appendix 1.)

- What skills am I selling? Is there a market for them?
- How can I bolster my own skills by joining forces with others?
- Can I support myself for three to six months while I check out the market and land my first contract?
- Can I handle periods of isolation interrupted by brief spurts of client contact?
- Am I good at multitasking and dealing with competing demands on my time?
- Am I resilient?

Source: Adapted from Maynard, 1992. Reprinted with permission.

Consulting is not a career choice for everyone, but if you see a market for your skills and want to be your own boss, if you have the financial resources and personal stamina that this career requires, then read on. Your intellectual capacity, self-confidence, moxie, adaptability, and endurance will give you the building blocks you need.

❖ NOTE

1.   Adapted from Rona Maynard, The Guru Gambit. *The Globe and Mail, Report on Business* magazine, October 1992, p. 66. Name of consultant is changed.

❖ USEFUL RESOURCES

- The Independent Consulting Bootcamp website provides a wealth of information and free resources to assist you in starting and growing your own consulting business. http://www.independent-consulting-bootcamp.com/index.html
- Dr. Barbara Moses is an international work-life expert. On her website she shares many of her articles on the work world, career strategies, career change, advice to women, and age-related dilemmas. http://www.bbmcareerdev.com/booksarticles_articles.php
- There are several excellent competency frameworks available for management consultants and evaluation professionals, including the following:

The Management Consulting Competency Framework, at http://www.imcusa.org/?page=CONSULTINGCOMPETENCY

Competency Profile for Federal Public Service Evaluation Professionals, prepared by the Research and Development Division, Personnel Psychology Centre for The Centre of Excellence in Evaluation, Treasury Board of Canada Secretariat, at http://www.tbs-sct.gc.ca/cee/stud-etud/capa-pote00-eng.asp

❖ DISCUSSION QUESTIONS AND ACTIVITIES

1. Identify three consulting colleagues with whom you might collaborate on a project. How do their skills complement yours? How might you approach them to discuss future collaboration?

2. What personality traits identified in this chapter are strengths of yours? Describe situations where these characteristics have been particularly useful. Which of the suggested characteristics do you need to develop to a greater extent? What strategies might you use to do that?

3. Think of several times in your life when you have shown courage, energy, and vision. What can you learn from these experiences that can help you cope with the challenges that consulting is likely to provide?

❖ REFERENCES

Bureau of Labor Statistics. (2009). *Career guide to industries, 2010–11 edition: Management, scientific, and technical consulting services.* Retrieved from http://www.bls.gov/oco/cg/cgs037.htm

CBS News (Producer). (2002, June 11). Personality traits linked to birth order: Place on family tree to shape personalities [Video webcast] [Television series episode]. *The Early Show.* Retrieved from http://www.cbsnews.com/stories/2002/06/10/earlyshow/living/parenting/main511694.shtml

The Centre of Excellence for Evaluation, Treasury Board of Canada. (2002). *Building community capacity: Competency profile for federal public service evaluation professionals.* Retrieved from http://www.tbs-sct.gc.ca/cee/stud-etud/capa-pote02-eng.asp

Church, E. (2000, April 17). Forget money, think passion. *The Globe and Mail,* p. M1.

Cronbach, L. J., Ambron, S. R., Dornbusch, S. M., Hess, R. D., Hornik, R. C., Phillips, D. C., Walker, D. F., et al. (1980). *Toward reform of program evaluation.* San Francisco, CA: Jossey-Bass.

Dreher, H. M., Donnely, F. G., & Naremore, R. C. (2005). Reflections on the DNP and an alternate practice doctorate model: The Drexel DrNP. *Online Journal of Issues in Nursing, 11*(1). Retrieved from www.nursingworld.org/MainMenuCategories/ANAMarketplace/ANAPeriodicals/OJIN/TableofContents/Volume112006/N01Jan06/ArticlePreviousTopic/tpc28_716031.aspx

Greiner, L. E., & Metzger, R. O. (1983). *Consulting to management.* Englewood Cliffs, NJ: Prentice-Hall.

Harris, C. (2001). Consulting and you. *Consulting to Management, 12*(1), 45–52.

Jakob-Hoff, M., & Coggan, C. (2003). Core competencies for evaluators. In N. Lunt, C. Davidson, & K. McKegg (Eds.) *Evaluating Policy and Practice: A New Zealand Reader* (pp. 132–137). Auckland, New Zealand: Pearson Prentice Hall.

Katz, D., & Kahn, R. L. (1978). *The social psychology of organizations* (2nd ed.). New York, NY: Wiley.

Maynard, R. (1992, October). The guru gambit. *Report on Business Magazine,* 58–68.

Moses, B. (2002, March 4). Unlock the door to self-employment. *The Globe and Mail,* p. C1.

Moxie. (2010). In *Merriam-Webster Online Dictionary.* Retrieved from http://www.merriam-webster.com/dictionary/moxie

Patton, M. Q. (2008). *Utilization-focused evaluation* (4th ed.). Thousand Oaks, CA: Sage.

Rosener, J. B. (1990, November-December). Ways women lead. *Harvard Business Review.* Retrieved from http://hbr.org/1990/11/ways-women-lead/ar/1

Von Oech, R. (2008). *A whack on the side of the head: How you can be more creative.* New York, NY: Hachette Book Group.

3

Essential Values

Highlights:

- Discover why an ethical stance is the number one value for consultants.

- Learn ways to support positive social change while implementing objective, fair, and balanced research.

- Understand how to keep your personal and professional agendas separate yet complementary.

- Find out how collaboration can enhance your reputation and create marketing opportunities.

- Uncover the secret about adult learning that you can use for the rest of your life.

The beliefs you hold about right and wrong define who you are and govern your work performance and day-to-day behavior. In a tough and sometimes unscrupulous world, you will need to be clear about your own personal bottom line. Here are five values that I believe are essential for an independent consultant.

❖ 1. AN ETHICAL STANCE

For the independent consultant, having an ethical stance is the most important value of all. When an ethical dilemma arises, and it surely will, there will not be time to weigh the pros and cons, look for advice, or consult with colleagues or mentors. Ethical issues emerge rapidly and require an almost knee-jerk response that is both intuitive and appropriate. You must react to requests to reveal data sources, fudge the numbers, and change recommendations. You must deal with demanding clients and overbearing stakeholders, and the requests they make that can be unethical or downright illegal. You need to be able to take a stand and say, "I go no farther."

I have found that there are three ways to do this. First of all, read deeply into the ethical guidelines and standards provided by your profession. Adopt the wisdom offered by the Guiding Principles for Evaluators (American Evaluation Association, 2004), the Guidelines for Ethical Conduct (Canadian Evaluation Society, n.d.) and the Program Evaluation Standards of the Joint Committee on Standards for Educational Evaluation (2010). Make them your own. Envision potential scenarios in the field. Role-play and brainstorm with trusted colleagues and friends. Plan to be prepared, because sooner or later your ethics will be challenged.

While the moral problems that accompany our work require skills in moral reflection (Bebeau, 1995), for those of us who make research our business, ethics gets a lot more complicated. Remember Enron? This energy giant lied about its profits, and world confidence was shaken. The company filed for bankruptcy, and many of its executives were later sent to prison. The connecting story is that its auditing and consulting firm, Arthur Anderson, was found guilty of deliberately destroying evidence for its client (BBC News, 2002). The firm later collapsed as a result of the scandal.

At about the same time, a Canadian government advertising and publicity campaign known as the "sponsorship program" broke into the news due to allegations of conflict of interest, bid rigging, and political interference in the contracting process. The program had awarded up to CAN$100 million to advertising firms that did little or no work. In particular, one marketing firm received CAN$550,000 for a report that was nearly identical to another one it had already delivered—right down to the same spelling mistakes. The auditor-general of Canada found that the program had been administered with complete disregard for federal contracting rules and procedures. Many high-ranking government officials were fired, several consultants were convicted of criminal charges and sent to jail, and a federal election was called (CBC News Online, 2006).

"What does all this have to do with me?" you ask. "I'm only a consultant." Well so were they. It is only a matter of scale. So my second piece of advice is to learn to say "no" to a client and feel good about it. It is easy to feel overpowered when you are the sole consultant in a room filled with strong and opinionated people. Here's what I do. In any client–consultant relationship, I remember that I represent my stakeholder group, the evaluation community. This gives me the leverage to begin a "no" statement by saying, "As a member of the evaluation community, I agree with my colleagues that X or Y is not appropriate because (state the reason) and I will not be able to do that." Hearing the choir singing behind you is a welcome sound indeed when you are in a tough or lonely spot. So I can say, "No, I will not release the data until the funder has reviewed it." "No, I will not suppress the negative (or positive) findings." "No, I will not write your thesis/chapter/article under your name." And "No, I will not continue to work for you if you pressure me in this way." *Independent* does not have to mean *alone.*

Thirdly, come to understand that while you are undoubtedly a nice person, there is no reason why clients should trust you. Learn what is meant by good business practice, because it is your reputation in the business community that will ultimately shape your success. It is not an acceptable excuse to say that you weren't aware of your responsibilities as a consultant and business person. For example, did you know

- you have a duty of care to your client and must provide your services with integrity, objectivity, and independence?
- you should accept only assignments for which you have the appropriate knowledge and skills?
- you should reach a mutual understanding with your client about project objectives, scope, work plan, costs, and fee arrangements before accepting the assignment?
- you should not work for two clients simultaneously that are in potentially conflicting situations without informing them in advance and getting their agreement to proceed?

- you should not take advantage of a client relationship by encouraging a client's employee to seek alternate employment, including working for you?
- you should not benefit financially from your assignment with your client apart from your agreed-upon fees?
- you should not use colleagues' proprietary information or methodologies without permission?

Management consultants have thought extensively about these and other ethical issues, and adherence to a code of ethics is a condition of membership and certification for those who use the Certified Management Consultant designation. It assures clients of members' professionalism and high ethical standards. Whether or not you decide to pursue such a designation, you should be fully aware of what an ethical consulting practice entails.

❖ 2. A SOCIAL JUSTICE PERSPECTIVE

As House (2005) has written, the principles of social justice are used to assess whether the distribution of benefits and burdens among various groups in society are appropriate, fair, and moral. It doesn't take long for an evaluator or applied researcher to become aware that benefits are definitely not appropriate, fair, or moral for many. Because you spend so much of your time interacting with target groups that embody some kind of deficit, you are likely to become an advocate for their cause. When you interview transient workers, women living in poverty, or victims of tainted blood transfusions, for example, your sense of social justice will inevitably be aroused, and you will come to believe that your work can "make a difference."

However, some theorists have been disillusioned with their work's perceived lack of impact. Weiss (1993) was disheartened by the limited impact of her evaluation findings on policy change, concluding that "the assumption is no longer tenable that evaluation research of one program at a time can draw useful implications for action or that piecemeal modifications will improve effectiveness" (p. 105). Yet others have been more optimistic. As Rossi, Lipsey, and Freeman (2004) commented, "There is considerable evidence that the findings of evaluations do often influence policies, program planning and implementation, and the ways social programs are administered, sometimes in the short term and other times in the long term" (p. 371).

How can you support positive social change while implementing objective, fair, and balanced research? Here are some solutions that have worked for me:

1. Ground your work in appropriate theories and methodology, and stay current in your field. You are not the only one that is wrestling with these thorny issues, and someone else may be able to help you. Document your work, leave a paper trail, and take extensive field notes. Don't forget to record your personal observations and feelings, and revisit them as you prepare your final report.

2. Be thoughtful in your study designs. Incorporate time into the end of your projects for knowledge translation, keeping in mind ways to accelerate the benefits of your research, the types of messages to be transmitted, the kinds of activities to recommend, and the audiences and users to target. Help your client think about how to move from study findings to action.

3. Acknowledge your own background and propensities. Be sensitive to divergent points of view and to issues associated with ethnicity, race, culture, gender, age, class, and disability. Avoid the misunderstandings and miscommunications that arise from stereotyping and lack of awareness. Examine your own values and beliefs, and obtain guidance from those more knowledgeable about the population you are working with. Present your evidence in as unbiased a way as possible. Involve your client in the interpretation of findings and in generating conclusions and recommendations.

If we can make a difference, in even a small way, our work will have value, not only for our clients and ourselves, but for society at large.

❖ 3. AUTHENTICITY

To be credible, you have to be authentic. As a student teacher, I quickly learned that kids could spot a fake a mile away. Clients have that same sixth sense. If you want their respect, you need to tell them the truth even if it puts you at a disadvantage. Building trust with a client not only leads to success, it leads to more work. If you are consistent, clients will rely on you to deliver the same kind of service the next time. I recently received a call from a client I had not heard from in ten years. "Darren," I exclaimed, "I haven't heard from you in ages. How's it going?" "Oh, fine" he said. "We just haven't needed an evaluator, but now we have a new grant and we need to talk. . . ."

Being genuine, however, does not mean that you have to share your life with your clients. To be honest, they are not interested in your kid, your marriage, your renovations, or your health. What they want is a good researcher who keeps his or her personal issues under wraps; they have enough issues of their own. Keeping your professional life separate from your personal one only adds to the respect and credibility you generate.

Keep this in mind when you travel. Have a personal agenda as well as a work agenda. Don't just stay in your hotel room and work; this would be a lost opportunity. And if you have to work all the time, question your time management skills. Maybe you are afraid to go out on your own. I recently overheard two business women in a hotel elevator. They nearly flew into each other's arms they were so glad to see each other. One said, "I'm so glad to see you. I have been eating in my room all week." She had yet another takeout box in her hand.

Teach yourself to eat in a restaurant by yourself and enjoy it. Don't work on your laptop, talk on your phone, or text people at home. Enjoy the food and the ambiance. Eavesdrop. Talk to someone. Look up some colleagues. Develop some new favorite haunts. You can have fun in any city, and you will find that by fueling your own interests, you will do a better job for your clients as well.

❖ 4. COLLABORATION

While theorists promote collaboration as a good research approach, it is not an option for me, it is a necessity. You may be the research expert, but your client and your client's clients are the program experts. How can you conduct an evaluation that is "good enough" to answer the questions under study (Rossi et al., 2004, p. 371) without their help and guidance?

When I meet a potential client who says, "Just tell me when it's over," I run the other way. In one of my early evaluation projects, the client refused to participate in any of our meetings. I could not obtain any feedback from her throughout the project, and when I presented the final report (after sending her several drafts that went unnoticed), she said, "This is the worst evaluation report I have ever read." It was then easy for her to distance herself from the recommendations. It was also easy for me to distance myself from her organization, and I never worked for them again.

Valuing the collaborative process will enhance your reputation and create more opportunities than you thought possible. Consultants often build teams to bid on projects that are too large for them to handle on their own. It works both ways. Sometimes I subcontract with colleagues to acquire their specific competencies, such as focus group facilitation, quantitative analysis, or language skills; and other times they provide the geographic breadth I need for data collection. Alternatively, they may ask me to subcontract with them. Consultants are not only your potential competitors; they are also your potential colleagues and clients. Treat them with respect, because you may need each other in the next project that comes along.

❖ 5. LIFELONG LEARNING

A consultant once told me he did not have time to read anything except what he needed for his current project's literature review. He also never attended professional conferences, because he was too busy. I envisioned him slipping farther and farther downstream as his knowledge and expertise grew out of date. There is a common saying among consultants that you are only as good as your last project. If you are not keeping up with the latest ideas, methods, and technologies, someone else will get your next contract instead.

The biggest secret about adult learning is that adults learn what they need when they need it. Adult learning gained a lot of attention with the growth of community colleges, and Knowles (1970) popularized the concepts of informal adult education, andragogy, and self-directed learning (Smith, 2002). By early in the 21st century, informal learning had become recognized as an economic driver. The Commission of the European Communities (2006) published a document entitled *Adult Learning: It Is Never Too Late to Learn.* It stressed the importance of lifelong learning for competitiveness and employability as well as for social inclusion, active citizenship, and personal development.

Lifelong learning is based on your own needs, curiosity, tastes, and hunger for information (Gross, 1977). While the prospect of running your own consulting business may seem overwhelming at first, you will soon find yourself excited and stimulated by it. Your learning will happen both incrementally and incidentally, and your learning needs will change as your business develops. To start with, you will probably want to focus on such basic business skills as business planning, business structures, marketing, managing cash flow, and hiring the right people. Over time, other topics may arise based on your current business and financial needs. Learning opportunities have never been better, and an extraordinary array of resources is at your fingertips. This book can give you a place to start, but you are your own curriculum designer. You will learn what you need when you need it.

Use the five critical values examined in this chapter to help you define and develop your consulting style. Then use them for life. An explicit understanding of your ethical stance will define your personal bottom line and will provide you with backup when you need it most. Understand how you can support positive social change while doing fair and balanced research, and don't shortchange either yourself or your client. See beyond the end of your project, and think of ways to apply the knowledge you generate for a broader social benefit. Be authentic, and value your own interests as well as those embodied in your current project. When you travel, enjoy the unique nature of each location, and make it your own. Treat both clients and colleagues as collaborators, and let them know you value working with them. Finally, never stop learning. As you bootstrap your consulting practice into reality, you will find serendipitously that you are growing as an individual as well.

❖ USEFUL RESOURCES

- For an excellent book on ethics that provides case-study scenarios and commentaries by evaluators on a suggested course of action, see Michael Morris's *Evaluation Ethics for Best Practice: Cases and Commentaries* (Guilford Press, 2008).
- The American Evaluation Association provides a helpful statement that affirms the significance of cultural competence in evaluation and identifies several essential practices for cultural competence. See *Public Statement on Cultural Competence in Evaluation* at http://www.eval.org/.

- There are many online resources for lifelong learners. Here are a couple of good places to start:

  The OpenCourseWare Consortium, which is a collaboration of higher-education institutions and other organizations that provide open educational content: http://www.ocwconsortium.org/.

  The U.S. Small Business Administration, which provides online training on many business topics: http://www.sba.gov/category/navigation-structure/counseling-training.

❖ DISCUSSION QUESTIONS AND ACTIVITIES

1. Can you describe an ethical dilemma you have faced while conducting research in the field? How did you respond to this situation? What might you do differently next time?

2. Identify a social issue that you learned about through your research. Did your research findings lead to any positive social change? How could your research have had a greater impact?

3. Choose the essential value for consultants described in this chapter that is most important for your clients or potential clients. For what reasons do you favor this value over the others presented here? How might you determine if your clients agree with your choice?

❖ REFERENCES

American Evaluation Association. (2004). *Guiding principles for evaluators.* Retrieved from http://www.eval.org/GPTraining/GP%20Training%20Final/gp.principles.pdf

BBC News. (2002, August 22). Enron scandal at-a-glance. *BBC News World Edition.* Retrieved from http://news.bbc.co.uk/2/hi/business/1780075.stm

Bebeau, M. J. (1995). *Developing a well-reasoned response to a moral problem in scientific research.* Retrieved from http://openedpractices.org/resource/developing-well-reasoned-response-moral-problem-scientific-research

Canadian Evaluation Society. (n.d.). *CES guidelines for ethical conduct.* Retrieved from http://www.evaluationcanada.ca/site.cgi?s=5&ss=4&_lang=an

CBC News Online. (2006). Federal sponsorship scandal. *CBC.ca News.* Retrieved from http://www.cbc.ca/news/background/groupaction/

Commission of the European Communities. (2006). *Adult learning: It is never too late to learn.* Retrieved from http://ec.europa.eu/education/policies/adult/com558_en.pdf

Gross, R. (1977). *The lifelong learner.* New York, NY: Simon & Schuster.

House, E. R. (2005). Social Justice. In S. Mathison (Ed.). *Encyclopedia of evaluation* (pp. 393–396). Thousand Oaks, CA: Sage.

Joint Committee on Standards for Educational Evaluation. (2010). *The program evaluation standards: A Guide for evaluators and evaluation users.* (3rd ed.). Thousand Oaks, CA: Sage.

Knowles, M. S. (1970). *The modern practice of adult education: Andragogy versus pedagogy.* New York, NY: Association Press.

Rossi, P. H., Lipsey, M. W., & Freeman, H. E. (2004). *Evaluation: A systematic approach* (7th ed.). Thousand Oaks, CA: Sage.

Smith, M. K. (2002). Malcolm Knowles, informal adult education, self-direction and andragogy. *The encyclopedia of informal education.* Retrieved from http://www.infed.org/thinkers/et-knowl.htm#andragogy

Weiss, C. H. (1993). Where politics and evaluation research meet. *Evaluation Practice, 14*(1): 93–106. doi: 10.1177/109821409301400119

4

Political Skills

Highlights:

- Identify the players in the political drama using Machiavelli's characters.

- Understand the policy environment, its history, and the conventional wisdom associated with it.

- Enhance your awareness of the political dimension by developing your savoir faire and understanding of organizational culture.

- Access the power of communication through such tools as status reports, feedback loops, reports, presentations, and knowledge dissemination strategies.

- Consider the importance of timing when making research decisions.

While evaluation is a research activity, much has been written about its political context (for example, Chelimsky, 1997; Cronbach et al., 1980; Patton, 2008). For the independent consultant, being politically astute is a sixth sense that can serve you well. Political proficiency will continue to grow throughout your career, but a good place to start is by observing and reflecting on the small-*p* political currents that you will find in any client's organization. Here are five political skills that I have learned.

❖ 1. KNOW THE PLAYERS[1]

First, it is important to identify all the players in an evaluation or research endeavor. While we have been trained to identify stakeholder groups, sometimes a fresh perspective can be useful. In his article "The Politics of Expertise" (1972), Benveniste used Machiavelli's book *The Prince* (1532) as a template to describe the key actors. The Prince is the individual ultimately in charge of your project. He probably signs your contract. He needs advice, but he only wants it when and how he wishes. He is the politician, the CEO, the department or board chair, the president, or the manager. He has both stated and unstated reasons for using your services.

To Machiavelli, the political ruler is interested in the acquisition of power to maintain the status quo. He is not motivated by a sense of goodness or of being right. Political activity is defined by the rules of political power, and power is needed to make individuals obey. Only then can the ruler maintain a safe and secure state (Nederman, 2009). Some things may have changed since Machiavelli's day, but the rules of power remain.

As you begin to work with an organization, the concept of power can help you see the research context more clearly. How does the Prince interpret and implement his power? Who makes the decisions? Who holds the purse strings? How does he get people to do the work he wants them to do? By understanding what makes the Prince tick, you can see how your project fits with his objectives.

While you may rarely meet the Prince in person, his staff will interpret his wishes. These are the *Lieutenants,* the bureaucrats or program managers who surround the Prince and control the machinery of administration. As key stakeholders, they will either foster or impede your work, and so you need to get them on board to move your research forward. In complex programs, there can be several Lieutenants, with each one representing a different department. They may well have competing interests, and you will see this being played out at team meetings. However, it is likely that one specific Lieutenant is responsible for your project, so it will be essential to make this individual a key partner.

While neither Machiavelli nor Benveniste identified this next group of players, there is another important group of stakeholders in large program contexts, the *Program Implementers*. These individuals are responsible for conducting program activities in the field, and they often work at the state or local level. They are the gatekeepers to program participants, and without their support, you will not have access to collect the data you need. They also control the implementation of your recommendations, so their needs should be addressed as you design your research. Patton's utilization-focused approach (2008) is particularly helpful when interacting with this group.

Finally there are the *Beneficiaries*, or those whose lives are affected by the program under study. Sometimes, as Benveniste suggests, they are actually the *Victims*. Too often, the evaluator or researcher has no direct access to them and has to rely on the program implementers instead. Indeed, program staff can be fiercely protective of their participants, believing that they speak on the participants' behalf, but sometimes this belief is unfounded.

The Beneficiaries can be seen as replaceable cogs in the organizational machine. In many health care contexts, they are never consulted at all, yet in a study on hospital readmission rates, I found that it was quite powerful to talk to the Beneficiaries directly. Those with chronic readmission rates talked to me about their need for follow-up support. As one individual commented, leaving the hospital was like stepping into outer space. We found that when someone knowledgeable followed up with them, they were able to stay out of the hospital longer.

Similarly, school children are often ignored, even though their perceptions are keen and valid and can be captured easily if you use the right tools. A preliterate child is perfectly comfortable circling a happy face or a sad face and can willingly offer advice to a child pictured in a specific scenario.

While Machiavelli did not have a researcher in his cast of characters, he did have an advisor or sage, known as the *Pundit*. This is the independent consultant who is hired for his or her expertise. While we all operate within a cultural framework, I believe that our consulting ideology should be as apolitical as possible. Not all researchers keep their political views under wraps, and some market to a specific ideological niche. However, there is the danger of confusing one's own political agenda with that of the client's, or of interpreting the results through a particular ideological lens. In my opinion, the researcher needs to tread carefully, to be impartial, and to focus on the evidence at hand. Personal political views are for after hours.

As the demands of the research become paramount, the Pundit may find that he pays too much attention to the Prince, too little to the Lieutenants and Program Implementers, and none at all to the Beneficiaries. I remember hearing a consultant say, "Well, the partici-pants will just have to do a survey. It's what the government wants." That may be true, but unless the Beneficiaries see a reason for their compliance, they may participate with their feet. When you see a sur-vey with a low response rate reported in the literature, ask yourself what political issues were playing out behind the scenes. If you work closely with all of the program players and understand what really motivates them, your knowledge of the political landscape will change, and your research design will be enriched.

❖ 2. KNOW THE POLICY ENVIRONMENT

Chelimsky (1987) has argued that evaluators must understand not only the information needs of the policy makers but also the policy environ-ment in which the research or evaluation is situated. You must under-stand the policy question asked by the Prince, because this is the reason the study was commissioned. Your research questions must flow from this original policy question, but Chelimsky warns that this translation is "one of the most sensitive and important political interactions in the entire process, fraught with risks" (p. 27).

To ensure that your policy translation is accurate, a clear under-standing of the program's history and philosophical underpinnings will help you understand what has shaped the program you see today. For example, to evaluate a Canadian health promotion program, I had to explore the social determinants of health, their role in a population health approach, and the framework of factors used by stakeholders to determine health status (Lalonde, 1974). Only with this background knowledge could I begin to talk to stakeholders in their own language.

Client perceptions are also important, and the corporate memory, conventional wisdom, folklore, and mythology that surround a program should be brought to the surface. For example, one program I evaluated came about as a result of a golf game conversation between a community college president and a university professor. A school–industry partnership program came about because a school trustee read about a similar program in an in-flight magazine. A northern government program was initiated by the former employee of a fur trading company. By the time I wanted to interview him, he had "returned to the land." While these wonderful stories won't help you frame your research, they color the collective memory and help to define stakeholders' perceptions of success.

Looking at an organization's policy environment inevitably leads you to its broader social context and its ability to adapt and survive. Changes in technology, legislation, government structures, politics, economics, the marketplace, demographics, social conditions, cultural influences, and the physical environment create a complex web that exerts pressure on the organization. Policy decisions are required to respond strategically to these issues. Thus, scanning the organization's environment can help you understand the policy question at hand and may lead to the design of more appropriate research questions. Recently, complexity theory has encouraged us to use situational thinking to understand systems. A developmental evaluation approach is one way of responding to a dynamic environment (Patton, 2008, p. 139; Westley, Zimmerman, & Patton, 2006, p. 174).

Ultimately, when your research is complete, ask yourself if the original policy questions have been answered, or if the research took on a life of its own. The Prince will not be happy if your results have not addressed his information needs.

❖ 3. KNOW THE POLITICAL DIMENSION

To understand politics, you need some political savoir faire. This skill is not taught in school; rather, exposure and experience are the best teachers. Select some role models to observe in action, and hone your political skills. Watch investigative journalists and interviewers on TV. Attend local political debates. Track CEOs from industry, finance, and the not-for-profit sector. See how they interact with staff, shareholders, and the public. Ask yourself what you would do in their shoes.

Mentorships or job shadowing with a well-regarded professional can provide an excellent way to develop new skills, overcome barriers, and develop confidence. The mentors also can benefit from sharing their learning, demonstrating their skills, gaining a grassroots perspective, and renewing their own energies. The problem is in the implementation. Few volunteer organizations are able to find the resources or set up appropriate guidelines and maintain a structure to manage the application, matching, and accountability processes for mentoring programs.

Even on an individual level, it can be difficult to find an independent consultant with the time to mentor someone. A good alternative is to act as a subcontractor on a project managed by an expert. While you may have lots of experience in your field, working in a supporting role for an experienced independent consultant can be an invaluable learning experience. Watch how this individual looks, dresses, acts, and responds in a particular environment. Even if you disagree with the individual's approach, there are valuable lessons to be learned about what not to do.

You also need to be aware that each sector and each organization within that sector has its own culture. I felt comfortable working in an education setting, but when the marketplace led me into the field of health care, I knew I was ill prepared. My initial moments of culture shock were only softened by saying, "I'm not a health practitioner. I'm really going to need your help to understand what is going on here."

Don't assume that you understand the undercurrents; you may not even be aware that they exist. Sometimes the initiation of an evaluation is a political statement in its own right and can be perceived as a threat. If you sense a fight-or-flight response from program implementers, or if no one will talk to you, look you in the eye, or sit beside you in the lunch room, your political sensors should go into overdrive. You may have stumbled into a work environment made toxic by management issues that have nothing to do with your research, but on the other hand, you may be perceived as the axe man. This would be a good time to have a serious talk with your contract manager to clarify the purpose of your project. While your client's interests need to be protected, so do yours. If you feel that your work is being compromised, you may need to withdraw. Never do this lightly, but never allow yourself to feel victimized by an untenable situation.

You should also consider the possibility that your research could end up in the media. The specter of front page exposure will add a degree of caution to your work. One of my clients experienced serious labor issues during our study. Every morning I had to walk through the television cameras to get into the building. Every night as I left, I would practice saying, "No comment. Please contact my client if you want further information." Fortunately, no journalist ever contacted me. However, it became difficult to separate study findings from the impact of the turbulent work environment, and ultimately, the results were inconclusive. This project taught me about the power of the media, and since then it has been my fervent wish to stay out of the limelight.

Know that you step into the political arena every time you take on a research project. The politics and organizational culture will affect the quality of your research. Rather than being oblivious to the political undercurrents, make sure you try to understand what is really going on so that the context can inform your research.

❖   4. KNOW THE POWER OF COMMUNICATION

Some clients need more communication than others. It is your job to determine what their information needs are and why they need what they need. Often their anxiety is related to the pressure for information that other stakeholders are exerting on them. To keep them apprised of study progress, a good strategy is to provide a monthly status report. I develop a brief report template that mirrors study objectives, and then I provide an update of activities conducted since the previous month and a short commentary on emerging trends and issues. This policy of "no surprises" is appreciated by clients. It helps them look good when their superiors ask them how things are going.

Some clients prefer more frequent updates, particularly if the study is of a short duration or requires a rapid turnaround. In these cases I use an informal weekly e-mail report. I follow up on either type of report with a telephone discussion with my client to answer questions and strategize next steps.

Feedback loops are an essential way to communicate with stakeholders. Make sure that all the necessary players respond to draft versions of logic models, tools, reports, and recommendations. The extra time required to solicit this feedback will pay off in enhanced study ownership. It will also improve the overall quality of the study.

While a final report may not be the best way to communicate your results, it is still the one deliverable that clients want the most. If nothing else, a report has a shelf life, and while staff may turn over, the report remains a witness to your study activities and findings. As report writing can take up at least 30% of your time and resources, it is important to do it well. Researchers in health technology assessment have developed a useful ratio for reports, namely 1:3:25 pages. For every one page prepared for the Prince or politicians, three pages are written for the Lieutenants or administrators, and 25 pages for the Program Implementers. Thus, the executive summary provides a high-level synopsis and focuses on the policy question. The body of the report provides simple tables and useful quotations that can be readily interpreted by staff. Details about methodology, procedures, and data are left to the appendices, because only other Pundits or researchers will find them interesting.

Presentations can be useful, but it is better to prepare them yourself rather than letting someone on the client's staff reinterpret your findings As a consultant, you may submit your final report and never be invited back to make a presentation. Internal staff members may extract the information they deem pertinent to send up through the organization to their superiors, and you have no control over the content. Something is always lost in translation, so it is better to include a slide show with your final report that represents the key points as you see them. At least you can hope that this material will be disseminated.

While slide shows are common, most of them are too long, too detailed, and too boring. Our short-term memories can only hold five to nine items. Viewers' critical thinking skills quickly dull as you rush through 45 slides of data; instead, aim for 10 slides. Answer the policy questions simply and clearly with a few critical numbers and some interesting quotations. If you are going to present the material yourself, follow your slides with two or three key discussion questions to stimulate stakeholders' thought processes and to move them forward.

You may be able to structure a knowledge dissemination phase into your project following the completion of the research. This will allow time to reflect on ways to tailor findings for different audiences and to translate knowledge into action. Working with your client, you can assess the potential impact of news releases, online articles, webinars, blogs, and social media as well as the more traditional mechanisms of conference papers and journal articles.

There are many ways to communicate with your clients, but rather than letting it happen incidentally, articulate your communication strategy from the outset. If you pay more attention to the power that is unleashed by effective communication, your research will have a greater chance of effecting change.

❖ 5. KNOW THE IMPORTANCE OF TIMING

Timing can make or break a study's outcomes. Chelimsky (1987, p. 31) cautions that the fit of the final report with policy cycles has a definite impact on its eventual use. Sometimes the goal of research perfection has to be sacrificed to the competing goal of timeliness. An adequate report that brings the findings to bear on the policy issue will always trump a better report that is produced too late for implementation.

The data collection calendar is often more limited than it seems. In education studies, for example, surveys of teachers will have lower return rates in September (school start-up), December (the lead-up to Christmas holidays), January (examinations), March (spring break), and June (burnout time). There are not so many good months after all. Decisions that will have an impact on next year's school program have to be made no later than March of the prior school year. If you miss that deadline, it will be another year before implementation can occur, and by then the study may have lost its relevance.

An evaluation of a program for seniors with substance abuse issues provides another example. The client suggested that we should not try to access participants in the week following receipt of their pension checks, because they tended to binge drink until their money was gone and so were not fit to take part in a survey during that period. Thus despite our advance planning, in reality, only half of the time allotted for data collection was actually usable.

Another critical timing factor is the organization's financial year. In Canada, the government's fiscal year is April 1 to March 31. This results in what we call March Madness. Government employees often call me close to year-end, because their budget surplus cannot be carried over to the next year. They often have unrealistic deadlines and suggest a variety of ways to work around this difficulty. Perhaps they can pay me in advance, or maybe I can do a quick and dirty study, or maybe I can prepare a brief report as a "place holder."

When you are hungry for work, it is hard to say, "No." The short-term desire to please a prospective client and to supplement your income has to be weighed against your sense of good business practice. While I understand their dilemma, I have learned that none of these options works for me for the following reasons:

- I am probably already overcommitted trying to complete current work for the year-end deadline.
- I have to wonder about their decision-making environment if their planning cycle is so delayed that they have only realized now that they need this research.
- It may not be possible to conduct the study at all for reasons yet to be determined, or I could miss out on valuable design opportunities because I am in a hurry. The client will not be happy with the suboptimal result and will quickly forget about the time constraints I had to deal with.
- The study may cost more than anticipated, but it will be impossible to renegotiate in a new fiscal year, and I will be left to cover the shortfall.
- The study could cost less, and if so, what should I do with the unaccounted-for profit? Declare it a windfall? Send it back?
- I could set up special accounting procedures for moneys paid in advance and draw down project costs as they are incurred, but while this solution does work, it also enables a poor system to continue being poor at my expense.

You can see that I have already explored these options and learned that none of them work for me. It is now easy to respond to these last minute requests and say, "No. I wish I could help you out, but I am pretty well booked to the end of the year. Maybe we can talk again in April?"

Awareness of timing draws us toward a longer-term view. Our work is cumulative. What may languish in one administration may come to the forefront in the next. Over time, good decisions can be made. As Chelimsky says (1997, pp. 67–68), the challenge for us is "to understand the strengths and vulnerabilities of both politics and evaluation, and to use both to help us contribute to public policy in meaningful and enduring ways."

Political skills are so important to consultants because they need to get up to speed as quickly as possible in each new organization. A heightened sense of context and dynamics can help interpret the political terrain. Think about the power perspective, and watch for the key players in our little Machiavellian drama. Be aware of the larger policy environment, and look for changing conditions that can affect your research. Observe how other evaluators behave, and use them as role models. Understand the power of the media, and stay out of the limelight. Look for better ways to communicate with your clients, and to help them communicate with their audiences. Know that timing is everything. Sometimes perfection will have to be sacrificed so that your research can have any impact at all. Be realistic with yourself and your clients about the critical and intersecting topics of power, politics, time, and money, and you will hone your consulting skills as you go.

❖ NOTE

1.   An earlier version of much of the material in this chapter first appeared in Barrington (1992).

❖ USEFUL RESOURCES

- For more on Machiavelli and his thoughts on political realism, check out http://plato.stanford.edu/entries/machiavelli/.
- For more on Eleanor Chelimsky's pragmatic approach to program evaluation, see this list of her relevant articles: http://scholar.google.com/scholar?q=%22author%3AChelimsky%20author%3AE.%22.
- For more on complex relationships, systems, and social change, see Westley, Zimmerman, and Patton's excellent nontechnical book: *Getting to Maybe: How the World Is Changed* (Random House Canada, 2006).

❖ DISCUSSION QUESTIONS AND ACTIVITIES

1.   Identify some role models who could help you refine your political skills. How might you go about learning from these individuals?

2. Think of a sector or program area that is currently experiencing substantial change. What environmental forces are exerting an influence on its sustainability? Outline how this turbulent context would affect your research design.

3. Imagine that a client has asked you to conduct an attractive research project, but it has an unrealistic time line. Identify the client's interests; identify your interests. Write the dialogue you might have with this individual to arrive at a satisfactory resolution for you both.

❖ REFERENCES

Barrington, G. V. (1992). Evaluation skills nobody taught me. In A. Vaux, M. S. Stockdale, & M. J. Schwerin (Eds.), *Independent consulting for evaluators* (pp. 69–84). Newbury Park, CA: Sage.

Benveniste, G. (1972). *The politics of expertise.* Berkeley, CA: Glendessary Press.

Chelimsky, E. (1987). The politics of program evaluation. *Society, 25*(1), 24–32.

Chelimsky, E. (1997). The political environment of evaluation and what it means for the development of the field. In E. Chelimsky & W. R. Shaddish (Eds.), *Evaluation for the 21st century: A handbook* (pp. 53–68). Thousand Oaks: CA, Sage.

Cronbach, L. J., Ambron, S. R., Dornbusch, S. M., Hess, R. D., Hornik, R. C., Phillips, D. C., & Weiner, S. S. (1980). *Toward reform of program evaluation.* San Francisco, CA: Jossey-Bass.

Lalonde, M. (1974). *Perspective on the health of Canadians.* Retrieved from http://www.phac-aspc.gc.ca/ph-sp/pdf/perspect-eng.pdf

Machiavelli, N. (1532). *The prince* (N. H. Thomson, Trans., Vol. XXXVI, Part 1). *The Harvard Classics.* Retrieved from http://www.bartleby.com/36/1/

Nederman, C. (2009). Niccolò Machiavelli. *Stanford Encyclopedia of Philosophy* (Spring 2010 ed.). Retrieved from http://plato.stanford.edu/entries/machiavelli/

Patton, M. Q. (2008). *Utilization-focused evaluation* (4th ed.). Thousand Oaks, CA: Sage.

Westley, F., Zimmerman, B., & Patton, M. Q. (2006). *Getting to maybe: How the world is changed.* Toronto, ON: Random House Canada.

5

Survival Skills

Highlights:

- Learn to engage in reflective practice to avoid burnout.

- Unblock your creative self through journal writing and solitary activities.

- Let your curiosity guide some personal research activities.

- Get involved in your community to make important connections and enhance your skills.

To survive in the world of consulting, you need first to look after yourself. The hours are long and the work is taxing, so you need stamina and staying power. The nature of your work provides part of your stress. The daily challenges of getting projects, dealing with stakeholders, and meeting deadlines keep you on your toes. However, even more stress is associated with society's expectations for you as a consultant. You have to be an expert, a knowledgeable methodologist, a rigorous researcher, a quick study, a problem solver, a mediator, and a judge; all this coupled with an amazing ability to disappear between projects and to have no need for a private life whatsoever. Above all, you must never, ever make mistakes.

This is a tough call, especially when you are standing on the far side of the River of Experience and are uncertain how to cross over. How can you survive in this demanding environment, stay mentally fit, avoid burnout, and keep asking for more? The purpose of this chapter is to discuss four survival strategies that have worked for me. The surprise is that it is not really about survival at all; it is about personal growth.

❖ 1. BE A REFLECTIVE PRACTITIONER

You will not be surprised to learn that consultants are the low man on the science totem pole. Schön[1] (1983) explored the science hierarchy and explained, "Applied science is said to 'rest on' the foundation of basic science. And the more basic and general the knowledge, the higher the status of its producer" (p. 24). Thus the top level of professional knowledge is a basic science or discipline, the second level is the applied science from which many solutions are derived, and the third and lowest level is the actual performance of services for a client through the use of basic and applied knowledge.

Even more disturbing is the fact that consultants are expendable. In government, as well as in large education and health organizations, "the consultant" is a replaceable cog in a purchasing machine. Your quality is judged on a point system, and your relative strength comes from your expertise. As a result, your CV must continue to grow. Each new project adds nuances to your knowledge and new understanding to your practice. You will be selected because you are very good at what you do.

At the same time, becoming an expert has its risks. As long as our practice involves the same type of projects, Schön (1983, pp. 60–61) suggests that we come to expect what to look for and we develop a repertoire of techniques. Eventually, as we become more specialized, we also become less surprised and increasingly automatic in our responses. We begin to pay less attention to phenomena that do not fit our preconceived categories, "a parochial narrowness of vision" (p. 61) that can lead to boredom and burnout.

The environment in which we work is confusing, messy, and fraught with complexity (McDavid & Hawthorn, 2006, p. 403). Our technical expertise is limited by situations of uncertainty, instability, uniqueness, and conflict (Schön, 1983, p. 345). Textbook solutions and standards of rigor rarely apply. We seldom have enough resources, time, or control over the phenomenon being studied to conduct even a quasi-experimental design. Instead, we are expected to fit our research into existing administrative processes, acknowledging that it is unlikely we will produce a definitive answer. At best, "our findings, conclusions, and our recommendations, supported by the evidence at hand and by our professional judgment, will reduce the uncertainty associated with the question" (McDavid & Hawthorn, 2006, pp. 408–409).

In the particularly turbulent environment of medicine, Dr. Atul Gawande, a writer, surgeon, and consummate practitioner, has commented as follows:

> You go into this work thinking it is all a matter of canny diagnosis, technical prowess, and some ability to empathize with people. But it is not, you soon find out. In medicine, as in any profession, we must grapple with systems, resources, circumstances, people— and our own shortcomings, as well. We face obstacles of seemingly unending variety. Yet somehow we must advance, we must refine, we must improve. (2007, p. 8)[2]

In order to do just that, we have to become aware of our own decision-making processes, observing the way we respond to our environment through the lens of reflection. We become researchers of our own practice and thus engage in a continuing process of self-education and renewal. Schön (1983, p. 299) explains, "The recognition of error, with its resulting uncertainty, can become a source of discovery rather than an occasion for self defense."

To be a reflective practitioner, you need to practice a form of reflective conversation. This is more effective during a project than at a postmortem (Schön, 1983, p. 268). However, this reflexive approach is not always seen as a legitimate form of professional knowledge, although Patton (2008) has explored it from the perspective of organizational learning.

In the important framework, Essential Competencies for Program Evaluators, developed by King, Stevahn, Ghere, and Minnema (2001, p. 235), reflection is a competency area where disagreement exists on perceived importance. Clearly, we need to become more comfortable thinking about what we are doing and better able to talk about it with our colleagues.

Here are some topics that Schön has suggested to start this reflective conversation (1983, pp. 62–63, 270):

- The language, repertoires or usual practice, and case examples we use to describe our reality
- The appreciative systems or ways we reframe situations and the methods of inquiry we use to describe the problem we are trying to solve
- The role we construct for ourselves in the larger organizational context
- The overarching theories we use to make sense of phenomena and patterns of behavior
- The feelings and intuitions we have about a situation that lead us to a particular course of action
- The tacit or inferred norms that underlie our judgment

❖ 2. NURTURE YOUR INNER ARTIST

Young children treasure their imaginations and use those princesses, monsters, and other imaginary friends to guide their play. All too quickly, they learn to conform, and they put away their childish selves and innate creativity. As adults, we often carry a nameless sense of loss and look for external stimuli to make us feel better, but all the while it is our unconscious creativity that is striving for expression. A good way to nurture this "inner artist" is through journal writing. Cameron (1992) and her colleagues Bryan and Allen (Bryan, Cameron, & Allen, 1998) have developed a journal-writing technique that they have used to train over a million participants in their creativity workshops.

This method, called the Morning Pages, is an important way to foster self-reflection, provide insight, and heighten a sense of self. Every morning, as soon as you wake up, you must produce three pages of longhand, stream-of-consciousness writing; this is not after coffee, not after breakfast, not on the way to work, but first. It means you have to set your alarm 30 minutes earlier than you would normally wake up. "Oh, no," you say, "couldn't I do it later in the day?" Cameron (1992) and Bryan et al. (1998) maintain that, consciously or unconsciously, you are setting your course for the day ahead. The free-form nature of the exercise allows your waking mind to slip easily from subject to subject before your inner critic awakes.

Unlike typical journaling techniques, this one has no set topic. You simply write as fast as you can about anything that comes into your mind, in the order that things pop up. Your thoughts are likely to be scattered, trivial, negative, or full of self-doubt. You may find yourself writing a "to do" list, or writing, "I have nothing to say," over and over, but you must produce three pages every day. Some thoughts tend to linger in your subconscious mind, and, at a minimum, you will soon find that you are getting more done. Over time you will find that memories, emotions, and your untapped intuition begin to surface. Because we lead stressful lives and try so hard to keep everything under control, we have no safety valve. Our very professionalism can also be our undoing. Morning Pages provide an outlet that is safe and surprisingly revealing.

Having used this personal form of reflection for more than 10 years, I find it both simple and powerful. Whole paragraphs will pop into my mind, opening sentences for my current report, conclusions for the data I have just analyzed, subtexts for recent stakeholder comments, connections and patterns not apparent before. Some decisions seem to get made by themselves. These types of thoughts happen so often that my journal frequently migrates from my bedside table to my computer in order to capture them verbatim. They are never as good the second time around. Of course, your reflection is not limited to your work life, and so you will find that personal insights arise as well. Go ahead, try it. Buy a blank journal and get started.

Cameron (1992) and Bryan et al. (1998) provide several other useful tools to unblock your creative self. Another one I particularly like is the idea of the Time Out. At first glance it seems counterintuitive to take one or two hours a week away from work and let yourself play. The Time Out has to involve a solitary activity that you consider to be fun, something that you have wanted to do for a long time but never had the time to do it. In practical terms, it is your creative off-switch (Bryan et al., p. 25). After concentrating hard at work, give yourself time to relax. Ideas will percolate in your unconscious mind. It may be hard to get away from the others in your life, but this is not an opportunity to socialize. Instead, go on your own to a play, a movie, a concert, an exhibit, or a book store, or take a long nature walk. Follow your interests and you will feed your soul. I found that the hardest part was knowing what I wanted to do. I spent so many years in the role of mother, daughter, wife, consultant, and teacher that I really did not know what I wanted to do. That revelation shocked me into my own journey of self-discovery, and this book is one of the results.

❖ 3. CONDUCT RESEARCH FOR YOURSELF

It was a physician who taught me to be my own client and conduct research for myself. Gawande (2007) encourages us to study something that interests us. As consultants, we are good at asking questions and finding answers for others, but where does our own curiosity fit in? How often do we get involved in a project and feel the sudden pull of a thought that begins, "I wonder if . . ." or "I wonder why. . . ." Of course we don't have the time to pursue these interesting questions, and so, regretfully, we let them pass.

But what if we took the time to explore our own interests as well? In Gawande's case, he started by counting. He wondered how many surgical procedures resulted in an instrument or sponge being left inside a patient. He began to count how many times these errors occurred. Then he got a little more sophisticated and compared those patients with such mishaps to those without. Eventually he found that mistakes were more likely to occur in urgent or unexpected circumstances. He and his colleagues began to develop a device to automate the tracking of sponges and instruments. He comments, "It doesn't really matter what you count. You don't need a research grant. The only requirement is that what you count should be interesting to you— the result will be that you learn something interesting" (pp. 254–255).

As researchers we are used to talking to strangers, but so often we just stick to the protocol. Why not learn something else about them at the same time? While this idea seems easy enough, we all have busy jobs. People sense we are busy and leave us alone. Gawande (2007) suggests that we take that extra moment to ask an unscripted question: "Where did you grow up?" or "Did you watch the hockey game last night?" or "What did you think about that weather yesterday?" It doesn't have to be a deep or important question; you just have to make a human connection (pp. 251–252). When the individual responds, challenge yourself to keep the conversation going for at least two more sentences. You will be surprised where you end up.

Thus the conversation I had recently with the grocery checkout clerk quickly moved from the weather to the 10-kilometer run for breast cancer she had done on the weekend. How proud she was of her accomplishment. I felt proud too just thinking about it. These sidebar conversations allow us to see others as individuals instead of just through the lens of our own distraction. They can provide a quick form of stress relief and enhance our attachment to the world at large.

As researchers for hire, we write a lot of reports, but how much writing do we do for ourselves? Our professional journals are full of articles on theories, frameworks, case studies, and ways to improve our methodology. These are written mainly by our academic colleagues, and while they encourage us to write about practice, few of us take up the challenge. There are several reasons for this gap in the literature. In the first place, unlike our university-based colleagues, we do not get rewarded for writing articles or books. While academics publish for advancement, tenure, and profile, we focus on our cash flow and upcoming deadlines. Writing is a luxury.

Second, there is the issue of intellectual property and proprietary information. When an organization enters into a research agreement with a university-based group, the issue of ownership is hashed out and clarified in a contract. Somehow the research expectations of the university carry a lot of weight, and usually, the researchers' future articles and publications are guaranteed. So when university researchers turn to consulting, they are often surprised to discover that their work belongs to their clients. They can only write about a project if they have client approval. One way they can get around this problem is to collaborate with their clients. Jointly published articles please everyone's egos, but typically clients will only agree if the findings are positive and the study casts them in a good light. As a result, the real lessons to be learned are seldom shared and rarely studied.

Finally, we are reluctant to take the time to prepare an article for publication only to have it turned down by peer reviewers. We are insecure about our writing styles, because we write in plain business language; in fact many clients do not like anything that is "too academic" in tone. They want short, crisp reports, preferably ones that focus on findings, so we learn to write in bullet points, executive summaries, and slide shows. We worry that our writing style will be inadequate for the academic context.

However modest our contribution may be, Gawande (2007) urges us to write something, to add some small observation about our world to the collective storehouse of wisdom (p. 255). He says,

> Most of all, by offering your reflections to an audience, even a small one, you make yourself part of a larger world. . . . An audience is a community. The published word is a declaration of membership in that community and also of a willingness to contribute something meaningful to it. So choose your audience. Write something. (p. 256)

Posting to the AEA 365 Blog, for example, is a good way for us to share hot tips from the field. There are lots of other informal ways to describe our experiences, and once we get started, we may be encouraged to write more formally as well. A few years ago, the journal *New Directions for Evaluation* produced an issue on independent evaluation consulting (Barrington & Smart, 2006), and a number of independent consultants collaborated in this project. It provided us with an opportunity to conduct research on ourselves, and the result was both professional and informative.

❖   4. GET INVOLVED IN YOUR COMMUNITY

Evaluators complain that they don't have enough time for their personal lives, let alone time to get involved in their community. I would suggest, however, that community involvement is a survival strategy, and there are not one but two communities waiting for your support.

Your professional community is an excellent place to start. Attending conferences and getting to know your colleagues give you a sense of professional identity. Seasoned evaluation consultants value organizations such as the American Evaluation Association and the Canadian Evaluation Society and have described them to me as their community (Barrington, 2006). While it may be difficult to find balance in their busy lives, because they work alone a great deal of the time, they see their professional organizations as "a fabulous networking and learning opportunity" (Barrington, 2006, p. 40), providing them with the contacts and connections they need. They routinely act as mentors for other evaluators, seek out teaching roles, or develop courses and workshops on evaluation topics. For them, to present at a conference is a way to continue their own learning.

The second community is in your own neighborhood. Being on a volunteer board, for example, pays huge dividends. You can work with the recipients of social programs without wearing your research or evaluation hat. You are simply there to help out, and while you are at it, you will gain in several ways.

The first benefit is learning. More than three quarters (79%) of volunteers surveyed by the Canadian Centre for Philanthropy (2004) said that their volunteer activities helped them with their interpersonal skills, including understanding people better, motivating others, and dealing with difficult situations. Over two thirds (68%) said that volunteering helped them to develop better communication skills, and 63% reported increased knowledge about agency-specific issues. The more hours they contributed, the more gains they reported (Canadian Centre for Philanthropy, 2004).

Since I have been an independent consultant, I have served on five different boards (three professional boards, one foundation board, and one community board), and these experiences have taught me many things. Here's a partial list of things I've learned through volunteering.

- Audits and annual reports
- Awards processes
- Budgets and year-end statements
- Crisis management
- Fund-raising campaigns
- Membership issues
- Obtaining charitable status
- Policy governance
- Relations with a national agency
- Site renovations and the sale of a property
- Searching for and hiring a CEO
- Service provision issues
- Staffing issues
- Working with funders, community stakeholders, and politicians

None of these topics relates directly to either my research or my consulting firm, yet all have broadened my understanding about how organizations, particularly nonprofits, interact with their communities.

A second equally important benefit is marketing. Volunteering gives you the opportunity to connect with high-profile individuals in many walks of life. You can learn from their example, gain their friendship, and develop higher visibility yourself. All these things lead to greater credibility and ultimately more contracts.

Take my book club, for example. To be a member of this august group, you had to serve on a certain community board during a particularly challenging decade. Our shared philosophy and collective history have bound us together, and of course we also love to read, so we are never at a loss for conversation. The truth is, though, that I have obtained a number of research projects through my association with these women. Some of these contracts have had significant budgets, and some have spanned several years. This group has become one of my main social outlets, but I also know that when the members think about research, they think about me.

A final benefit to volunteer work is that it adds the sense of satisfaction that is often missing in the work we do. Very often when we finish a project we never hear what happened afterward. Community work provides some continuity, and by helping out in a direct way, we see firsthand the impact that programs can have.

As you begin your consulting career, your energies will be focused on earning money and building your business. Take the time now to reflect on the way you work, to nurture your inner artist, and to unleash the researcher within. Explore what your communities can offer you in terms of skill development and personal connections. Become more self-aware, and be open to the wealth of learning opportunities around you. In doing so, you will find that this is not about survival; it is about the joy of self-fulfillment.

❖ NOTES

1.   Quotations from Donald Schön are Copyright © 1984 Donald A. Schön. Reprinted by permission of Basic Books, a member of the Perseus Books Group.
2.   Quotes taken from the book *Better: A Surgeon's Notes on Performance* by Atul Gawande. Copyright © 2007 by Atul Gawande. Reprinted by permission of Henry Holt and Company, LLC.

❖ USEFUL RESOURCES

- If you want guidance on how to start journal writing or need advice on ways to unblock and enhance your creativity, follow the 12-week program of self-exploration in either of these books:

  Cameron, *The Artist's Way: A Spiritual Path to Higher Creativity* (Tarcher/Perigee, 1992)

  Bryan, Cameron, & Allen, *The Artist's Way at Work: Riding the Dragon* (William Morrow, 1998)

- This book is a favorite with the members of my book club:

  Gawande, *Better: A surgeon's notes on performance* (Metropolitan Books, 2007)

- Check out your readiness to be a volunteer and find more information on volunteer centers in your community:

  In Canada, see http://www.volunteer.ca.

  In the United States, see http://www.serve.gov/ or http://www.volunteermatch.org/.

❖ DISCUSSION QUESTIONS AND ACTIVITIES

1. In the next few conversations you have with random acquaintances, practice asking an unscripted question. Make a mental note of the direction the conversation takes following this question. When you get the opportunity, record your observations. What can you learn from this approach? Did anything surprise you?

2. Journal writing is one way to practice reflexivity. For the next week, practice writing three pages of longhand stream-of-consciousness text as soon as you wake up in the morning. What did you enjoy about this process? What did you find the most difficult?

3. Schön (1983) outlines some of the demands for competence that society places on the expert and provides suggestions for the reflective practitioner's response (p. 300). For example,

Expert:	*I am supposed to know [this topic], and must claim to do so, regardless of my own uncertainty.*
Reflective Practitioner:	*I am supposed to know [this topic], but I am not the only one in the situation to have relevant and important knowledge. My uncertainties may be a source of learning for me and for them.*

   Consider the impact of these different stances on a consultant's interactions with a client. List some of the advantages and disadvantages for each stance, and determine what your own response might be.

❖ REFERENCES

Barrington, G. V. (2006). The evaluation consultant's life cycle: Theory, practice, and implications for learning. *New Directions for Evaluation, 111,* 29–40. doi: 10.1002/ev.194

Barrington, G. V., & Smart, D. H. (Eds.). (2006). Independent evaluation consulting [Special issue]. *New Directions for Evaluation, 111,* 1–113.

Bryan, M., Cameron, J., & Allen, C. (1998). *The artist's way at work: Riding the dragon.* New York, NY: William Morrow.

Cameron, J. (1992). *The artist's way: A spiritual path to higher creativity.* New York, NY: Tarcher/Perigee.

Canadian Centre for Philanthropy. (2004). The benefits of volunteering. *2000 national survey of giving, volunteering and participating (NSGVP).* Retrieved from http://www.givingandvolunteering.ca/files/giving/en/factsheets/benefits_of_volunteering.pdf

Gawande, A. (2007). *Better: A surgeon's notes on performance.* New York, NY: Metropolitan Books.

King, J. A., Stevahn, L., Ghere, G., & Minnema, J. (2001). Toward a taxonomy of essential evaluator competencies. *American Journal of Evaluation, 22,* 229–247. doi: 10.1177/109821400102200206

McDavid, J. C., & Hawthorne, L. R. L. (2006). *Program evaluation & performance measurement: An introduction to practice.* Thousand Oaks, CA: Sage.

Patton, M. Q. (2008). *Utilization-focused evaluation* (4th ed.). Thousand Oaks, CA: Sage.

Schön, D. A. (1983). *The reflective practitioner: How professionals think in action.* New York, NY: Basic Books.

PART II

Entrepreneurial Skills

"Just tell me about marketing," people say to me. "I'll worry about the rest of it later. Once I get a contract, everything will fall into place." Well, the truth is that if you are lucky enough to land a contract without any preplanning, things won't fall into place, because you will be too busy working on your research project and won't have any time to think about your business. Bergholz and Nickols (2000) suggest that managing a small business is the skill set that is the weakest for most would-be consultants. Many of those who fail do not have an orientation toward running a successful (i.e., profitable) small business.

Here is the big conundrum. If you focus too much on your research, your business will suffer from lack of attention, and you may soon be out of business altogether. On the other hand, if you spend too much time on business management and not enough on your research portfolio, your skills and experience will become obsolete, and you will run out of clients. Obviously, a fine balance is required between research and small business management.

Part II is about the critical entrepreneurial skills you need to start your business. We will look at some basic decisions about where to work and what to call your business and how to develop and use your business plan. To make this plan, you need to set your fees and learn to manage and track your time. Then the rest of Part II takes a serious and detailed look at finding work. We will examine some of the many informal marketing strategies available and will then look at writing proposals, both the informal letter proposal and the formal response to a Request for Proposals (RFP). You will discover why it is important to use any down time you have in the early days of your business to set up your office systems. Then when you get busy, your business will roll along like a well-oiled machine, and it will keep on rolling for many years to come.

6

Getting Started

Highlights:

- Consider the pros and cons of having a home office.

- Review possible location options available in the community.

- Understand what to ask for when negotiating an office lease.

- Have fun selecting inexpensive office furniture and equipment.

- Explore the art and science of selecting your business name.

You may have done consulting "on the side" and now feel ready to take it on full time, or this alternative may have been thrust upon you by employment circumstances. Whatever the reason, setting up your own consulting practice now seems like a good career choice. Even if you don't recognize it yet, you have an entrepreneurial streak that will grow exponentially along with your experience, so let's try to get your business up and running. In this chapter we will look at making some preliminary decisions about where you will work and what you will call your firm.

❖ LOCATION

You have heard it many times: "Location, location, location!" This is certainly true for your business as well as your home, so take the time to make an informed choice. Visualize yourself in your future office setting. You can work at home, or you can work in the outside world where a variety of options await you. Your decision will depend on both your personal and your economic situation. Remember that as your business circumstances change, you may need to change your office as well, so make your plans with some flexibility in mind.

The Home Office

Many consultants start their businesses at home, especially if they are consulting on a part-time basis, but it is a good idea to review the pros and cons before committing to this choice. Locating your office at home has several advantages.

The most important benefit is that this is the most economical option. You can save on the cost of going to work. Say good-bye to expenses such as gas, parking, other transportation costs, and the time expended commuting to work. You can save on your business wardrobe too, because although you will need some appropriate, high-quality clothes to attend client meetings, you can work in your jeans for the rest of the week. You can save on lunch costs and the incidental expenses associated with lunch hour shopping. You can save on child care or elder care, as long as you can coordinate your business needs with those of the rest of your family. You can increase your tax benefits by writing off a proportionate amount of your rent, heat, power, and water costs using the area of your office compared to the overall floor space of your home. However, be careful of the lure of tax write-offs. Your write-offs may not exceed your total business income. You need to generate enough business income to be able to deduct your operating expenses from that total.

The second advantage of a home office is personal flexibility. You can set your work hours to integrate with family needs. For example, if you have school-aged children, you can work while they are at school and do your parenting when they come home. Or you can work at night and sleep during the day. Your pets can keep you company. I love the fact that my cat saunters by and offers unsolicited advice. My dog sleeps under my desk. He even takes me for walks at noon and I often come back with a new idea for the afternoon's work.

A third advantage is that it is easy to work from home, or from anywhere else for that matter, thanks to enhanced connectivity. The Internet, Skype, e-mail, smartphones, social networks, blogs, twitter, and other recent technology and software let you stay in touch, do your research, and present a professional image. I work with clients I never meet in person, teach graduate students I only see at graduation, and keep in touch with colleagues I only socialize with once a year. The world of work has changed so much in the past few years, and no one benefits more than the independent consultant.

Still, there are some disadvantages to working at home. Not surprisingly, the biggest is the potential impact on you and your family. Can you separate your personal or family lifestyle patterns from your work life? Are either you or they going to be distracted by your working at home? Will demands on your time actually increase as you are perceived to be more available for household tasks? Will family members resent your mental inattention? Will you turn into a workaholic because the work is always there? Will weekends lose their magic?

According to McConnon (2008), "The support of family members is extremely important to the success of your business." He stresses,

> It is essential that each member of the family be given the chance to share his or her thoughts and feelings about starting a business in their home. Family members need to be kept informed of plans likely to affect the family. Take time to establish an atmosphere of open communications within the family to help generate trust and support, which will help you grow your own business.[1]

On the plus side, operating your business at home may well encourage you to set priorities, develop good time management skills, and limit your office hours to specific times of the day and week. In order to meet the challenges you face in a home-based office, you may find that your self-discipline is strengthened and your overall productivity enhanced.

Another possible disadvantage to working at home is your business image. While your business address may seem like a small thing, it can be very important. A residential address may connote a hobby job, a perception you definitely do not want to promote. Nor is it wise, for reasons of privacy and security, to make your home address widely known. An obvious solution may be to obtain a post office box, but according to Gray (2008, p. 19), a longtime expert on starting and running a consulting business, this can have a negative impact on business credibility and reliability. I must say, though, that since I moved my office home and opened a post box at my local shopping mall, I have not noticed any negative impact apart from the need to provide a street address from time to time for courier deliveries.

Another drawback to the home office is the lack of good meeting space. Somehow your dining room table or patio may not project the business image you need. I find that most of my meetings occur at my client's offices, but it is also possible to meet them in a restaurant, coffee shop, or another public location. When you need a larger space, you can rent a board room at a local hotel or at your chamber of commerce.

Other considerations for the home office relate to infrastructure requirements, and these may come as a surprise to you, especially if you are used to working in a professional office. It is not just a question of plugging in your computer and going to work. According to Ward (2008), commercial space is designed for better quality electrical support than most residences. Especially if your home is older, the circuitry may be eccentric or oversubscribed. Even a small laser printer consumes 300 to 400 watts of electricity, and plugging in a kettle at the same time may blow the lights. No matter how minimal, your office power needs will increase your overall use of electricity. You will need to protect your equipment from power outages or surges. I lost one telephone system due to a bad electrical storm. My server was destroyed when construction workers accidentally dug into neighborhood power cables. A good backup system is a necessity.

We tend to ignore lighting and ventilation issues, but few homes are designed for fluorescent lighting. You may need to install more lights in your office to ward off eyestrain, headaches, or neck and shoulder pain. Your office equipment also generates heat, and this can damage PCs or servers. If your office is in a small room, it can become a "hot box," and you may need to install fans or an air-conditioning unit.

It is a good idea to consult with an electrician about these types of infrastructure needs as you set up your home office, because in the long run it will probably save you money.

Eventually, as time goes by and your business expands, you may find that you don't have enough room to work. Indeed, it may be at this point that you decide to move away from home. Some of the advantages of an office outside the home include more credibility, more self-esteem, and more space. Of course, there are also more costs. Once you decide to move out, there are several location options to consider ranging from less expensive to more expensive. Over the years, I have tried most of them myself.

The Client's Office

While this is a temporary solution at best, working from a client's office may tide you over in the short term. It allows you to be close to the action and the key players associated with your research project. You can use some of your client's infrastructure, as long as you can demonstrate that you are not acting like an employee. This distinction is important for tax purposes, so check with your local tax department about the differences between an independent contractor and an employee before selecting this option. (See Chapter 15.) Be aware that your presence may cause resentment among staff. On the other hand, your familiarity may cause them to think of you as just another staff member. If that happens, you will have to choose: become an employee or move on.

The Sublease

Sometimes, small firms rent too much space and are happy to sublet some of it to you. This arrangement is usually a good temporary solution. You sign a sublease agreement that sets out your rent, the duration of the agreement, and any arrangements to cost-share services such as reception or the use of certain equipment. The main benefit is that your sense of professionalism is enhanced by the business environment. One drawback is that you may find yourself isolated, as you are not part of the regular staff in this office. One of my colleagues who tried this option found that when clients came to call, they were confused because her company's name was not on the door. A sublease arrangement may seem temporary or unstable, and this is not good for your business image. Further, you are at the mercy of your landlords' business plans, and should they decide to merge, move, or fold, your office space will be collateral damage.

Shared Space

Another low-cost office arrangement is to share space with other professionals or business tenants who pool rent and reception expenses and prorate other costs based on use. The advantages provided by this arrangement are opportunities for networking, collaborating, and marketing. The moral support provided by other new entrepreneurs is also an important feature. The main disadvantage is that you are relying on the goodwill, positive chemistry, and success of the other tenants in your space to keep the office afloat.

The Small Business Incubator

Many cities have small business incubators sponsored by the local chamber of commerce, a university, or other business agency. For example, in collaboration with the private sector, the educational community, and various levels of government, the U.S. Small Business Administration offers many types of assistance to small business owners through their Small Business Development Centers. This option addresses many start-up issues. Business incubators often provide a graduated list of services that can be tailored to your stage of business development. You can begin with a professional identity package that includes a mail drop or street address and a telephone answering service. Then as your business grows, you can use their equipment (photocopier, fax machine, mail meter), facilities (reception room, board room), and services (secretarial, bookkeeping, and desktop publishing). Finally, if you want to move in, they generally offer short-term individual office leasing arrangements, and you can even rent furniture. The beauty of this approach is that the incubator's business is serving you, the small business client, and this tends to validate your role as an entrepreneur.

Gray (2008, p. 20) recommends this option, and my own experience in two different incubators supports it as well. For five years I rented space in a business incubator with a month-to-month rental agreement. During that time I moved in and out of three or four offices in the building based on my project mix and related staffing needs. Then I moved to a high-tech business incubator that was located close to my home and to my son's school and stayed there for another five years. I had an annual lease there, but again, was able to move within the building as my business needs grew. While sometimes it seemed that my office was on wheels, my moves reflected the natural growth and retrenchment process of a project-based business model. These incubators gave me the flexibility I needed. Many useful business relationships were also forged during that period.

Leased Space

It is the "big time" when you sign a commercial lease, because the commitment is typically for three to five years. You need to know you will have the revenue to cover this ongoing financial commitment. It is important to consult with an accountant and a lawyer before you sign anything. It may also be worthwhile to hire an experienced commercial realtor to help you negotiate your lease. As Gray (2008, pp. 21–22) comments, all leases are negotiable—you just need to know what to ask for. In particular, he suggests that you attempt to negotiate the following concessions:

- Obtaining a one-year lease with two additional one-year options. This minimizes your risk in case you have to move out for any reason.
- Offering a security deposit of the last two or three months' rent. Then if you default and leave before the end of the term, you are freed of further liability. Try to negotiate interest at a fixed rate on any security deposit.
- Ensuring that any alterations or improvements to the space that you require are done at the landlord's expense. If this is not possible, try to recoup a portion of the improvement costs from the landlord—after all, you are improving the space not only for yourself but for other tenants who may follow you.
- Obtaining the first few months' rent free as an incentive to sign the lease.

Gray also cautions that you should watch for restrictive clauses in a proposed lease such as the following:

- Restricting your ability to sublet or assign your lease
- Limiting your ability to make alterations or improvements

- Defining the liabilities and duties of the landlord and tenant in ways that could be more restrictive than current commercial real estate law in your area
- Accelerating payment if you default on your rent
- Requiring a personal guarantee even if you are doing business as a corporation

It is important to know that the rent is much less straightforward than it appears, and it may be difficult to budget for more than a year in advance. Some leases are "net" or all-in, but many are "double net" or "triple net." This means that there is a base rent that relates to your square footage, but the operating costs that are covered by the landlord are passed on to the tenants on a proportionate basis. You may be asked to cover part of the costs of the common areas such as the parking garage, elevators, and hallways. You must share the landlord's other costs such as taxes, insurance, maintenance, repairs, security, improvements, and management and administration fees. Even the landlord can't predict taxes in future years, so any tax increases can result in additional unexpected overhead for you. Changes in commercial real estate regulations or zoning during your tenure can also affect your bottom line. The economy in your area has a significant effect on the availability of office space and going rates. You need to be conscious of the point in the economic cycle at which you enter the market, because it will have a significant impact on your ability to negotiate a favorable lease.

This whole discussion may be way out of your comfort zone. Someday, however, you may realize that leasing space is just what you need to do next. When I leased office space, I was managing some large multiyear federal projects, had a staff of 20, and was billing more than CAN$1,000,000 annually in revenues. The more informal arrangement and limited space at the office incubator could no longer meet our needs, and it was time to move on. I leased space close to downtown for nearly six years. Eventually even those needs changed, this time in a negative way. Many of my long-term contracts wound down, and the government contracting environment no longer favored smaller firms like mine. I had to downsize. Fortunately I found an insurance company that wanted to take over my space and I was able to end my lease. I finally moved into my home office and find that it fits my current business and personal needs very well.

Your clients' perception of the stability and quality of your business is really important to your business image and to your likelihood of winning contracts. As a result, think carefully about these location decisions. For example, while locating your office in an industrial area, near the airport, or over a restaurant may have its advantages from a cost perspective, the location may not portray a professional image. Do you have easy access to services such as your bank, post office, courier depot, and office supply store? If you don't have a board room, is there one you can access nearby?

Frequent address changes can have a negative impact on your business contacts and relationships. While my own story is one of many office relocations, I minimized address changes to about once every five years. Even so, despite notifications, change of address forms, and letters explaining reasons for relocation, clients continued to be confused about where to find me. Their databases are seldom up to date, and they tend to rely on word of mouth. I found that maintaining a consistent e-mail address was helpful, as was my website. I would encourage you to change your location as your business needs dictate but always be aware of the impact that relocation has on your image and accessibility.

Furniture and Equipment

One of the fun parts of setting up shop is selecting your furniture and equipment. I don't mean to suggest that you should buy a lot of expensive oak furniture, as one of my incubator neighbors did. Sadly, he was out of business two months later. Rather, if you find that clients rarely come to your premises, do what I did, and develop a bargain basement approach to decorating. All kinds of office furniture are available at auctions, government surplus sales, secondhand stores, and going-out-of-business sales. You can create a warm and pleasant work environment even on a shoestring.

Office equipment is cheaper than ever. You can get a printer, photocopier, scanner, and fax all rolled into one small, economical machine. Internet and telephone are often combined, and long distance charges in North America can be free if you shop around. Skype is also free for your international calls. My mini notebook computer weighs under three pounds, but it has far more power than my first PC. Every youth you see is hooked into texting, Internet, Facebook, twitter, and a host of other services, and you should be as well. Your client expects instant feedback, and these days it is easy to oblige.

❖   YOUR BUSINESS NAME

Developing your business name is both a science and an art. You need to register your business name so that you can complete any required government forms, applications, licenses, or permits or to obtain an employer tax identification number if you plan to hire staff. In many states you can operate your business under your own personal name, so, for example, Mary Smith can operate a business called "Mary Smith," but as this is likely to be confusing, she will probably want to register her business name as "Mary Smith Consulting." This is known variously as a *trade name*, a *doing business as* (DBA) name, or a *fictitious name*, depending on where you live. Typically, you register this business name with the county clerk's office (United States), state government agency (United States), or corporate registry office (Canada).

At the same time, you want to project a certain image, so if your business card reads "Mary Smith, PhD, Applied Research Analyst," the use of your own name implies that you are a one-person service. Clients may wonder if you have the capacity to complete a project on your own. They may worry about what would happen if you became incapacitated. To counteract this problem, consultants often add "and Associates" to their name, implying that there is a whole group of consultants out there that can be called upon as needed. The business name becomes "Mary Smith & Associates."

While it is important to describe your services, you don't want to be too restrictive, especially when you are starting out. You may be unsure of the market direction that will be the most successful for you, so while it may be informative to identify a specific sector, such as education, this can be problematic if funding for educational research dries up. Research is difficult to describe, and so some business cards present a list of choices such as "Consultants in Education, Research & Planning, Program Evaluation, and Policy Analysis." This can work against the specialist image you may be trying to project. In my experience, the words *program evaluation* are often misinterpreted. When my card and telephone directory advertisement read, "Program Planning and Evaluation," I used to get calls to evaluate everything from real estate to used cars.

Eventually Mary Smith may want to hire a staff member. This individual may not feel comfortable saying, "Hi, I'm Ted Jones from Mary Smith & Associates." Clients may wonder if they are dealing with a second stringer and may want Mary instead. To create a more inclusive business name, do some brainstorming. Try out your tentative choice with long-suffering clients, friends, family, and colleagues before you finalize it in print.

Some things to consider when choosing a business name (Ward, 2010, pp. 1–2) include the following:

1. It should be memorable but easy to spell.

2. It should have a visual or metaphoric element.

3. It should have positive connotations.

4. It should provide some indication of the service you provide.

5. It should be short, memorable, fit on a business card, and look good online.[2]

When you go to register your business name, have a second option in mind in case your first choice has already been taken by someone else.

Just like decorating your office, you need to think about signature business colors. Read up on color theory, or get help from a graphic artist or an art student. Students often have assignments to design a business logo; it might as well be yours. Germuth (2009), an independent consultant and program evaluator, suggests that you should go one step farther and brand yourself so that you convey your business personality and what you stand for in everything you do. Good branding builds prospective clients' confidence in your ability to deliver. Some of the things you can brand include the following (Brand Strategy, 2010):

- Your proposals, marketing literature, and report covers
- Your e-mails, website, business cards, and stationery
- The way you answer your phone, the way you respond to voice mail, and the messages you leave
- Your customer service policy and the way you treat your clients
- Your day-to-day interactions with your market and the business community

Start small, try out some of your ideas in the field, and see what kind of response you get. As your confidence grows, and as you receive feedback from your clients, you can enhance or reposition your branding strategy accordingly.

Having thought about these start-up decisions, you should be getting excited about the possibilities ahead. You can see yourself in your future office environment, and you have a business name that works for you, so it is time to attend to the many other critical activities needed to get you up and running.

❖ NOTES

1.   Reproduced with permission. James McConnon, "Starting a Business in Your Home: Weighing the Pros and Cons." Bulletin #4190 (Orono: University of Maine Cooperative Extension, 2000). You can find an HTML version of the bulletin at http://extension.umaine.edu/publications/4190e/

2.   © 2011 Susan Ward (http://sbinfocanada.about.com). Used with permission of About, Inc. which can be found online at www.about.com. All rights reserved.

❖ USEFUL RESOURCES

- The U.S. Small Business Administration provides lots of information about starting a business. Check out the following resource: http://www.sba.gov/category/navigation-structure/starting-managing-business/starting-business/thinking-about-starting
- Get inspired and look at ways to decorate your home office: http://www.hgtv.com/topics/home-office/index.html
- Look into registering your business name:

  In the United States: http://www.sba.gov/content/register-your-fictitious-or-doing-business-dba-name

  In Canada: http://www.canadabusiness.ca/eng/guide/1280/

❖ DISCUSSION QUESTIONS AND ACTIVITIES

1.   Select the home office and one other office location discussed in this chapter and prepare a list of pros and cons for each. Consider their feasibility based on your current situation.

Which option is more appropriate for you? What do you need to do to make it a reality?

2. Remember that small is beautiful, so think secondhand. Make a list of the furnishings and equipment you need, and search online for bargains available near you. Attend a going-out-of-business sale or auction. Are you surprised at what is available?

3. Brainstorm possible business names for your consulting firm. Rate them using the criteria suggested by Ward (2010). Test your top three names with some colleagues and friends, and then search online to see if these names exist elsewhere. See if you have a winner; if not, go back to the drawing board.

❖ REFERENCES

Bergholz, H., & Nickols, F. (2000). The independent consultant as "equilateralist." *Consulting to Management, 11*(2), 26–27.

Brand Strategy. (2010). *Marketing M.O. Process, tips and strategy for business marketers*. Retrieved from http://www.marketingmo.com/strategic-planning/brand-strategy/

Germuth, A. A. (2009, November). *Becoming a consultant: Key questions to consider*. Paper presented at Evaluation 2009, the annual conference of the American Evaluation Association, Orlando, FL.

Gray, D. (2008). *Start & run a consulting business* (8th ed.). Bellingham, WA: Self-Counsel Press.

McConnon, J. (2008). *Starting a business in your home: Weighing the pros and cons* [Fact sheet]. Retrieved from http://www.umext.maine.edu/onlinepubs/htmpubs/4190.htm

Ward, S. (2008). *The basics of small or home office design*. Retrieved from http://sbinfocanada.about.com/cs/homebusiness/a/officedesign.htm

Ward, S. (2010). *5 Rules for choosing a business name: How to create a winning business name*. Retrieved from http://sbinfocanada.about.com/od/startup/a/createbizname.htm

7

Your Business Plan

Highlights:

- Consider the reasons why a clear business plan is essential.

- Explore the 10 topics you need in your business plan.

- Identify some useful resources to help you get started.

As a researcher, you already know about the importance of design. In a way, completing a business plan is similar to preparing an application for an institutional review board. You are forced to consider all the objectives, activities, and resources required to do a good job before you know how the project will unfold. Some people think that they need to write a business plan only when they are applying for a loan. Actually it is much more important than that, because the process of preparing your plan allows you to crystallize your thoughts around your proposed venture and to test the viability of your idea. The surprising news is that preparing your business plan is a lot of fun, because it's all about you. Don't skimp on the time and attention needed to prepare it. Never let someone else do it for you.

Writing your business plan is a process of self-examination and development. You will probe your dreams and desires to determine how they can be realized. At the same time, you will also be preparing a financial plan, a marketing tool, and an accountability framework. You are creating the first product that shows your managerial skills to the world. As independent evaluator Kathryn Bowen (2005) commented, "The Business Plan is the blueprint for your business and the single most important thing you will do in establishing your business on a sound footing." The likelihood and speed with which you will achieve your objectives will increase dramatically if, as she suggests, "you have a well-thought out plan and execute it flawlessly."

There are so many resources available to help with this process. You just need to find the ones that work for you. Check your chamber of commerce, the small business development centers or continuing education departments at your local university or community college, the U.S. Small Business Administration offices, associations of retired business executives, women's business centers, and minority business associations. It seems like everyone wants to help the small business person succeed, so don't be afraid to ask for advice.

Take a personal retreat for a long weekend and begin to outline your business plan. Create your vision statement, and define the purpose and values of your organization. Develop your mission statement, and identify your primary objectives. Think about the values that you hold most dear. These statements will inspire and motivate you and will remind you on a daily basis about why you are creating your own future. Identify the type of business you want to run, and decide how you will go about achieving your goals. Develop a template for your plan, and then over the next few weeks fill in the gaps by doing the additional thought, footwork, and research required. Developing your business plan should take approximately two months if you dedicate about 10 hours a week to it. However, if you find your energy flagging, it may be because you have some reservations about this career path. If so, explore them now.

Package your plan as you would any proposal. After all, it is a proposal to the world at large. Don Martin, a small business counselor and trainer, suggests that your business plan should be between 6 and 12 pages in length, excluding appendices (Johnson, 2009). About half of it should focus on your marketing plans. (See Chapter 10.)

Like any proposal, the final product reflects a lot of effort but is represented in as few words as possible. Soon you will be taking it to meetings with your banker, insurance agent, lawyer, and accountant. You will be quoting it in your proposals. You will be discussing it with prospective clients who in turn will be pleased to know that you mean business.

Here are 10 topics you need to cover in your business plan. This chapter provides an overview, but some of these topics are covered in more detail in later chapters in this book.

❖ 1. TITLE PAGE, TABLE OF CONTENTS, AND EXECUTIVE SUMMARY

Like a research proposal, your presentation style will be crisp and businesslike. Your title page should include your name and that of your company, your contact information (address, phone and fax numbers, e-mail address, and website if you have one), and the purpose of the document. If you have developed a logo or a marketing tag line, put them here as well. As with any final report, the executive summary will be written last but is presented first. Martin suggests that this one-page summary should show your passion for this enterprise, the uniqueness of your product, the identification of your target market, and the key points of your financial plan (Johnson, 2009).

❖ 2. INDUSTRY OVERVIEW

Briefly define the consulting industry, and summarize the national and local trends for this sector. Provide its economic outlook. You can review Chapter 1 of this book to get an idea about some of this information, but update it, and add information that is particularly relevant for your field of expertise and geographic area. Indicate where your business fits into the consulting landscape, and identify your market niche (e.g., a boutique consulting firm offering senior expertise in program evaluation and performance measurement for the health care sector). Highlight your specialties and indicate what differentiates your business from others in the marketplace. (See Chapter 10.)

❖ 3. YOUR BUSINESS VENTURE

Describe the nature of your consulting services and the types of clients you anticipate serving. Include your vision statement, your mission, your values, and a brief overview of your goals and plans (Bowen, 2005). Be very specific so that potential clients can understand what it is that you are offering. You should also add a paragraph about your background, expertise, relevant experience, and unique skills. In addition, provide a two-page résumé in an appendix.

❖ 4. MARKET ANALYSIS

Scan the current research environment, and identify your target market. To gain the information you need, interview five to seven potential clients in your general geographic area who contract for the types of services you want to offer. How are they currently meeting their research needs? Are they satisfied? Are there any gaps that you can fill? Do they know of anyone else who might require your services?

You may find that your competition is not as strong as you thought. For example, university professors offer applied research and evaluation services but are limited in terms of available time by university requirements. Psychologists conduct standardized tests but seldom get involved in organizational development. Market research firms conduct opinion polling but don't take on longer-term projects. Management consulting firms study performance measurement but tend to rely on popular business tools. Your market intelligence will help you determine if you have a competitive advantage or if you need to focus your services more clearly to find your niche. With increasing demands for accountability and organizational effectiveness, there may be a lot of room for your services if you can identify areas of need.

❖ 5. MARKETING PLAN

Your business plan needs some realistic, growth-oriented marketing objectives. Provide a list of the organizations you have identified that can use your services, and indicate, if possible, how they are similar to clients you have worked with in the past or projects you have already conducted. Indicate how you will price your services. (See Chapter 8.) Outline your marketing strategy by month, quarter, and year. For example, your promotional plans for the next month might include the following:

- Contact four decision makers (specify organizations) for information interviews.
- Take two colleagues (specify names) to lunch to explore joint business opportunities.
- Take a seminar on (specify topic and course) provided by (name provider).
- Join the local chapter of a specified professional organization.
- Submit one abstract for a presentation at an upcoming conference, or arrange to be an invited speaker for a local group.
- Evaluate the effectiveness of these plans using a rating scale to indicate their relative success, and track feedback and potential marketing leads. Plan to make course corrections in the following month based on this analysis.

You can prepare a sales forecast for each month and each quarter in the first year. Include the number of expected projects and their projected dollar value. Of course, as you are just starting out, this is difficult to do, but your information interviews should give you a sense of some likely prospects. Sometimes these turn into projects very quickly. As each month goes by and as more information becomes available, you need to update your plan. If you find that you have nothing new to add at the end of a month, ask yourself, "Why not?" Are you serious about this enterprise? If so, follow through. Planning is not enough.

Provide a thumbnail marketing plan for Years 2 and 3 to track, in more general terms, your targeted organizations and sectors. Each year, the projected value of new sales plus the income for work already contracted has to support your ongoing business activities, including marketing, and leave you with at least a small profit. If the money coming in and the money going out do not, at a minimum, balance, you will be out of business very soon. What is remarkable, though, is that when you have a clear goal, such as "I need to gain $3,000 in new contracts by the end of the month," and you do everything you can to make it happen, it usually happens.

When I registered my business, it was November 1, 1985. I had a grace period of two months left in the calendar year, and so I called it Year 0 and focused on start-up and marketing activities. I rented an office in a small business incubator and furnished it (with furniture from my basement), put an announcement in the business section of the local newspaper, created a brochure and printed business cards, planned a letter-writing campaign, joined a professional society, had several networking lunches, searched for potential associates, and attended seminars on small business management. Meanwhile I continued to work on my one ongoing research contract.

As Year 1 got under way, I sent out my brochure and targeted letters to key contacts, attended networking activities, was a guest lecturer at the university, submitted a paper to a professional conference, joined the chamber of commerce, and was nominated to a volunteer board of directors. I pursued potential projects by conducting information interviews with my project's steering committee members and expanded the design of my current project.

By the end of that year, I had prepared seven proposals and had won one of them, obtained three small projects through informal means, and had published three articles. Overall I had spent 15% of my time on marketing activities. My total contract revenue was CAN$33,137 in 1986 dollars, which is approximately CAN$65,530 in 2010 terms (Gail V. Barrington & Associates, 1991). It was not a stellar year, but it was a beginning. I was encouraged enough to keep going. Keeping track of my successes and failures allowed me to see where my energy was best spent. I had learned some important marketing lessons and began to refine my approach.

❖   6. MANAGEMENT PLAN

This section of your business plan demonstrates that you have set up systems to ensure that good management is part of the way you do business. Lenders always look at management ability, so this will add to your credibility even if you are not yet thinking about a line of credit or a bank loan. (See Chapter 12.) If you have registered your business name or obtained any licenses or other legal documents required to operate in your area, list them here and attach copies as an appendix. You need to describe your ownership structure. (See Chapter 13.) List the owners, officers, and corporate directors. Any related documentation, such as partnership agreements, articles of incorporation, shareholder agreements, management contracts, service contracts, or leases should be appended.

Describe your management approach, and provide a quick sketch of your management capabilities. Even if you have never run a business before, you probably have a lot of managerial experience already. You may have managed research projects with significant budgets and several staff members, or you may have managed a department in a large organization, or you may have worked as a volunteer, managing a fund-raising campaign. What you need to do is demonstrate that you know how to manage both money and people.

If you plan to have some external guidance, such as an advisory group, a business mentor, or a coach, identify your guides and explain their role in your management process. If you plan to use contract services for bookkeeping, data entry, or other routine needs, indicate that here. Generally, you are demonstrating that you have given your work processes some serious thought and are ready to leap into action.

❖ 7. OPERATING PLAN

Outline your plans for the next three years. Bowen (2005) suggests that you provide a brief physical description of your building and office site, as this can be useful for insurance purposes and demonstrates that you have thought about security and other issues associated with managing risk (see Chapter 14). If you need to do any renovations or improvements to your office space, describe them briefly here. Indicate what equipment you need to purchase.

If you plan to hire staff or contractors, indicate their roles and where they will be located. Will they be working in your office or from their homes? Describe how you plan to hire and manage them (see Chapter 16). Of course you may not know your staffing needs yet, but give it some thought, and project when you may need a student, research assistant, administrative assistant, research associate, or statistician if your upcoming marketing plans come to fruition.

To highlight major business development events, consider presenting a flow chart or Gantt chart by month or quarter. Identify checkpoints where you will be reviewing your progress and making course corrections.

❖ 8. FINANCIAL PLAN

Your banker will immediately turn to this section, so make sure you have thought it through carefully. The information you present here is an essential guide to the survival and profitability of your firm. Gray (2008) suggests that although this section should be brief, it represents a lot of background work on your part. As the forecasts you present here are based on current assumptions and the information you have now, you will constantly be revisiting and reworking them as time goes by. You may work with an accountant to get your statements set up, although many accounting software packages are easy to use. What is important is that you must be willing to commit the time needed to understand and know in detail what your financial statements contain. (See Chapter 12.) Because it is your money, you will find that the whole topic of finance suddenly becomes a lot more interesting, but I strongly suggest that you take a course on small business accounting to give yourself a head start on this critical aspect of your business.

You should include the following statements in your business plan:

- Capital cost estimates (any costs related to facilities, materials, and equipment)
- An opening balance sheet (current assets and liabilities as well as owner's equity)
- A forecast of income and expenses or a profit and loss statement (the revenue and expenses you expect for the first year of operation)
- A cash flow forecast (shows the flow of money in and out on a monthly basis and identifies when cash shortages may occur)
- A break-even analysis (at what sales volume your business will break even)

Once you have completed these statements, you will be in a position to see what your sources of funding are and when the money will become available. This may help you decide if you need to apply for a line of credit or a loan.

❖ 9. REFERENCES

You need to identify your key business advisors. These include the following:

- Your bank and account manager, to help you navigate and manage your cash flow
- Your accountant, to prepare your financial year-end statements for tax purposes
- Your lawyer or attorney, to review your contracts and help you with incorporation when the time comes

In order to include their names in your business plan, you need to find them first. Shop around and ask your colleagues for suggestions, or work through small business agencies, as they probably have lists of resources. Once you have some names (at least three per category), conduct your information interviews. Look for individuals who understand small business and who take the time to show an interest in your plans. You will probably have to explain your research services, so the clear description in your business plan will come in handy. Remember that you are the consumer, and keep looking until you find advisors that you will be comfortable working with.

❖ 10. APPENDICES

Finally, append any other useful documents such as your two-page résumé, a recent business photo, pertinent legal agreements, and other support materials that enhance your credibility.

Preparing your business plan is a lot of work, but by the time it is complete, you will already see yourself as an entrepreneur. The plan will clearly outline the kind of business you plan to run. Its content will demonstrate the care with which you will handle all the work that comes your way. Be proud of your accomplishment.

However, preparing your business plan is not an end in itself. Instead it is the beginning of your ongoing business planning cycle.

Spend three to four hours a month updating your plan, measuring your progress, and correcting your course. This will save you considerable time and money in the long run, and, as Gray (2008) suggests, it may save your business altogether. He says, "It is essential to develop a habit of planning and reassessment on an ongoing basis as an integral part of your management style" (2008, p. 54). Lack of planning is often cited as one of the top reasons for small business failure. Make sure it isn't yours.

❖ USEFUL RESOURCES

- For quick references to developing your business plan, see the following:

  See the U.S. Small Business Administration's business plan outline at http://www.smallbusinessnotes.com/starting-a-business/small-business-administration-sba-business-plan-outline.html or at http://www.sba.gov/content/templates-writing-business-plan.

  In Canada, see http://sbinfocanada.about.com/od/businessplans/Business_Plans.htm

  Webinars are available on developing your business plan at http://www.youtube.com/watch?v=tEL_17klIY8.

- Strategic planning materials to help you develop your mission, vision, and values statements are available at http://www.mindtools.com/pages/article/newLDR_90.htm and http://managementhelp.org/plan_dec/str_plan/stmnts.htm.

❖ DISCUSSION QUESTIONS AND ACTIVITIES

1. Recall your life experience to date in areas where you were able to manage people and/or money. Describe those experiences, and identify the management skills you gained that would be useful in running your own business.

2. A critical part of your business plan is the description of your business venture. Prepare a one-page description of your proposed consulting services and the types of clients you anticipate serving. What background research was needed to prepare this description?

3. Your market analysis is essential to define your consulting landscape. Conduct three information interviews with potential users of the consulting services you might offer. Determine how they are currently meeting their research needs. Develop a list of key players and potential competitors based on the market intelligence you gather. Are there any gaps in service that you might fill?

❖ REFERENCES

Barrington Research Group, Inc. (2010, April 4). *Mission statement*. Retrieved from http://www.barringtonresearchgrp.com

Bowen, K. (2005, October). *Developing a business plan*. Presentation delivered as part of Intermediate Consulting Skills: A Self-Help Fair, a think tank session conducted at the joint conference of the Canadian Evaluation Society and the American Evaluation Association, Toronto, ON.

Gail V. Barrington & Associates. (1991). *Three-year plan* [2nd version]. Calgary, AB: Author.

Gray, D. (2008). *Start & run a consulting business* (8th ed.). Bellingham, WA: Self-Counsel Press.

Johnson, R. (Producer). (2009, May 18). *Small Business Administration, Small Business Training Network: Interview with Don Martin*. [Podcast transcript]. Retrieved from http://www.sba.gov/index.html

8

Setting Your Fees

Highlights:

- Determine what information you need to calculate your fees.

- Calculate your start-up and monthly business costs.

- Determine your salary and profit levels.

- Calculate your daily rate.

- Review a variety of price-setting methods, and determine which ones fit for you.

We feel uncomfortable talking about money, yet small business failure rates are high, and money, or the lack of it, is generally a root cause. So let's get the topic of money out on the table right away. You need to make enough money to stay in business, because only then can you continue to do what you love. This chapter looks at setting your fees.

To be an independent consultant, you need to understand the very direct relationship between work and money. You need to be able to ask for money, manage it, and spend it, and in doing so you will see that you have become part of the huge, invisible machine that drives our economy.

❖ CALCULATING YOUR FEES

When you set up your business, you will find that there are many business expenses that are not covered by your research contracts. Clients will only pay for the tasks required. Most of the behind-the-scenes costs are left up to you. Thus the first key question related to setting fees is, "What can I charge for?" Coming on its heels is the second question, "How much can I charge?"

The answers are not straightforward. They are hidden within two important calculations. First, you need to determine how much time you actually have in a year to work on clients' projects. This is called billable time. Then you need to figure out how much it costs to run your business for a year. This is referred to as overhead. Once you have these two important calculations in hand, and have determined a couple of other important variables, namely salary and profit, you can figure out your daily fee.

Billable Time

Kubr (2002) provides a good way to determine the number of hours available in a year for billable time. Just because there are 365 days in a year, don't assume that you can do client work on all of them. As my management consultant colleague, Ken Philip, commented (1994), the reality is "that there are a large number of non-revenue producing activities which must continually be completed before one hour of time can be devoted to fee-producing client work" (p. 1). You need to consider general administration time to run your business as well as time for marketing, networking, research, and your own professional development. You need weekends off, vacations, public holidays, and time to be sick (though hopefully, not much). The result is that there are probably fewer billable days than you expected. (See Exhibit 8.1.)

In this example, out of a possible 260 working days in a year, only 190 of them are billable days. Recovery rate is a useful indicator that compares billable time to total working days in a year. In this example, if you divide the total billable time by the total time available (or 190/260), you are looking at a recovery rate of 73%. Over time you can use this indicator to measure your marketing effectiveness and your productivity.

Exhibit 8.1   Annual Billable Time Analysis

Item	Weeks	Days
Total time	**52 weeks**	**260 work days**[a]
Annual vacation	4 weeks	20 days
Public/statutory holidays	2 weeks	10 days
Sick time	1 week	5 days
Time available	**45 weeks**	**225 days**
Administration & professional development	2 weeks	10 days
Marketing & research	5 weeks	25 days
Billable time	**38 weeks**	**190 billable days**

[a] Excludes weekends.

SOURCE: Adapted from *Management Consulting: A Guide to the Profession* (p. 683), by M. Kubr (Ed.), 2002. Geneva, Switzerland: International Labour Office. Copyright © International Labour Organization 2002. Adapted with permission.

You may want to adjust Kubr's hypothetical example to suit your own needs, but it gives you an idea of the maximum billable days in a year for the average consultant. Kubr (2002, p. 684) cautions that independent consultants who take care of their own marketing and administration may well achieve a recovery rate of only 55% to 65% because of the need to spend up to 25% of their time on marketing. In the example I provided in Chapter 7, I spent only 15% of my time on marketing during the first year, but I already had one multiyear contract in place.

In a start-up scenario like yours, you need time to figure out what to do. So let's begin with a relatively safe number, say 125 billable days. This would make your recovery rate 48% (125/260) for your first year. This realistic goal would allow you to keep your priorities straight, your productivity at its peak, and your stress at a minimum. You can work out your available billable time on the worksheet provided in Appendix 2.

Overhead

Nothing focuses the mind like thinking about money, especially when you have to spend it. As a result, a good way to make some hard decisions about your proposed consulting business is to look at your operating costs. There are two main types of operating costs: start-up costs and monthly expenses, although some start-up costs will become annual ones, such as professional memberships or business licenses, for example.

Start-Up Costs

You have already thought about whether you are going to work at home or elsewhere, how you will acquire furniture and equipment, and if you will need staff or contractors in the immediate future. As Gray comments (2008, p. 14), "Your individual finances and needs and your shrewdness and negotiating ability will clearly affect your overhead." So based on the choices you make, he suggests that your start-up costs will vary anywhere from about $1,800 to just over $9,000, depending on the use of a home office versus a rented office and office support services (e.g., secretarial or telephone answering service) versus a half-time support person. The following list of start-up costs is a place to start, but you will have to do some homework to find out specific costs in your area. Consider whether you need the following:

- Answering service (may require a deposit) or voice mail
- Bank account start-up (e.g., printed checks)
- Business announcements or brochures
- Business registration, licenses, and permits
- Equipment or equipment rentals (computer, printer/scanner/ fax machine, color printer)
- Furniture
- Rent (first and last month or deposit as required)
- Start-up legal and/or accounting fees
- Office supplies and stationery (including business cards)
- Professional and/or business memberships
- Utilities, Internet cable and/or telephone, cell phone/Blackberry deposits and installation charges
- Website development and domain name registration
- Miscellaneous or contingency

In my case, the miscellaneous category included moving truck rental, gas, breakfast for the movers, a deposit for a photocopier key (to track shared use of the machine), the cost of some equipment repairs, a couple of reference books, and a business photo. These start-up costs should be funded by a nest egg that you have put aside for this purpose. They should not be included in your monthly calculations, because they are one-time expenses.

It is important to keep a record of your estimated and actual expenses for this start-up period, because this information will help you refine your cost projections for the coming year. Work out your projected start-up costs using the sample worksheet provided in Appendix 3, and enter them into a spreadsheet program to facilitate tracking and updates.

Monthly Expenses

Once your office is set up, you will have ongoing operating costs. It is a good idea to estimate costs by month and year. Most expenses are paid on a monthly basis, but some expenses are paid quarterly or annually (e.g., insurance). These can be prorated by month to give a more accurate month-by-month picture.

For the purposes of this costing exercise, do *not* include your anticipated salary, but do include every other cost, including other projected staff costs if needed. Here is a list of possible categories for your monthly expenses. Think carefully about each item to see if it is a potential cost for you. If not, delete it from your list of projected expenses.

- Accounting fees (e.g., preparation of financial statement formats, tax returns, and other accounting expenses)
- Advertising, webpage
- Automobile costs
- Bank charges
- Books and reference materials
- Business services
- Business taxes
- Communications (e.g., telephone and fax lines, cell phone/ Blackberry, long distance charges, cable/Internet charges)
- Conferences, courses, and professional development
- Donations
- Equipment leases or monthly purchase payments
- Interest on loans
- Insurance prorated by month (e.g., health,[1] life, general liability, theft, automobile, and professional liability; see Chapter 13)

- Legal services (e.g., contract review)
- License renewals prorated by month
- Loan payments
- Marketing, entertainment, and promotion
- Membership renewals prorated by month
- Office rent
- Office supplies
- Printing costs
- Postage, courier, postal box rental
- Repairs and maintenance
- Retirement savings
- Subscriptions/journals
- Taxes prorated by month (e.g., business income tax, social security, pension plans, sales or service tax)
- Travel not covered by your contracts (e.g., attending conferences)
- Storage
- Utilities
- Salaries, wages, and benefits (staff only, not yours)
- Miscellaneous/contingency

As an example and for the purpose of our calculations here, my office and administrative costs (excluding my salary and any subcontractors' fees) in a home office setting were just under CAN$38,000 in 2009. We will be using this amount as an example to calculate daily rates in Exhibit 8.2 on page 94.

Work out your projected monthly and annual costs using the sample worksheet provided in Appendix 4, and enter them into a spreadsheet program for future tracking purposes.

❖ SALARY

Of course, you are not going to do all this work for free. You expect a reasonable income to support your lifestyle, but if you are just starting out as a consultant, you may not know what "reasonable" is. A good place to start is to ask yourself what you need to maintain your personal and family expenses. Your needs also vary depending on your life stage. For example, I found that day care costs were a lot cheaper than tuition and living expenses for that same child once he went to college. The support of your family members, including your spouse or partner, is essential for all aspects of this career choice. This may be a particularly good time to review your family budget and other sources of income.

When in doubt, start with your previous base salary. You need to make at least as much as you did in your last job, otherwise why are you doing this? You can also check online to determine average salaries and pay scales for consultants and evaluators, but you will see that they vary widely by industry, level of experience, and employer.

In 2003, the median personal income for full-time self-employed independent evaluation consultants was $75,000 (Jarosewich, Lynch, Williams, & Doino-Ingersoll, 2006, p. 14). The range was from $12,000 to $350,000. Half of the group reported that they were making "just above" or "well above" an adequate living. The researchers found that the category with the largest personal income was the solo consultant who worked from home and had low overhead expenses. Evaluators with several employees likely worked fewer billable hours, because they had to spend time on supervision and administration and had higher overhead costs. However, Jarosewich and colleagues concluded that having a larger number of employees could also provide more personal income if billing rates covered the additional overhead (p. 20).

For now, determine a reasonable and realistic salary for your first year in business and use it for your calculations. You may wish to change it in future years, but remember that you will have to come back to the drawing board to redo your calculations before you increase your fees. For the purposes of our exercise, we will use $75,000 as a starting salary.

❖ PROFIT

Talking about profit can be tricky, because, as Kubr (2002, p. 615) suggests, it is not always easy to call a spade a spade. Some professionals may be embarrassed to admit that to some extent they are actually in sales, and some clients, especially the less-experienced ones, may feel that the consultant should not make a profit at their expense. As a result, the whole topic has to be handled with delicacy. However, the truth is that consulting is a business that provides services to clients for a fee, and profit is a natural part of this equation. Your firm has to finance its expenses and build its capacity. To keep your business healthy, it is okay to make a profit.

Profit depends on many variables—some under your control (e.g., quality of service), some not (e.g., market demand). Profit planning and the use of profits, once they materialize, are important considerations. When you start as a sole practitioner with talent, experience, a small amount of working capital, and the desire to work hard, you are investing in your own future, and profit is your reward. Of course, I am not talking about gouging anyone or taking more than is your fair share. A profit margin of anywhere between 10% and 30% is generally acceptable, so see what you are comfortable with, and plan for it. If you make it, celebrate your success. If you don't, find out what happened, and make some changes. In our example, we will use a start-up profit rate of 10%.

❖   YOUR DAILY RATE

Armed with all this financial information, at last you can determine your daily rate. We will use the above examples for demonstration purposes, using the consultants' fee calculation formula as described by Burns (2001) (see Exhibit 8.2).

Exhibit 8.2   Fee Calculation Process

Step	Calculation	Estimated Amount
Step 1	Determine desired salary	$75,000
Step 2	Determine overhead costs	$38,000
Step 3	Total costs	$75,000 + $38,000 = $113,000/year
Step 4	Cost for 125 billable days	$113,000/125 = $904.00 base daily rate
Step 5	Profit @ 10%	$904.00 x 0.10 = $90.40
Step 6	Final daily rate	$904.00 + $90.40 = $994.40 Round it up to $1,000.00
Step 7	Hourly rate	$1,000.00/8 hours = $125.00/hr

Now use your own figures from the worksheets to calculate your actual daily rate. (There is a worksheet for this purpose in Appendix 5.) If you are uncomfortable with the result, review your assumptions. Change your desired salary, change your profit margin, change your overhead—play with the numbers until you come up with a formula and an amount that works for you—but don't sell yourself short.

❖ PRICE-SETTING METHODS

Now that you have calculated your daily rate, you probably think that price setting is going to be straightforward. Not so. While the "science" of determining your rate is formulaic, there is also an art to setting the price for your services. Pricing is not static. It is a process, and the factors affecting it are changeable and require constant adjustments on your part (Higgins, 1998). There are a number of price-setting methods that you should be aware of. Each has advantages and disadvantages for the consultant.

Hourly/Daily Rate

Sometimes called the *per diem*, this method is the traditional price-setting method for consultants, and, for me, it is certainly the preferred one. Many consultants consider this the only correct way to charge for professional services. Easy and clear fee calculations and straightforward billing procedures are the main advantages to this method. The client is billed after an agreed period of time (usually a month) for time actually worked during the previous month. If you are working toward a total amount stated in a proposal, this method offers the challenge of coming in as close as possible to the proposed budget by the end of the contract. That way, little or no money is left on the table. At the same time, you are also working to ensure that you do not have to cover extra costs out of your own pocket to complete the project.

If clients feel that they are being billed for time used without any evidence that it was time well spent, they might raise an objection to the amount of time on the monthly invoice. I have two solutions to this issue. The first is to track your time. (See Chapter 9.) The second is to provide monthly accountability in the form of a status report that lists the activities conducted during the month and identifies progress made toward project goals. Generally, everyone is happy with these solutions. The client has an update on project progress, and in preparing the report, you are reminded of where you stand in relation to outstanding activities and the project's bottom line.

Fixed Fee

Many consultants believe that they make more profit on a fixed fee or flat rate than on an hourly basis. Some consultants collect half their fees up front and half upon completion of the consulting project. Kubr (2002, p. 688) suggests that this approach benefits clients, because they can withhold the final payment until they are satisfied with the result. On the other hand, if the client doesn't like your work, at least you get paid something. My son, who is a portrait artist, uses this method. The amount of work he puts into a picture is generally the same from project to project, but the client can be influenced by the outcome. Sadly, there have been a few occasions when the client has been dissatisfied with the product, and the second installment has not materialized. This is a tough way to earn a living, especially if you are not always compensated for your work.

A consultant can also be disadvantaged if the project costs more than was originally anticipated. This can easily happen, and then you have a dilemma. Should you pick up the additional costs for free, rather than ask for an additional payment? Does it reflect poorly on your planning ability or on your management skills? Did events beyond your control result in cost overruns or time extensions? Typically, clients are not pleased if there are unexpected additional costs, unless they have specifically asked for additional work. In a case like that, your contract should be changed to reflect the additional work, and at that point, the opportunity exists to change the total amount (see Chapter 15).

While the potential exists for lots of problems with a fixed fee method, some consultants work this way all the time. Others tend to work for a flat fee for small engagements such as quick surveys, workshops, or preparing grant proposals. To protect yourself on fixed fee assignments, prepare a one-page letter agreement, limit the scope of your engagement, and use a phased approach. Breaking down an assignment into smaller parts allows you to estimate costs more accurately, limits your financial exposure, and allows you to judge your client's willingness to pay.

Standing Offer

Government departments sometimes hire consultants through a standing offer arrangement. In this process, you submit an extensive proposal, not to bid on a project, but to be on a short list of consultants whom they will call up whenever they need consulting services. The offer is usually good for a set period of time (often three years). You are required to prepare an exhaustive document that describes your skills, research methods, former projects, and team members. You provide rates for each individual, usually with a cost of living adjustment for each year of the offer. If you are selected, you sign a standing offer agreement to provide work at the set rates. When clients have projects, they circulate a quick invitation to bid (often to only three or four firms) with a short turnaround time, and you submit a brief proposal that focuses directly on methodology and total price. You have to have the time, energy, and resources to survive the initial selection process, but afterward, as one of the in-group, you have the opportunity to bid on a number of projects. This approach has worked well for me, and I have received a lot of interesting work this way. Sometimes though, after getting on a list, I have never heard from that department again.

Retainer

Historically, retainers were a popular arrangement between organizations and their consultants, but this is less the case today. The consultant's fee is calculated on the basis of a number of days of work in a given period (e.g., four days a month) at the consultant's normal daily fee. This provides the consultant with steady income and some security. It also saves marketing time. For these reasons, the consultant may even agree to a slightly reduced daily rate. The retainer is paid even if the client makes less use of the consultant than foreseen by the contract. Criticisms of the method include the fact that there is no defined scope of work, there is rarely a tangible deliverable, and good relationships may be hard to maintain. It is also important to make sure that you are not perceived as an employee, either by internal staff or by the tax department.

However, this type of relationship can also work very well. Bloom (1992, p. 29) was a successful advisor to the U.S. Navy for a number of years. He found that by documenting all meetings and phone calls, providing monthly status reports, and maintaining close communications with his client, he was able to provide the accountability needed for his monthly fixed fee billing. The assignment was also an investment in his own business development, because he learned a lot from the engagement. Over time, he was not only able to sustain his position, but he also increased his fees.

Colleagues of mine often go into small agencies or government departments on a retainer basis to assist with such research-related activities as developing (or cleaning up) databases, providing management for a specific research or evaluation project, developing policy in a new area, or supervising and mentoring new staff. However, they have found that they have to be careful, or the arrangement can turn into a part-time job, and their independence can be compromised.

Contingency Fee

A contingency approach means that the fee is paid only when specific results are achieved. It can also mean that the size of the fee is dependent on the success level of those results. The client pays only for a positive outcome (Kubr, 2002, p. 689), so you can imagine the impact this approach would have on research ethics. Business situations where contingency fees are used include mergers, acquisitions, real estate deals, and joint ventures. The consultant can receive a percentage of the value of the business transaction that he or she facilitates. While motivation to succeed is obviously high on the part of the consultant, the risks are significant.

The form this often takes for applied researchers and evaluators is when the client asks you to write a funding proposal for free and then "guarantees" you the research or evaluation component of the project if they get the funding. Many of my colleagues do this routinely. I do not, because early in my career, I tried it a couple of times with disastrous results. The first time, the client became very elusive when I called and asked about the proposal outcome. I found out later that he used my "free" research design for his own purposes. The second time, the client did not receive the funding and blamed my research design for not getting it. I felt my reputation suffered for something beyond my control. These lessons led me to conclude that I would work only for pay. I seldom write proposals for clients, because I can't guarantee the outcome, and when I do this kind of work, I negotiate a small fee for my efforts. Still, some consultants are extremely successful at proposal writing and often work this way. One of my colleagues draws up a brief agreement with the client stating that if the client obtains the grant, she will be hired for the research component, but I am not sure how enforceable this arrangement would be.

Contingency fees have a darker side, and they have fueled a long-standing controversy in management consulting circles. For many years, the use of contingency fees was banned by the code of ethics for management consultants, but as Kubr (2002, p. 690) explains, "This ban has been lifted in most countries and contingency fees are no longer regarded as unethical. This, however, does not remove the technical problems associated in their use." He cites the following problems:

1. The consultant is tempted to focus on short-term results regardless of future impacts.

2. It can be difficult to identify and measure real results achieved specifically from the consultant's intervention as opposed to other results achieved by the client, or it may take a long time for the results to materialize.

3. The client and the consultant may disagree on the nature, extent, or quality of the results achieved, and conflict can ensue.

4. Through no fault of the client, projected results may not be achieved, and the consultant can do nothing about it.

5. If the client is in or gets into financial difficulty, projected results may not be attained, and the consultant is not compensated at all. (pp. 689–690)

Other Market-Based Pricing Methods

There are a variety of other pricing methods that are tied to market issues. The first is to find out how your competitors calculate their fees, what pricing policy they follow, and what their clients think about their fees. This is easier said than done, however, because many consultants consider their rates to be a closely held secret. You may be able to find out what fees are charged by other professionals and or by colleagues whom you do not consider to be competitors. One way to find out what competitors charge is to work with them on a joint project.

You also have to be careful not to compare yourself to a consultant in a larger firm or one with more years of experience, or you will price yourself out of the market.

Once you find out your competitors' rates, you could choose to set your rate below that of the competition. In this case you need to control the service you provide closely, because it can be difficult to sustain service at a lower-than-market rate. On the other hand, if you price above the competition, you are asking for a premium, and you will need to justify this increase. For example, I know a management consultant who specializes in business turnarounds. His clients are in desperate straits when they come to him, and he often "saves" their businesses. He bills at a premium rate, but I must say he works in a highly charged and stressful environment. Clients may be willing to pay more for your speed, knowledge, quality of service, or proprietary product or technology, but be sure that your rate is perceived to be a fair value.

Another approach is to charge different fees for different segments of your market. For example, you may want to charge lower fees to nonprofits and small or start-up organizations and higher fees to foundations or government departments. Some consultants feel that it is fair to have the big fish help the little fish in this way. I find it confusing and difficult to keep the accounting records straight. Generally, I have discovered that most nonprofits prefer to pay market rates, or they feel they may be getting a lesser service. Another choice made by many of my colleagues is to do pro bono work. This means they work for free for organizations they support. For example, one of my colleagues is deeply committed to the Canadian Cancer Society and is happy to do pro bono work for them.

A few very well-known consultants become highly sought after for their skills and can charge more than the going rate. Some become celebrity consultants, either because of their former political profiles or because of their status as best-selling authors. These individuals live in the stratosphere and can basically charge whatever they think the market will bear.

In this chapter, we have taken a look at the nuts and bolts of setting your fees. If you take the time to complete the worksheets and determine your billable time along with start-up and monthly costs, and if you decide on an adequate salary for your needs and a profit level that seems realistic, you can determine your daily rate. Once you know

what you need to charge to stay afloat, you can prepare realistic proposals and enter the marketplace with confidence.

❖ NOTE

1.   Note that health insurance costs vary widely depending on where
you live.

❖ USEFUL RESOURCES

- For all management consulting topics, nothing beats the well-
known text by Milan Kubr. My third edition is nearly worn out
but was well worth the money: *Management Consulting: A Guide
to the Profession*, 4th ed. (Geneva, Switzerland, International
Labour Office, 2002).
- Similarly, the first edition of this popular book by Douglas Gray
helped me resolve many practical start-up issues and his 8th
edition is just as useful today: *Start & Run a Consulting Business*,
8th ed. (Self-Counsel Press, 2008).

❖ DISCUSSION QUESTIONS AND ACTIVITIES

1.   Imagine that on January 1st you will formally begin your consulting practice. How much time will you allot over the year
for vacation, public holidays, sick time, administration and
professional development, marketing, and research? As a result
of these decisions, how many billable days will you have available? Is this appropriate, or do you need to make adjustments?

2.   Based on the fee calculation modeled in Exhibit 8.2, conduct
your own fee calculation. You may wish to use the worksheet
provided in Appendix 5. What is your hourly rate? How appropriate do you feel this rate is in your local consulting marketplace? What research have you done to support this conclusion?

3.   Churchill (2006) suggests that many entrepreneurs do not have
a grasp of the business end of their operations: "This is where
many companies get sidelined because a big part of running a

successful business is developing pricing models and contracts that work well" (para. 3). Of the pricing models described in this chapter, which ones seem to be the most appropriate for the services you plan to offer? What are the advantages or disadvantages of each?

❖ REFERENCES

Bloom, F. B. (1992). Managing the ongoing fee relationship. *Journal of Management Consulting, 7*(1), 28–34.

Burns, K. (2001). *The consultants fee calculation formula.* Oracle PeopleSoft Planet. Retrieved from http://www.peoplesoft-planet.com/The-Consultants-Fee-Calculation-Formula.html

Churchill, C. (2006). *Pricing models for the small SEM shop.* Search Engine Watch. Retrieved from http://search enginewatch.com/3623293

Gray, D. (2008). *Start & run a consulting business* (8th ed.). Bellingham, WA: Self-Counsel Press.

Higgins, C. (1998). A primer on pricing. *The Micropreneur Mentor: Small Business Advisory, News and Views, 1*(4), 1–5.

Jarosewich, T. V. L. E., Lynch, C. O., Williams, J. E., & Doino-Ingersoll, J. (2006). Independent Consulting Topical Interest Group: 2004 industry survey. *New Directions for Evaluation, 111,* 9–21.

Kubr, M. E. (2002). *Management consulting: A guide to the profession* (4th ed.). Geneva, Switzerland: International Labour Office.

Philip, K. (1994). *The good, the bad and the ugly, or making it on your own in the epoch of the twenty-first century.* Unpublished manuscript.

9
Managing Time

Highlights:

- Find out what tools can help you record your time.

- See the important differences between billable and nonbillable time.

- Examine the many kinds of information your timesheets can provide.

- Learn to use your timesheets as an essential management tool.

Exhibit 9.1   Adman Gosselin Given Two-Year Jail Term

On November 20, 2009, an advertising firm president and one-time journalist, Gilles-André Gosselin, was given a two-year jail term because he had frequently charged his client, the Canadian federal government, for more than 24 hours of work in a single day. Over a four-year period he defrauded taxpayers of $655,000. Now bankrupt, he pled guilty. "I'm sorry, I apologize," he said in tears, unable to add anything else as he was led sobbing from the courtroom. While he suffered from depression, heart problems, and sleep apnea, the judge was unsympathetic, commenting that he had been well aware that he was committing fraud.

(Daniel Leblanc. *The Globe and Mail*. November 21, 2009.)

The object lesson provided by Gosselin's experience may be an extreme case, but keeping track of your time is critical for any consultant. If research and evaluation service is what you sell, time is the unit of measurement you use to track it. Even if you don't choose to use your daily rate for billing purposes (see Chapter 8), you still need to track your time for internal monitoring. As Gray (2008) points out,

> Accurate time records are extremely important to ensure that clients are promptly charged and that you have accounted for all the billable time expended. . . . Time records also reflect the expenditure of time for the benefit received, and whether or not your efficiency and profit are improving or [if] certain activities or clients should be reconsidered. (p. 86)

If you do have a dispute with a client over time expended, accurate records could make the difference between winning and losing a law suit (and likely your business). Gray believes that the odds are in favor of you having to provide such evidence at some point in your consulting career.

❖ RECORDING TIME

So how do you record your time? It is easy to forget what you did this morning, let alone yesterday, so here are some tools that may help.

A Day Book

Whether electronic or paper based, you need a day book or daily calendar with you at all times. Because you will be recording your time for the rest of your consulting life, scraps of paper are not sufficient. You need an enduring record of your activities. So for example, I have a box of old day books in my storage locker. I could easily tell you what I was doing on September 16, 2005. So far I have not had to provide this type of evidence, but I have still used this information in many other ways.

Think in terms of quarter-hour segments. Every time you change your activity, record the time spent for that specific project in your day book. Do it immediately. If you spend eight minutes on one project and seven on another, assign the time to the first project; over time it will even out for the second project. Don't leave your desk at the end of the day without making sure that you have documented all your activities in your day book.

A typical day might look as shown in Exhibit 9.2.

Exhibit 9.2   A Typical Day

Time	Activity	Hours
8:30–9:00	Office administration	.50
9:00–10:30	Client meeting (conference call) (Project 1)	1.50
10:30–10:45	Accounts (banking online)	.25
10:45–11:00	Marketing (phone call)	.25
11:00–12:00	Content analysis (Project 2)	1.00
	Lunch break	
1:00–3:30	Report preparation (Project 3)	2.50
3:30–5:00	Telephone interview (Project 2)	1.50
7:00–9:30	Travel (Project 1)	2.50

You can see that both billable and nonbillable time are recorded here. The habit of time tracking may be difficult to instill, but once it is there, it is hard to break. One of my former staff members told me that she still keeps track of her time many years later, it has simply become a habit. Be assured that the lawyers and accountants you know already track their time routinely. It is the way they calculate their bills, and it will be the way you will probably calculate yours.

A Spreadsheet Workbook

Although there are many time tracking software programs available, and you have the option of subscribing to an online tracking program, a spreadsheet program with a workbook function is all you really need. For example, you can create two workbook masters, one for the first half of any given month and one for the second. This approach reflects the pay periods we selected in our office (i.e., two per month) but the half-month timesheet also provides a useful unit of analysis. It is easier to make course corrections in the second half of a single month rather than waiting until the end of the month. At that point you will find that you have a much bigger problem on your hands, and it will be harder to catch up or make significant changes.

Apart from the different dates (i.e., 1–15 and 16–31), the two masters are identical. At the beginning of each pay period, you copy the master into a new file and save it for the specific individual and period (e.g., Your Name—August 1–15, year). This way the master is available to be copied again next time.

Each workbook has three different kinds of sheets.

Billable Project Timesheet. The first sheet is the Billable Project Timesheet. You can make multiples of this sheet, one for each of your billable projects. The sheet has four sections.

1. General information includes the project name (using an acronym such as the CHHP Evaluation), the name of the individual whose time is being tracked, and the pay period (e.g., August 1–15).

2. A breakdown of project tasks mirrors the tasks outlined in your project proposal or work plan. In this way you can track the time expended on each of your planned activities.

3. A row is provided for each day in the pay period. At the end of the day, enter your total time worked per task, using the totals from your day book. It is easy to do this if you use your scroll bar and bring the row for today's date to the top of the screen. Daily totals in terms of hours are summed automatically at the end of the row and hours per task are summed at the bottom of the column.

4. The number of task hours is automatically divided by 8 (as 8 hours = 1 work day) to give you the total days worked on this project in this pay period. (See Exhibit 9.3.)

The timesheet tells the story of project activities during this period. In this example, 7.96 days were worked on the CHHP evaluation

Exhibit 9.3   Sample Billable Project Timesheet

Billable Project:					Project 1. CHHP Evaluation				
Your name here:					Date: August 1–15, (year)				
Task:	Evaluability design	Interim Report preparation	Meetings	Data collection	Analysis	Final Report preparation	Communications & administration	Travel	Total
Date									
1									
2					6.25	4.75			11.00
3					0.50	3.75			4.25
4					6.75	0.25			7.00
5						0.50			0.50
6					4.50				4.50
7									
8					3.25				3.25
9			2.00			3.75			5.75
10						4.00			4.00
11						6.25			6.25
12			2.25			4.75			7.00
13						6.25			6.25
14									
15						3.75			3.75
Total hours	0.00	0.00	4.25	0.00	6.75	51.75	0.75	0.00	63.50
Total days	0.00	0.00	0.53	0.00	0.84	6.47	0.09	0.00	7.94

project. The focus was on final report preparation, as the report was due at the end of August. You can see that many planned activities were already complete, and little time was spent on client meetings and administration. The project total rolls forward to the Summary Timesheet (see below).

Nonbillable Projects Timesheet. You just need one copy of the Nonbillable Project Timesheet for each pay period. It allows you to track all of your business-related activities that are not tied to specific projects. The sheet has four sections.

1. General information includes the name of the individual and the pay period.

2. A breakdown of nonbillable activities is provided under the general headings of Office Administration, Marketing, Service, and Professional Development. You can change the master sheet to reflect your current nonbillable activities.

3. A row is provided for each day in the pay period. At the end of the day you enter your total time worked per task. Your daily total is summed automatically at the end of the row, and hours per task are summed at the bottom of the column.

4. The number of task hours is automatically divided by 8 to give you the actual number of nonbillable days in this pay period. (See Exhibit 9.4.)

The story told by this timesheet is that very little nonbillable time was expended, due to the focus on the final report, although some administration, planning, accounting, office management, and volunteer tasks were completed. Overall, less than one day was spent on nonbillable activities during this period. The totals roll forward to the Summary Timesheet (see below).

Summary Timesheet. The Summary Timesheet is very important. You need one copy for each pay period. (See Exhibit 9.5.)

This sheet has five sections.

1. General information includes the name of the individual and the pay period.

2. Total time worked is compared to the calendar days available. As this sheet is for the first two weeks in August, there are only 9 working days, because the first Monday is a civic holiday. You

Exhibit 9.4   Sample Nonbillable Projects Timesheet

Task	Office Administration					Marketing		Service	Professional Development					Total
	Administration	Planning	Accounts	Personnel	Office management	Proposal preparation	Other marketing	Volunteer work	Courses/seminars	Conference attendance	Conference presentation	Technical reading	Article/publication	
Your name here:						**Date: August 1–15, (year)**								
Date														
1														
2	0.50				0.25									0.75
3								1.00						1.00
4	0.25													0.25
5	0.25							0.75						1.00
6														
7														
8	0.25													0.25
9	0.25													0.25
10	0.25													0.25
11	1.25													1.25
12	0.25													0.25
13	0.25													0.25
14														
15		1.00	1.00											2.00
Total hours	3.50	1.00	1.00	0.00	0.25	0.00	0.00	1.75	0.00	0.00	0.00	0.00	0.00	7.50
Total days	0.44	0.13	0.13	0.00	0.04	0.00	0.00	0.22	0.00	0.00	0.00	0.00	0.00	0.94

Exhibit 9.5   Sample Summary Timesheet

Name:		Date: August 1–15 (year)			
# Calendar working days	9.00				
Total time worked	9.93				
Difference/overtime	.93	Vacation:			
Brought forward	2.50	**Total**	**# Taken to Date**	**# Taken This Month**	**Remaining**
Total Accumulated Overtime	**3.43**	20	14	0	6

Total Time on Nonbillable Projects:	*# Days*	*% of Total Time*
Office management	0.72	0.07
Marketing	0.00	0.00
Service	0.22	0.02
Professional development	0.00	0.00
Total Nonbillable Time	**0.94**	**0.09**

Total Time on Billable Projects:	*# Days*	*% of Total Time*
Project 1. CHHP Evaluation	7.94	0.81
Project 2. CCT Consulting	0.00	0.00
Project 3. PR Evaluation	0.49	0.05
Project 4. ISHP Research Design	0.54	0.06
Total Billable Time	**8.97**	**0.91**

can see that 9.93 days were worked, although there were only 9 working days in the period, so some overtime was calculated. It was added to the overtime brought forward from the previous period to make an accumulated overtime total of 3.43 days.

3. The third section tracks vacation time. As this individual planned to have four weeks of vacation during the year, and as 14 days had already been used, there were six days left.

4. The totals from the Nonbillable Projects Timesheet are automatically brought forward to this section, and the proportion of nonbillable time expended compared to total time is calculated by category and overall.

5. The totals from each Billable Project Timesheet are also brought forward. Again, the proportion of total billable time worked compared to total time expended is calculated by project and overall.

❖ USING TIME RECORDS TO MEASURE YOUR EFFECTIVENESS

Recording your time is just the first step. You will find that your timesheets are an essential management tool that will help to sustain your business, increase your efficiency, assist in the preparation of new proposals, and increase your competitive edge.

Using Your Billable Time

Now you can link project totals to your billing system to prepare your monthly invoices. If you have staff or subcontractors working with you, their timesheets can be linked as well. In addition, their timesheets will be needed for your payroll and tax records.

The number of projects you have at any time will vary. A review of my timesheets over the last seven years shows that I have worked on between 3 and 10 projects at any one time. My recovery rate has hovered between 60% and 70%. When I had many projects on the go, I also had subcontractors or staff working with me, so the time I needed to spend on many of those projects was limited. I would often work less than one full day per period on each of those projects, and that was mainly in a supervisory role. Meanwhile, I would focus my attention on 2 to 3 of the projects and would do critical design work, maintain client contact, or write reports. Now that I work by myself, I never have more than four or five projects on the go at a time, but I still tend to focus on one or two projects in any given period.

In order to keep your work under control, you need to have your projects at different stages of development. In the natural course of things, because you tend to write one proposal at a time (which you may or may not win), work usually starts on a broken front, but sometimes it comes in bunches. A second factor to consider is project length. Some projects are three months long; some last three years. You need to balance project tasks so that different activities are happening in the same period; thus you can be waiting for data to be returned on one project while you are conducting interviews on another. My worst-case scenario would be to find myself writing two final reports at the same time. I know from experience that I could not divide my attention in this way, and so should this happen, I would hire someone to help me through this critical period.

Looking at Nonbillable Time

You need to set goals for your use of nonbillable time. In your first year, if you decided to have a recovery rate of 48%, that would leave 52% for nonbillable activities. You need to decide how much time to spend on marketing, administration, professional development, and volunteer work. With clear targets in mind, it is easier to make adjustments as you go. If you set 25% as your goal for marketing time, this only leaves 27% for the many other nonbillable activities. How much time can you afford to spend on office management? You need to plan, answer e-mails and correspondence, go to the bank, pay bills, and send invoices—there is always a lot to do. Perhaps you will wonder if you should engage in volunteer work during your first year. Nonbillable time can quickly eat into your project time, so watch it carefully.

Analyzing Recovery Rates

As we mentioned in Chapter 8, recovery rate refers to how much billable time you work compared to the total working days available. This productivity measure is an important data point to track over time. In our example, the recovery rate was unusually high at 90.6% due to focused efforts to complete a final report. It also occurred during the summer period, and, as many clients were away, several projects were on hold. Such a high rate would flag the fact that other business and marketing activities were being neglected. On the other hand, if the recovery rate were very low (say 30%), you would wonder what had distracted you from billable work. By reviewing your use of time over several periods, you can see where adjustments need to be made. In the long term, you can determine if your recovery rate is increasing as your business gets established and less time is needed for nonbillable activities.

Comparing Planned and Actual Time

You will want to compare your actual time spent on a project with the estimates in your original proposal. To do this you can set up a spreadsheet for each project to compare your planned and actual use of time by project task. My colleague Kathryn Race (2007) has provided a sample spreadsheet of estimated time for a generic evaluation project; actual time would be added as tasks are completed. (See Exhibit 9.6.)

Exhibit 9.6   Estimated and Actual Project Time

Major Task/ Responsibility	Estimated and Actual Time (Hours)						
	Smith- Est.	Smith- Act.	Brown- Est.	Brown- Act.	Jones- Est.	Jones- Act.	Total
1.0 Project Management							
1.1 Finalize work plan for calendar year	8.0		0.0		0.0		8.0
1.2 Prepare monthly progress report	10.0		0.0		0.0		10.0
1.3 Maintain frequent contact with program staff via meetings, phone, & e-mails	6.0		0.0		0.0		6.0
Subtotal	24.0	0.0	0.0	0.0	0.0	0.0	24.0
2.0 Revise Program Model							
2.1 Meet with staff to identify key program changes	14.0		0.0		0.0		14.0
2.2 Review outcomes in light of program changes	8.0		0.0		0.0		8.0
2.3 Make final changes to program model Milestone #1	2.0		0.0		4.0		6.0
Subtotal	24	0.0	0.0	0.0	4.0	0.0	28.0

(Continued)

Exhibit 9.6   (Continued)

Major Task/ Responsibility	Estimated and Actual Time (Hours)						
	Smith-Est.	Smith-Act.	Brown-Est.	Brown-Act.	Jones-Est.	Jones-Act.	Total
3.0 Analyze Evaluation Data							
3.1 Data entry, clean & verify data	4.0		6.0		8.0		18.0
3.2 Obtain attendance & demographic data	2.0		6.0		4.0		12.0
3.3 Conduct preliminary analysis	14.0		8.0		2.0		24.0
3.4 Finalize analysis	16.0		8.0		2.0		26.0
Subtotal	36.0	0.0	28.0	0.0	16.0	0.0	80.0
4.0 Prepare Final Evaluation Report/Conduct Briefing Meeting							
4.1 Draft body of report & appendices	30.0		8.0		8.0		46.0
4.2 Share draft report with key decision makers	2.0		0.0		0.0		2.0
4.3 Revise report	8.0		0.0		0.0		8.0
4.4 Submit final evaluation report	4.0		0.0		0.0		4.0
4.5 Present key findings to stakeholders Milestone #2	8.0		0.0		0.0		8.0
Subtotal	52.0	0.0	8.0	0.0	8.0	0.0	68.0
Project Total	136.0		36.0		28.0		200.0

Note: This is a template that has been created to demonstrate how this time management tool can be used. The estimated hours to complete tasks are entirely contrived. Adapted with permission from "Summary of Major Tasks: ACTUAL for 2007 Calendar Year" by K. Race, 2007. Retrieved from http://www .raceassociates.com/materials/consulting_skills_workshop_race.pdf

Overall, 200 hours or 25 days (200/8) were planned for this project. As bimonthly timesheets are completed, the Actual columns can be updated, and total time per task tracked closely. No project comes to completion exactly as planned, but it is important to see if any particular tasks are getting out of hand. When many staff members are involved, project management software can be used to keep track of time lines and tasks. These comparisons can also be graphed. Sometimes the visual message received by seeing the "actual" task bars shoot up higher than the "planned" task bars is enough motivation for you to make the changes needed to bring your project in on time.

Planning Future Projects

Your timesheets provide a historical record of projects, so keep them for at least seven years. They are available proof of your firm's activities, should you ever be audited. However, their real utility becomes apparent when you are working on a new proposal. While every project is different, some components are usually alike. For example, data collection, focus groups, travel, or report writing might be similar to tasks in past projects in some way. How long did it take you last time? What can you do differently to make the process more efficient? Can you make those changes? Is the budget adequate? Should you bid on this project at all? These and other questions run through your mind as you look at future work. Your old timesheets can show you the way, so start tracking now.

Increasing Your Productivity

You can use your analysis of time to increase your productivity and profitability, and in this way, as Stalk (1988) suggests, use time as a strategic weapon to increase your competitive edge. By studying the time used to complete your work, you can identify where hold-ups are occurring and decide how to reduce delays. For example, report preparation could be taking too long because of poor computer speed, old software, inefficient file and data management, or slow client feedback. What can you do to address these issues?

You can also increase your innovation. For example, you may need a more rapid response to market requests. You could develop a proposal database, a flexible proposal template, or a proposal budget template. You could prewrite your biographical information and simply slot it into the proposal. On the other hand, you might determine that you need to improve your skills, and so you might take some courses in project management or database management. There are many ways to work smarter. Your timesheets are going to give you the evidence you need to make some changes.

Developing the time tracking habit will change the way you see your work. Although timesheets have very pragmatic roots, their use is limited only by your own imagination. If you are too busy to fill them in, you will be too busy to study your own work. If you don't have time to understand your consulting practice, you won't be able to make improvements. And if you don't grow and develop your business, it may not last very long.

❖ USEFUL RESOURCES

- For information on timesheet software, see reviews at http://www.softwareshortlist.com/products/timesheet_software_reviews_feb2010.html

❖ DISCUSSION QUESTIONS AND ACTIVITIES

1. Create a timesheet in a spreadsheet program, and over the next week, keep track of the time spent on your current projects and other daily activities. Were you surprised that you spent more or less time on certain activities than you expected? Why do you think this is so?

2. Managing time is like managing any other resource. How can time tracking lead to efficiencies for the independent consultant? Why do you think people may try to avoid using this important business tool?

3. Create a spreadsheet using the information provided in Exhibit 9.6. Based on your best guess, fill in the "Actual" columns with the amount of time you estimate it will take Smith, Brown, and Jones to complete their work. Compare planned and actual times, and prepare a graph to illustrate the comparison. What did you learn from completing this exercise?

❖ REFERENCES

Gray, D. (2008). *Start & run a consulting business* (8th ed.). Bellingham, WA: Self-Counsel Press.

Leblanc, D. (2009, November 21). Adman Gosselin given two-year jail term. *The Globe and Mail*, p. A6.

Race, K. (2007, November). *Intermediate consulting skills: A self-help fair. Time and budget management: A skills building workshop.* Workshop presented at the meeting of the American Evaluation Association Conference, Baltimore, MD.

Stalk, G., Jr. (1988, July-August). Time: The next source of competitive advantage. *Harvard Business Review*, pp. 41–51.

10

Getting Work

Highlights:

- Discover two important marketing secrets.

- Learn how to define your competitive advantage.

- Explore eight different business networks.

- Find out why referrals are the most valuable business generator.

- Learn how to build strategic alliances.

- Encourage repeat business.

❖ MARKETING SECRETS

There are two closely guarded marketing secrets that you should know. The first secret is that many of your marketing activities will not result in obtaining a project. Rather, think about marketing as planting seeds, so the first thing you need to know is how many seeds you need to sow for one positive result. When I had been in business for a while, I found that my filing drawer was filling up with unsuccessful proposals. There was little to show for my efforts, and I was getting depressed. Fortunately one evening as I attended a networking reception, a colleague confided in me that his well-established consulting firm had a success ratio of one in six: For every six proposals they wrote, on average they obtained one project. I rushed back to my office and started counting my proposals. I found to my delight that my ratio was one in five. In this way I learned that marketing is actually a numbers game.

The second secret may also be surprising. Most independent consultants get most of their work through informal channels, not through a formal bidding process. A 2004 survey of independent evaluation consultants (Jarosewich, Essenmacher, Lynch, Williams, & Doino-Ingersoll, 2006, p. 14) found that, of the 137 respondents who were self-employed and who had operated their business for at least a year, 59% ranked referrals or word-of-mouth as the most effective marketing method; and 30% ranked repeat business as the most effective method. For most of them (n = 111), the least effective marketing methods were responding to Requests for Proposals (RFPs) (16%) and having a website (14%).

These interesting findings led me to examine my own list of projects to see if my experience reflected this perspective. Of the 125 research and evaluation projects listed on my résumé, 87.2% were obtained through informal means. This group included the following types of projects:

- Repeat business, including different contracts for various stages of the same project, different projects for the same client, and spin-off work connected in some way to a particular client (33.6%)
- Referrals from previous clients, colleagues, former workshop participants, students, former staff, community volunteers, and friends (29.6%)
- General reputation based on previous work (16.8%)
- Networking and collaboration through professional organizations (7.2%)

Still, it is important to note that while projects obtained through formal RFPs and standing offers accounted for only 12.8% of the total number of projects I have obtained, they tended to be much larger in both budget and scope. They also tended to occur later in my career, when I had more experience and my business was well established.

It stands to reason, then, that if you are just starting out, you should pursue informal marketing strategies first to build your portfolio and your credibility. Later, as your confidence and experience grow, you can start to bid on larger projects through more formal means. In this chapter we look at five different informal ways to get work.

❖   1. DEFINING YOUR COMPETITIVE ADVANTAGE

If you are new to consulting, you may be uncertain about what you have to offer. Jansen (2003, p. 41) suggests that your first step should be to differentiate yourself and your services so that you can give prospective clients a good reason to choose you instead of your competition. Here are some features that may distinguish your work (Kubr, 2002, p. 624):

- Technical expertise
- A unique product
- A multidisciplinary approach to complex topics
- An intimate knowledge of a specific sector
- Speed and reliability of service
- Low fees
- Good reputation
- Good contacts with other agencies
- Excellent relationships with existing clients

You can analyze your strengths, weaknesses, opportunities, and threats by conducting a SWOT (strengths, weaknesses, opportunities, threats) analysis (Chapman, 2010). This popular strategic planning tool can help you assess your business in relation to your competitors, the marketplace, and the business environment in general. Your strengths are your internal assets, resources, and capabilities that give you a competitive advantage. Your weaknesses consist mainly of the absence of any of these strengths, along with anything else that may work against your business success. Opportunities are the circumstances or trends in the environment that favor demand for your services, while threats are the external forces and events that may be hindering your growth.

Once you have conducted your SWOT analysis and identified any critical issues standing in your way, put together an action plan. It should include a list of actions, who should be involved, what resources are required, when tasks need to be completed, and how success will be measured. Every few months, you will need to revisit your analysis to see what has changed, because determining your relationship to the marketplace is an ongoing process.

Kubr (2002, p. 624) suggests that you also need to incorporate your ambition, imagination, preferences, and personality, as well as your research training, into your strengths as an independent research professional. When thinking about your professional goals, ask yourself the following:

- What sort of professional firm do I want to establish?
- What will be my culture, consulting philosophy, and role in solving clients' problems and building their capacity?
- What kind of leadership do I want to demonstrate in terms of technologies, methodologies, and services?
- Can I offer these services without losing my identity or demonstrated level of competence?

For example, independent evaluator Amy Germuth (2009) explained what set her firm apart from other competitors, commenting,

We are recognized as a **woman-owned small business**. Many federal grants require a certain percentage of funds to be set aside for utilization of small businesses. This has made [large] organizations . . . interested in having us subcontract to them.

❖ 2. NETWORKING FOR LEADS

Networking is considered to be the most effective way to uncover and identify resources and leads, especially until most of your clients come to you through referrals (Jansen, 2003, p. 42). Networking is all about building relationships, and there are lots of ways to do this (Cramer, n.d.). Here are eight kinds of business networks to explore.

Key Contact Networks

Many business organizations facilitate making introductions and networking. They offer seminars and workshops on how to network effectively, and they coordinate networking events. In my community, for example, there are organizations for business owners, women executives, adult trainers, K–12 educators, futurists, and high-tech innovators, just to name a few. Whatever your background and skills, there is bound to be a circle of organizations where you feel comfortable. Whenever you attend one of these events, be sure to carry your business cards.

Speisman (2010) suggests that in order to take advantage of networking, you need to be able to articulate your competitive advantage, what you are looking for, and how others can help you. This may take some preplanning on your part. Rehearse what you want to say before you attend one of these events. Be a good listener, ask open-ended questions, and be a good resource for others, providing feedback and following through. Remember that the speed of your follow-up has a lot to do with your success. Most marketing material suggests that you have 48 hours to follow up, or your advantage will be lost. The 48-hour rule is good for all business communications. If you haven't e-mailed a response or returned a phone call within 48 hours, you have missed a potential opportunity.

Professional Networks

Professional networks provide critical connections for evaluators and applied researchers. They link us to colleagues, professional development opportunities, and speaking and writing opportunities. They keep us current in terms of new theories and methods and offer us ways to build our skills and develop our potential. Professional networks can also be a source of work. A lot of networking takes place between independent consultants and members of client organizations at the Canadian Evaluation Society (CES) and American Evaluation Association (AEA) conferences, for example. Colleagues tell me that another resource is the Association of Fundraising Professionals; individuals in the nonprofit sector refer to this organization when looking for freelance grant writers and evaluators. This type of sector-specific organization might provide a great opportunity to make connections and demonstrate your research skills.

Mentor Networks

Look around you and ask, "Who do I know who can offer me qualified advice and provide support when I need it?" Some obvious places to look include your university networks and small business circles, but family members and former clients may be useful resources as well. Ask them if they know of individuals who already have mentors, and then contact those individuals to find out how they set up their arrangements. When you attend events sponsored by professional organizations, you may be able to identify potential advisors. For me the Topical Interest Group (TIG) for Independent Consultants at the AEA has provided a network of colleagues to call upon. It may be that there is no one perfect person to mentor you, but maybe there are many people who can offer you parts of what you need.

Dynamic Networks

By their very name, dynamic networks are ever-changing and emerge from your most recent activities. For example, if you attend a workshop, the participants who attended with you provide a time-limited network that could be useful. You might want to contact some of them to follow up on a topic discussed at the workshop or to provide them with a resource that you think is relevant. You might consider offering a workshop yourself; the participants may be prospective clients. Or volunteer to speak at an upcoming lunch or dinner sponsored by a professional organization. The advantage of this type of activity is that the organization does the marketing for you. All you need to do is show up. You build your reputation by being out there, being knowledgeable, and being available. Sooner or later, someone in one of these dynamic networks will need your services.

Partner Networks

There are lots of ways to partner with businesses that offer services that are complementary to yours. In these partner networks, you have a shared sense of the issues associated with being in a service industry. As you are not direct competitors, it is sometimes easier to discuss your concerns. You many also find ways to collaborate. This will depend on your skill set, but here are two examples from my experience.

One interest area of mine is market research, so I joined the local chapter of a national a market research organization to learn more about their work and to meet local colleagues. I attended several events and spoke at one of their meetings. Eventually, when I was looking for survey researchers and focus group leaders, I was able to use this network to hire the support I needed. Since then I have worked collaboratively on a number of projects with one market research colleague I met in this way.

Another of my partner networks is the management consultant industry. Through their networking activities and conferences, I met several consultants who shared the same clients, although typically they were hired for different reasons. On several occasions they needed my skill set and so asked me to work on their projects. In turn, I have hired a few of them when I needed a business perspective.

Resource Networks

Online databases of approved consultants provide critical networks for consultants. These are usually sponsored by government departments, foundations, and nonprofits. Your goal is to get on these lists so that when these organizations need a consultant, you will hear about the opportunity. Sometimes identifying the appropriate databases can take some digging, so ask your colleagues for recommendations.

Find out who is currently funding research and evaluation, and then, as my lawyer husband often says, "Follow the money." Whoever is funding research could be funding you. Check out the federal government, provincial or state governments, local government, health departments and agencies, universities and school boards, research organizations, social service agencies, tribal councils, foundations, the United Way, and other charitable organizations. Don't forget to register with your professional organizations, because they often have sites at which members can register their services and potential clients can search for them.

What does it take to get on these lists? You have to see if you fulfill their screening requirements, which may specify the number of years of experience you must have in a specific field or the dollar value of contracts you have won. Then you can submit your credentials. In some cases the registration process is quite onerous, but in others it is simply a question of completing a series of check boxes. There is no way to predict which sites will respond, so get on as many lists as possible. Nothing is more encouraging than having an RFP show up unannounced in your in-box. Often these RFPs have a limited circulation, so you may have a better chance of winning.

At the same time, it is a good idea to develop your own database to track the resource sites where you have registered. Include each website's link and your date of registration so that you can update your information from time to time.

Client Networks

Every client has a unique set of networks. By working with your clients, you may be able to access their worlds as well. One particularly effective method, at the end of a successful project, is to offer to help them prepare a paper for a conference that they typically attend but that is not part of your circle. If you do most of the work, they are often happy to be involved. Prepare the abstract and presentation for their approval and feedback, and offer to deliver it jointly if they can cover your travel costs. Whether you attend or not, it is a good way to get your name out to a different professional network. One important tip: I have learned always to make sure that your client's name appears as first author on the paper or presentation.

Another strategy is to help clients prepare for cross-departmental or senior management presentations or for external presentations they may make to advisory groups and councils. You can even offer to attend to provide expert support. While the attendees may be familiar with your name on the final report, you make a greater impression by being there in person, not only for the formal session but also to circulate informally afterwards.

Social Networks

The concept of *weak ties* was developed and explored by Granovetter (1983). While each individual has a network of close friends, or strong ties, he or she also has a collection of acquaintances, few of whom know each other, and these are known as weak ties. Similarly, your acquaintances all have their own closely knit groups of friends as well as a broader group of acquaintances, and so it goes. Grant (2004) found that weak ties are more important than strong ties in fostering innovation and knowledge diffusion. In such areas as marketing and politics, weak ties can build bridges to populations and audiences not accessible through stronger connections. Hence the astounding success of social networks.

Social networking provides a fluid yet targeted Internet version of word of mouth. It can lead to new projects or job opportunities. Pinker (2009) suggests that if you rely on people you know well for new opportunities, you may make around 20 connections, but if you form weak ties through just three degrees of separation, using such social media as Facebook or LinkedIn, you can connect to 8,000 people. This huge network is purposeful, because each individual link has something in common with all the others. While you may not be comfortable with such an extensive social network, it is interesting to know that up to 300 online friends is considered "normal" for today's college student, according to research conducted by Stephanie Tom Tong, a doctoral candidate at Michigan State University (Pinker, 2009).

It may be that a weak tie provides the important spark you need to ignite your career. The investment of your time in social media may be minimal and, while the returns are unpredictable, they are probably the most useful marketing tools that are currently available. Macnamara (2010) believes that your consulting success can be advanced not only by Facebook and LinkedIn but also twitter, YouTube and blogs. He recommends that you separate your personal and business personas and have a different web address for each. Link your Facebook or LinkedIn home page to your website, where you can provide articles and tools in portable document format (PDF). Develop settings that protect your privacy, and set up a "friending" policy that reflects your business goals. Be prepared for the discipline of providing weekly updates of interest. Teach yourself the skills you need to take advantage of these fabulous, ever-changing marketing networks. If you have something important to share, there has never been a better time to do it.

❖ 3. GETTING REFERRALS

According to Bergholz and Nickols (2001, pp. 25–26), the referral is the most valuable business generator of all. After 25 years, 70 clients, and 400 engagements, they have never marketed to a potential client directly but have relied entirely on referrals. They provide four reasons for the power of referrals:

1. **A referral to someone else validates your value.** Confidence is critical in consulting, but it may be in short supply for those who are new or somewhat insecure. Few things build confidence faster than hearing how someone recommended you to someone else. When your confidence improves, your performance improves, and this then generates more referrals.

2. **When you walk in, the relationship is already half-formed and the engagement half-sold.** People are always looking for "someone good," and so when we use professionals whose services please us, we are happy to pass along their names. Your past clients will do the same

thing, so when you meet potential new clients, they will have been pre-sold on your desirability. How could this be any more perfect?

3. Referrals have the highest return on investment. Referrals are certainly cost effective; in fact they don't cost anything at all. As a result, they are the cheapest marketing strategy in the world, so refine your referral-generating skills.

4. Referrals generate high-quality clients and engagements. The referral comes your way because someone needed help and did not have an appropriate contact. The client had to ask someone he or she trusted for advice. The effort of looking for a referral demonstrates that the client has a strong need for your services. As a result, it is likely that these projects will be interesting, meaningful, and challenging.

It may not be easy to ask for a referral, but don't wait to be noticed. Be direct with your clients, and ask them to pass on the good word. Bergholz and Nickols (2002) recommend that, in your own words, your message to your client should include the following:

- You build your business through referrals, and so their help would be appreciated.
- They have appreciated your skills and services, and as others may need them as well, it would be helpful to all concerned if they passed on this information.

At the close of this conversation, ask your client, "Is there anything else I could do that would make it easier for you to refer me to others?" Bergholz and Nickols say it is surprising how often this discussion may also turn to the topic of repeat business. Your current client may be your next one as well.

Another referral strategy that has worked for me is to contact former clients when you are preparing a proposal for someone else. Ask if you may use their names as references. While this is certainly a business courtesy anyway, it also helps to refresh your talents in their minds.

❖   4. BUILDING STRATEGIC ALLIANCES

My management consultant colleague Jane Somerville (1995) has explored the increasing use of strategic alliances in the consulting industry. More small and specialized firms are emerging, while at the same time client demands are getting more complex. An effective way for you to work on bigger or more diverse projects is to create a strategic alliance with others. Some of the benefits include the following:

- Enhanced competitiveness by tailoring team skills to the unique needs of the project
- An opportunity to pursue larger, more complex projects
- Decreased competition by jointly pursuing projects
- Expanded team efficiency through increased manpower and more competitive scheduling
- Enhanced cost competitiveness by assigning tasks to team members with appropriate skill levels
- Access to an expanded network through team members' contacts
- Enhanced project quality due to the use of different perspectives
- Insight into the way other consultants work

Somerville stresses that successful strategic alliances are built on high levels of trust. They rely on positive team dynamics and good communications. The strengths of individuals have to be closely aligned with project responsibilities. Strong project management skills; well-defined roles and responsibilities; and clear budgets, schedules, and reporting requirements are essential. The team must be flexible and willing to accommodate unanticipated shifts in project requirements.

However, there are bound to be some issues associated with working with potential collaborators. Some things to consider include the following (Hendricks, Bond, & Bonnet, 2006):

- Determine potential team members' competencies, work standards, reputation, ethics, interpersonal skills, and abilities to be team players. Review samples of their work.
- Decide how much of your competitive information you want to share with these colleagues; they are sometimes your competitors.
- Develop a clear contract or memorandum of understanding (MoU) to describe your understanding of the collaboration and your working relationship. For example, who will liaise with the client? How will you handle deadlines? How will the team communicate? How will disagreements be resolved?
- Identify how project tasks will be divided. This should be clarified not only in the proposal and work plan but also in any subcontracts between team members and you. How many days of

work are proposed? What is the daily rate and total budget for their services? What needs to be done if requirements, time lines, or budgets change? What will happen if there are cost overruns?

- Review your own insurance coverage to determine if subcontractors working for you are covered for errors and omissions. What level of risk may be involved? Do they need to use their own vehicles? Do they have adequate coverage?
- Clarify the authorship of the final report and ownership of the study information.
- Determine how the team will debrief on the collaborative experience.

Strategic alliances are a great way to expand your consulting experience. Adequate planning can ensure that the collaboration works well and benefits all concerned.

❖ 5. ENCOURAGING REPEAT BUSINESS

Repeat business speaks to the quality of your work and the relationship you have already developed with your client. Once you have worked for an agency or organization, or even for a particular type of agency or organization, you have a significant advantage when you next bid on a similar project. You know the context, you know the players, and you are ready to hit the road running.

There are also some disadvantages to repeat business. Your client may be developing a dependence on your skills, and this can turn against you. People may perceive you as self-serving. You may stay on too long, and as the old saying goes, familiarity breeds contempt. There is also the danger of getting involved in the implementation of your own recommendations.

Nevertheless, I have obtained a lot of business this way, often through spin-off work or additional phases to a particular project. The strength of your commitment to your own independence will help you steer clear of potential pitfalls and will allow you to benefit from the opportunities that repeat business can provide. While repeat business is not a start-up strategy, it is a goal to strive for. In a sense it is a reward for all the effort you have invested in your practice.

There is a trajectory to the way you get work. It starts with positioning yourself in the marketplace and determining your competitive advantage. Then you can move into networking activities and gaining work. Once you have work, you need to ask for referrals. You can build alliances to broaden your scope and deepen your portfolio. Eventually, your good work will generate repeat business. Over time your marketing strategies will shift, but remember these words of advice: You will never be finished marketing as long as you are in business. It is a way of life. These informal marketing strategies will continue to help you get work, and your reputation and experience will continue to grow, project by project.

❖ USEFUL RESOURCES

- Chapman (2010) provides a comprehensive set of examples to consider along with a SWOT analysis template at http://www .businessballs.com/swotanalysisfreetemplate.htm.
- Check out Stephanie Speisman's 10 tips for successful business networking at http://www.businessknowhow.com/tips/networking.htm.
- Review this sample memorandum of understanding when considering a strategic alliance: http://www.ovw.usdoj.gov/docs/sample-mou.pdf.

❖ DISCUSSION QUESTIONS AND ACTIVITIES

1. Prepare a clear, simple message to describe your services and position yourself in the consulting marketplace, and practice it until you can say it in less than one minute. Find a partner and practice your statements together. Change your message as needed to make sure it is clear.

2. Select one of the eight types of business networks listed in this chapter and consider why it would be an appropriate place to start your marketing. What strategies would you use to take advantage of this network?

3. Conduct a SWOT analysis to assess your individual strengths, weaknesses, opportunities, and threats in terms of starting a consulting business. Identify any critical issues that stand in the way of your success. Prepare an action plan to deal with these issues.

❖ REFERENCES

Bergholz, H., & Nickols, F. (2001). Building your consulting practice through referrals (Part 1). The value of referrals. *Consulting to Management, 12*(3), 25–26.

Bergholz, H., & Nickols, F. (2002). Building your consulting practice through referrals (Part 3). Asking for the referral. *Consulting to Management, 13*(3), 24–25.

Chapman, A. (2010). *SWOT analysis method and examples, with free SWOT template.* Retrieved from http://www.businessballs.com/swotanalysisfreetemplate.htm

Cramer, G. (n.d.). *The magnificent seven: Manage your business network contacts* [Slide presentation.] Actif Communications.

Germuth, A. A. (2009, November 13). Becoming a consultant: Key questions to consider. In *Starting and succeeding as an independent evaluation consultant.* Panel session conducted at the meeting of the American Evaluation Association, Orlando, FL.

Granovetter, M. (1983). The strength of weak ties: A network theory revisited. *Sociological Theory, 1,* 201–233.

Grant, S. (2004). *Caves, clusters, and weak ties: The six degrees world of inventors. Q & A with Lee Fleming.* Retrieved from http://hbswk.hbs.edu/item/4516.html

Hendricks, M., Bond, S., & Bonnet, D. (2006, November 12). *Re: Some useful questions for maximizing both the effectiveness and the enjoyment of our collaborations with other independent consultants* [Electronic mailing list message]. Retrieved from evalbusiness@yahoogroups.com

Jansen, J. (2003). Ways smaller firms can gain clients. *Consulting to Management 14*(2), 41–44.

Jarosewich, T., Essenmacher, V. L., Lynch, C. O., Williams, J. E., & Doino-Ingersoll, J. (2006). Independent consulting topical interest group: 2004 industry survey. *New Directions for Evaluation, 111,* 9–21. doi: 10.1002/ev.192

Kubr, M. (2002). *Management consulting: A guide to the profession* (4th ed.). Geneva, Switzerland: International Labour Office.

Macnamara, D. (2010, October). *Using social networking tools to advance your consulting success.* Presentation at the 2010 conference of the Certified Management Consultants of Alberta, Calgary, AB.

Pinker, S. (2009). Social networks connecting online: Small investment, big return. *The Globe and Mail.* Toronto, ON, p. B20.

Somerville, J. (1995, May 16). *Strategic alliances: Making them work.* Institute of Certified Management Consultants of Alberta practice management workshop, Edmonton, AB.

Speisman, S. (2010, May 24). *10 tips for successful business networking.* Retrieved from http://www.businessknowhow.com/tips/networking.htm

11

Writing Proposals

Whether you hear about a potential project through one of the many informal marketing approaches discussed in Chapter 10 or through a formal Request for Proposals (RFP) process, you still need to write a proposal to secure the work. If you are the successful bidder, the proposal will structure your research activities and commit you to producing specific deliverables within a certain time frame and for a certain price. In a nutshell, if you win, this proposal will rule your life, so plan it well.

❖ SETTING THE STAGE

Long before you toss your proposal into the postbox or hand it to the courier, even before the RFP is prepared, the client may have gone through a rigorous planning process behind the scenes. The Financial Management Board Secretariat at the Government of the Northwest Territories (2008) suggests that its key preparatory tasks include the following:

- **Determine who will be project manager.** The role includes managing the search and selection process and providing ongoing supervision for the consultant. This individual must provide the direction, support, and internal linkages required to bring the project to a successful conclusion.

- **Identify financial resources.** An amount is usually set aside in the organization's budget for the research or evaluation project. Sometimes, the budget may stretch the costs across two fiscal years to minimize its financial impact on more routine costs.

- **Prepare staff for the evaluation.** Staff members need to be aware that an evaluation is being planned before the consultant is hired. If they are clear about the study purpose and process and about what will be expected of them, they will be more willing to participate, especially if they can see some potential benefits.

- **Inform key stakeholders.** The project manager should identify stakeholders and partners. They need to be informed of the project to gain their cooperation, ensure access to their constituents and data sources, and make them aware of study time lines.

- **Establish a steering committee.** A steering committee is often established at the beginning of a project to gain stakeholders' interest, give them a chance to provide input, facilitate access to data sources, increase ownership, and strengthen relationships. Appropriate representatives need to be identified and invited. A roster of meeting dates needs to be set up. Sometimes a project charter is developed. The committee may meet several times in advance of hiring the consultant to provide input to the project design.

• **Develop terms of reference.** The terms of reference for the study need to be developed in consultation with relevant staff and the steering committee and a formal document prepared to accompany the RFP. It should include everything that the consultants need to know in order to prepare their proposals. Any initial lack of clarity here will be compounded once the study gets under way.

❖ WHAT CLIENTS WANT

Clients want a good consultant who does not disrupt daily routines and who provides the best quality and most useful information in the least amount of time and at the best price. They are usually looking for four things:

• **Specific skill sets.** Clients are looking for up-to-date expertise which may not be available in-house. It may be appropriate to offer a multi-disciplinary team to accommodate their needs.

• **Independence.** Clients usually have a good reason for wanting an external person to conduct the project. They may feel that the results will have more credibility if an independent third party drives the process. It may also be easier for staff or clients to speak in confidence if they are unlikely to suffer reprisals.

• **Objectivity.** Working in a particular department or agency can produce in-depth understanding, but it also results in a biased view. Consultants arrive without emotional or historical baggage and so can provide a fresh and impartial perspective.

• **Focused attention.** Consultants bring their full attention to the issue at hand without having to deal with the day-to-day responsibilities, distractions, and politics experienced by the program manager. Typically, clients hire a consultant because they do not have the time to do the work internally.

❖ WHAT CONSULTANTS WANT

Consultants want a straightforward RFP with clear terms of reference, clear time lines, and clear reporting requirements. Most of all, they want a clear budget. However this is often the area of most contention. As the Financial Management Board Secretariat (2008, p. 8) cautions, while managers may not want to reveal the project budget in the hope that a consultant will provide a low bid, at the end of the day, it is unlikely they will get the project they want. The secretariat offers the following advice, "It is more important to get a good product for the evaluation money that you have set aside rather than saving a few dollars on the product. Buying an evaluation is not like buying office furniture. . . ." In their view, good consultants who are well aware of the budget will provide added value in their proposals to remain competitive. When this happens, it is the client who benefits in the long run.

Over the years I have had clients say, "Tell me how much it will cost, and then I will tell you how much I have got." Even worse, some have asked me to prepare a proposal for them so they can cost out their project. Sometimes they have then gone on to hire someone cheaper. Now, when the evaluation budget is not provided, I contact the client and say, "I can design a good evaluation for you for $10,000, and I can design a good evaluation for $100,000. I need to know your budget parameters so that I can create something that works for you." If this strategy fails, I refuse to bid on the project, because I believe it is unfair practice.

❖   THE ELEMENTS OF A PROPOSAL

Proposal requirements may vary slightly, but the basic elements are generally the same.

Project Purpose

There are many reasons for commissioning a research project or a program evaluation, but the project purpose always establishes the specific problem that the research project will address in one single, very clear statement. Many proposals fail because the researcher does not have a clear enough understanding of what is required.

Program Overview or Background

In a program evaluation, the program overview provides a brief history of the program and describes the following:

- Current structure
- Location and participants
- Achievements to date

- Staff complement
- Overall budget

In an applied research context, this component supports the study rationale by summarizing important background, citing other related studies, and reviewing recent events that have led to the current situation.

Scope

In order to design the research methodology, many factors need to be considered, such as the amount of background documentation, records, files, and other data; number and type of staff, participants, stakeholders, partners, and community groups; number of sites; timeframe; and many other variables. The clearer these are described, the better able the consultant will be to determine what resources are required to conduct the study.

Policy Questions

The questions generated in response to the study purpose should be listed here. These questions frame what the client wants to know and are often called *policy questions* because of their orientation toward organizational as opposed to research issues. As we know, translating these policy questions into research questions can be a delicate political process (see Chapter 4). The client needs to recognize his or her questions in the consultant's proposal, yet the consultant must combine them in a manageable framework that can inform the research.

Project Objectives or Intent

The entire research process needs to be encapsulated in a few clearly stated objectives. These explain what the project will achieve in order to address the client's research need. The success of your project will depend on your ability to achieve these objectives as fully as possible.

Statement of Work

This core component describes the research activities required to achieve the study's objectives. Each activity, method, and tool must be explained and data analysis methods outlined. Study limitations or anticipated risks should be identified along with mitigating factors. Other study issues need elaboration, including research ethics, adherence to privacy regulations, data security, and ownership of study tools, reports, and other deliverables.

Project Team

The team members, including subcontractors, must be presented in a priority listing by project responsibility. Their qualifications and recent relevant experience should be provided along with brief versions of their résumés. The roles, tasks, and number of work days required for each should also be specified.

Project Time Frame

In setting up the project schedule, the client often works backwards from an upcoming decision that awaits the results of the proposed research. This time frame then determines project duration. Contextual factors that could affect data collection need to be considered. Issues like stakeholder availability, operations schedules, vacation periods, and access issues due to weather, geography, and time of year can affect the consultant's ability to complete the work in the time allotted.

Responsibilities

To foster a successful project relationship, the responsibilities of the consultant as well as those of the project manager should be outlined. For example, it is the consultant's responsibility to adhere to the agreed-upon work plan and resources provided, to adhere to contractual agreements and confidentiality requirements, and to advise the client of any conditions that could affect the schedule or scope of work (Institute of Certified Management Consultants of Alberta, n.d.). The project manager is responsible for keeping staff and stakeholders informed about study progress; providing access to resources, data, and participants; providing feedback for drafts of tools and reports; and ensuring that the consultant's invoices are paid in a timely manner.

Deliverables

The deliverables are the product of the research or evaluation activities and are the most enduring part of any study. Because it is hoped that the deliverables will directly address the client's identified need for information, they are also what the client is interested in the most. Typical deliverables can include the following:

- Progress reports
- Tools and technical reports
- Interim and final reports
- Other documentation such as cleaned data sets
- Attendance at specified meetings or events
- Presentations, workshops, and other knowledge translation activities

Budget

The project budget must lay out personnel costs broken down by role, number of days required and daily rates, and disbursements, which includes any nonpersonnel costs associated with conducting the research. Typically no capital costs or other overhead will be supported by a project budget.

❖ THE MOST CRITICAL COMPONENT

While all of these proposal elements are important, one stands out for the independent consultant, and that is the project budget. It must be attended to first. I have learned that although the budget, like the *coup de grâce,* is presented last in a proposal, it is your starting point. The detail you need to identify project tasks, staff, numbers of days, and associated costs will determine the feasibility of proceeding with this opportunity. Do not be distracted by the siren song of an interesting topic, a fascinating client, or a new methodology. The cold, hard reality is that your planned activities and the dollars available have to balance. You need to grapple with the budget first.

As you will probably be in a hurry when the time comes to prepare your proposal, it pays to develop a proposal budget workbook in your spreadsheet program. Prepare a series of worksheets, one for each main project task, and a summary page that automatically calculates the number of days, rates per staff member or contractor, and associated costs. Here is an example of the summary sheet from a proposal budget that was developed by using a template (see Exhibit 11.1).

Exhibit 11.1   Sample Proposal Summary Budget

Personnel		Rate/Day	Planning, Communications & Admin. Days	Data Collection	Analysis	Report Preparation	Total Days	Total Cost
Project Director	PD	$1,000	3.00	7.00	2.00	4.00	16.00	$16,000.00
Senior Researcher	SR	$750	-	5.00	1.00	3.00	9.00	$6,750.00
Research Assistant	RA	$325	-	-	2.00	2.00	4.00	$1,300.00
Administrative Support	AS	$275	1.00	-	-	-	1.00	$275.00
Total Staff Time			**4.00**	**12.00**	**5.00**	**9.00**	**30.00**	**$24,325.00**
Disbursements								
Travel			-	5,387.19	-	-		$5,387.19
Long Distance			-	-	-	-		$0.00
Postage/Courier/Shipping			55.00	-	-	-		$55.00
Supplies/Materials			-	-	-	-		$0.00
Transcription			-	750.00	-	-		$750.00
Total Disbursements			**$55.00**	**$6,137.19**	**$0.00**	**$0.00**		**$6,192.19**
Grand Total			$3,330.00	$16,887.19	$3,400.00	$6,900.00		$30,517.19

This budget was developed for a proposal to conduct a program evaluation study involving case studies in three different geographic regions. As travel costs were significant and because I live in the West, I hired a colleague as senior researcher who was located on the East Coast. Our plan was to conduct the first case study together at the most central site, and then we would visit the other two sites separately. The research assistance and administrative support required were relatively minor in this project.

Working back and forth between the task worksheets and the summary sheet, I made changes as needed until I arrived at a total that seemed appropriate. Now if this RFP had stated that the maximum budget for this project was $30,000, some additional modifications would have been needed. If the total budget was actually $25,000, this would be my decision point. Unless I suddenly had a brainwave about a different methodology, I would now know that I couldn't bid on this project. This decision would save me time, because I would not continue to prepare the rest of the proposal. If I did continue, despite my own best advice, it would be at a projected loss. Why would I go into any project knowing that?

❖   THE LETTER PROPOSAL

The letter proposal is a particularly useful way to respond to the opportunities you identify through your informal marketing strategies. If a two- or three- page proposal is all that is needed, a letter proposal is the way to go, but do not confuse "informal" with "casual." Thinking through the budget and methodology takes concerted effort and attention. The amount of time required is dependent on the size and complexity of the project, but not all projects addressed by a letter proposal are small. I recently wrote a two-and-a-half-page letter proposal for a 20-month project worth just over $125,000. It took me between three and four days to write it.

Some suggested topics for your next letter proposal are provided in Exhibit 11.2. A sample letter proposal is also provided in Appendix 7.

Because time is short, and the client has an urgent need for your services, the format is understandably brief. However, once you are awarded the contract, your first task will be to develop a detailed work

Exhibit 11.2   Nine Topics for Your Letter Proposal

Use your firm's letterhead and a letter format.

1. Address the letter to the key decision maker or purchasing agent.

2. Thank the individual for the opportunity; provide an overview of your firm, your mission statement, and a brief comment about similar work for similar clients.

3. Provide a rundown of the special skills and experience that you can offer this project.

4. Prepare a one-paragraph description of your study purpose, objectives, and planned methodology.

5. Present a brief task analysis with schedule (in chart form).

6. Add a couple of sentences about your team members and their key strengths in this project. (Attach their two-page résumés to the letter.)

7. Provide a summary budget by cutting and pasting a minimized copy of your budget template summary sheet.

8. Review the total price, and mention any tax considerations as well as your invoicing procedures (e.g., monthly invoices accompanied by a status report).

9. Provide a final thank-you, contact information, and your signature.

plan. This will give you the time you need to conduct initial interviews, read key documents, and expand the brief methodology described in your letter proposal. You will have time then for appropriate consultation. I have found that some of the best designs are developed through this two-step process.

Sometimes a client will review your proposal and will make some suggestions for change. This kind of interaction is very welcome, because it ensures that the services you provide are the ones that are needed. You may also negotiate further with regard to the budget. In contrast, a formal response to an RFP is a one-shot deal. You have no recourse if you don't get it right the first time. So if the client contacts you and requests some revisions, consider yourself lucky. You will also know that you are close to finalizing the contract.

❖ THE FORMAL PROPOSAL

A formal proposal is like a tender. You have to follow the rules, meet the requirements, and get it in on time. Your proposal will be date stamped when it arrives. It will not even be considered if it is late. The demands are extensive, and preparation will take a significant amount of time and effort.

Consider the opportunity costs before embarking on this endeavor. How much paid project time are you sacrificing while working on this proposal? Consider the odds. How many other consultants do you think will bid on this project? Will your competitive edge apply in this case? Do not go into this process if you have only two days until the deadline, or if you are distracted by other pressing issues. It is a recipe for sleepless nights and ultimate heartbreak. The chances are that you will lose. But if you are confident in your proposal writing skills, feel positive about your fit with the project, and have the time to do an outstanding job, then write it.

Review the RFP as soon as you receive it, because there may be a period when questions will be entertained. Sometimes a bidders' conference is held to provide more information, and if you cannot attend in person, you may be able to link in by conference call. You will also receive the minutes of the session and a summary of any questions received and answers provided during this period. The key benefit to attending an information session is to see who else is bidding, but you can also get this information through the e-mail correspondence generated through these announcements. In addition, you can get a sense of the staff who may be involved. Often, however, these presentations are conducted because they are a requirement, and you may gain little by attending.

Make sure that you have all the necessary parts of the RFP, including appendices, annexes, attachments, and background reports. Read all the documents thoroughly, and make sure you understand the requirements. Apart from the actual work involved, there is usually a lot of regulatory material attached related to privacy, access to information, insurance requirements, any preferential selection processes (based on geographic location, cultural orientation, race, language, or gender), and the decision model to be used in making the selection, including the criteria, rating scheme, and number of reviewers. Sometimes a sample contract is also provided.

Exhibit 11.3 is a list of typical proposal topics along with some suggested strategies to consider when preparing your next formal proposal.

Exhibit 11.3   Topics and Suggested Strategies for Formal Proposal Preparation

Proposal Topic	Suggested Strategies
1. Cover letter	• Write this section last. • Include key points about your track record and accomplishments. • Include your mission statement. • Provide proposal highlights. • Indicate why you are interested in this study.
2. Front pages	• Include title page with contact information, table of contents, and executive summary. • List the proposal evaluation criteria (if available), and identify page numbers for reviewers to find relevant information.
3. Introduction	• Demonstrate your understanding of the issue with an overview of related literature. • The project size will determine how much effort you put into this section, but try to keep it short.
4. Study purpose, program theory, objectives	• Develop study objectives, or clarify those provided in the terms of reference, shaping them into something that is meaningful for you. • If appropriate, suggest a phased approach to the project, and provide the focus and objectives for each phase. • Provide a draft logic model, research framework, or other visual model to guide your work. Indicate that you will confirm this with stakeholders once the contract is awarded.
5. Corporate background	• Introduce your company, qualifications, number of years in business, and management structure. • Include relevant studies and experience, tailored to the requirements of this project. • Mention your approach to working with clients. • Refer to your website if more information is required.

Exhibit 11.3   (Continued)

6. Study team	• Introduce team members in decreasing order of responsibility for the project. • Provide one or two paragraphs per team member or subcontractor, and describe each member's education, experience, and responsibilities in this project. • If required, include signed forms from the subcontractors, confirming their availability.
7. Study methodology	• Demonstrate your understanding of the project. • Build a logical argument from problem to solution. • Describe proposed methodology carefully, matching your language to the interest and knowledge level of the client. • Ground your work in relevant literature, but be brief; this is not an academic treatise. • Explain how you will implement each study method, and estimate sample sizes. • Discuss feasibility and degree of success expected. • Enumerate any limitations, risks, or anticipated problems, and provide your plans to mitigate them. • Identify particular strengths of your research approach, such as ethics, data security, and confidentiality. • Identify team members by task, indicating their level of effort, number of hours, or days assigned for each. • Do not provide any financial information in this section.
8. Task schedule	• List the project tasks and critical dates for meetings and deliverables. • Use a Gantt chart or visual time line of activities broken down by weeks or months.
9. Deliverables	• Include the deliverables as stated in the RFP, and describe each briefly. • Indicate that your first deliverable is a detailed work plan, even if this is not required; suggest monthly status reports. These are "value added" deliverables. • Provide a draft version of the table of contents for the final report.

(Continued)

Exhibit 11.3   (Continued)

10. References	• Include references for three similar and/or recent studies, providing dollar amount, time frame, and contact names with current phone numbers and e-mail addresses. (Remember to ask these individuals for permission each time you use their names.)
11. Budget	• Include only the summary sheet from your budget workbook, or use whatever budget format is required. • Provide a budget narrative at the level of detail required. • Be particularly clear about travel costs, and cite the guidelines for travel and accommodations used by this agency. • Include only cost items that are identified in the RFP. • Identify any taxes.
12. Schedule of payments	• Specify your expectations about payment (e.g., net 30 days). • Indicate that you will submit monthly invoices along with your status reports to act as milestones.
13. Résumés	• Provide brief résumés for each member of the team. These are not your academic CVs, so be brief (suggested maximum length four pages). • In each résumé, include projects of relevance to this study, as well as others that are notable or recent. • Add professional designations and volunteer experience of interest to the client.

The length of your proposal will vary according to the specifications of the RFP, but typically they run between 20 and 50 pages excluding appendices. It is very time consuming to meet all of these requirements, and when working with staff, it often took us up to two weeks to prepare a formal proposal. We had to have both the time and the cash flow to support this activity. As these projects generally ranged from $60,000 to $500,000 and involved many levels of staff, it was worth the effort if we won. If we lost, we also lost a lot of money.

Writing proposals is both challenging and nerve-wracking, so start small. When you have time, create budget and proposal templates. Keep a proposal precedent file on your computer. Customize your résumé and those of your associates in preparation for upcoming opportunities. As one of the real stressors is the time-sensitive nature of proposals, this up-front work can ease last minute pressure. While each RFP is different, it is always helpful to prime the pump by looking back at other proposals you have written, but be careful to avoid a boilerplate style. All clients must be assured that you have taken sufficient time to understand their unique needs.

Unless you can deliver your proposal in person, the whole proposal delivery process is fraught with risk. Make particular note of the closing date, time, and location, and plan for at least two different courier strategies, depending on how long it takes you to complete your proposal. Be sure you know the time of the last courier pickup of the day, where drop boxes are, and where the client's central office is located for last minute deliveries. Make sure that the proposal reference numbers are clearly provided on the outside of your package, and indicate that the material is time sensitive. The last thing you want is to have this package sit unattended in a mail room for several days. Consider the weather, and add extra delivery time if storms are brewing. Determine which courier company or postal agency service is preferred by the client. Sometimes packages go astray, so be sure you obtain a tracking number. Always be aware that couriers guarantee far less than you may have been led to believe, so read the small print.

As you gain confidence in your skills and your ability to satisfy clients, and as your proposal precedents grow, you will find that you can write proposals for larger and larger projects. Remember that it is a numbers game. As the number of proposals you write grows, your success rate will grow as well.

❖   USEFUL RESOURCES

- For more information on government requirements for proposals and tips on bidding, see the following:

  In the United States: http://www.fedmarket.com/1/free_content/ newsletters/proposals   or   http://www.government-proposal -writing.com/government-proposal-writing-checklist

  In Canada: https://buyandsell.gc.ca/for-businesses/bid-on -opportunities/best-practices-for-bidding-a-checklist

❖ DISCUSSION QUESTIONS AND ACTIVITIES

1. Search online for a recent Request for Proposals (RFP) in your field. Read it carefully, and identify the following key elements: need for the research or purpose of the evaluation, program overview or background, scope, policy question, and project objectives.

2. Based on the RFP you identified in Question 1, review the statement of work, and prepare a proposed list of project activities. What types of staff would be required to complete these activities? Approximately how many days would each person require? Estimate their per diems. Do a rough calculation for the overall project budget. If you were a consultant, would you bid on this project? Why or why not?

3. Point-rated criteria are used to determine the relative technical merit of each formal proposal. Consider what criteria might be used to rate proposal submissions and the value you would assign to each. Determine the minimum number of points that a proposal would need to be included in your short list. Would any individual criteria require a higher minimum level? What has this process taught you about the relative importance of the components of a proposal?

❖ REFERENCES

Financial Management Board Secretariat, Government of the Northwest Territories. (2008). *Writing requests for proposals for an evaluation and working with evaluation consultants.* Yellowknife, NT: Author.

Institute of Certified Management Consultants of Alberta. (n.d.). *How to select and work with a management consultant* [Brochure]. Edmonton, AB: Author.

PART III

Business Skills

Once you have a few projects under your belt, your business will start to fall into a pattern, and routines will begin to surface. Take a huge breath. You are an entrepreneur now, and you deserve to celebrate your success. But there is an ongoing challenge. Every day you will need to keep a number of balls in the air. Handling multiple demands just got a lot more complicated. You will learn that no matter how interesting your current project is, taking care of business comes first.

Part III is about ways to develop your ongoing business management skills. We will look at how to manage your money, how to make the most of your cash flow, and what types of loans are available to you. We will explore four types of ownership structures and will learn why some independent evaluation consultants made the choice they did. We will look at the many risks we face each day, how to manage them, and what insurance we need to protect ourselves. As contracts are an essential part of our work, we need to know what to expect and what to ask for. Eventually, your success may lead to the need to grow, and so managing people will become important. We will explore ways to find help and discuss managing staff and subcontractors. Finally, as knowledge is our main product, we will consider ways to manage this valuable resource.

12

Managing Money

Highlights:

- Explore financial basics, and find out what you need to get started.

- Look at 10 ways to manage your accounts receivable.

- Manage your accounts payable, and beat the bill-paying blues.

- Understand why cash flow is the single most important indicator of business health.

- Learn about two key financial reports.

- Explore ways to get a loan.

- Identify common consultants' errors that can lead to cash traps.

Everyone loves money, but we love it more when it is coming in than when it is going out. While you are the brains of your small business, your money is the oxygen that circulates through your system. It is what keeps you alive. We all know that we need to manage our money, but the statistics on business failure are very telling. No matter where you read it, the list of reasons for small business failure always includes the same items: lack of working capital, inability to manage cash flow, failure to budget, poor financial controls, and inadequate financial monitoring. While managing money cannot make you, not managing money can break you.

Toncré (1986, p. 11) warned about the potential for business failure due to poor financial management. He found that

- only one in four business owners reviews accounting records carefully;
- less than 5% of business owners actually know their current cash position or know how it has changed since last month; and
- less than 2% of business owners have ever used a cash flow projection.

Take these cautionary words to heart, and learn how to manage your own money. This chapter will get you started with some tips about managing accounts receivable, accounts payable, and cash flow. It will look at two important financial statements and provide some information about common types of loans. Finally we will look at some of the reasons why consultants get in over their heads. Once you are aware of these issues, it will be less likely that you will have to deal with them.

❖ THE BASICS

Let's take a look at some financial basics. Visualize you, the private person, as separate from you, the owner and manager of your company. As soon as you begin to conduct business, you need to differentiate between these two entities. Separate your business finances from your personal ones, and arrange for a business checking account, savings account, and credit card. This will make it much easier to keep your finances and taxes straight.

Credit Card

Use your business credit card for project expenses such as travel and accommodations. Keep all credit card slips and cash receipts so that you can pass the appropriate costs on to your client, and keep a record of all your own business transactions as well. Of course you should use your credit card only if you can pay off your expenses on time, so keep a close watch on the due date. The last thing you need is credit card debt.

Banking

Set up Internet banking facilities to make it easy to check your account balances every day. Routine bill paying is cheaper and faster online than in person or through the mail. You can set the date on which payments are to be made to ensure that you don't have late payment charges.

When you open your bank accounts, read the small print before you sign. There will likely be an Operation of Account Agreement or a Verification Agreement that sets out the terms and conditions of day-to-day operations. Look for the following:

- **Accuracy of the monthly account statement.** Find out how many days you have from the date of the statement to notify the bank of any errors, irregularities, or omissions on your account statement. Otherwise the bank will assume that your balance is correct. If you find an error later, you will be unable to retrieve any lost funds. This is a really good reason to review your statement closely.
- **Interest on overdraft balances.** Overdraft rates are well above prime lending rates, so be careful to make sure you always have enough cash in your account. Overdraft protection is a good idea.
- **Service charges.** Your account will be debited for the usual service fees and charges. These can vary by bank, so shop around.
- **Credit information.** The bank will ask if they can provide your credit, banking and loan information to other financial institutions and consumer reporting agencies. It is your choice whether or not you want to release this information.
- **Printed checks.** Get checks printed with your business name and address on them. When you fill in a check, do it on your printer to look more professional. Buy window-style envelopes so that you don't have to retype the payee's name and address. Your business image starts with such small decisions, and maintaining it will become a way of life.

Financial Year

One final basic consideration is to determine your financial year. Your financial records are organized into 12-month periods. It may be easiest to use the calendar year or your government's financial year, but it also can depend on when you start to conduct business and have financial transactions. An early discussion with your accountant should help you clarify what is appropriate for you. Although you can change your financial year later, you will want to make it as easy as possible to do trend analyses across financial years.

❖ ACCOUNTS RECEIVABLE

Accounts receivable are composed of all the invoices you prepare for your clients in a 12-month period. You may not be aware that as soon as you have completed the agreed-upon work for the month, you are beginning to extend credit to your client. It is a business convention to allow clients to wait 30 days before they pay you (i.e., "net 30 days"), but as they are now holding money that belongs to you, the objective is to get it as professionally, but as quickly, as you can. Here are some tips on how to manage your accounts receivable.

The Creditworthiness of Your Potential Client

Before you enter into a contract with a potential client, consider the client's ability to pay. Whitlock (2003, p. 30) suggests that you think about the 5 C's of credit:

- Character—the reputation of the client's organization
- Conditions—how changing economic or industry conditions may impact the client's business
- Collateral—the security or guarantee that commitments will be met
- Capacity—the client's financial strength to repay obligations
- Capital—your sense of the client's overall financial health

Credit and Payment Policies

Being reasonable with your clients is important, but remember you have a business to support. While giving a client 30 days seems adequate to me, there may be extenuating circumstances. Some of my colleagues wait considerably longer for payment, particularly at the beginning of a contract.

Some businesses offer a discount for prompt payment. If, for example, you see "2% 10, Net 30," it means that 2% will be deducted from the invoice if it is paid within 10 days; otherwise payment is expected in 30 days. However, many professionals would never dream of offering a discount, because they want to be seen as self-sufficient and successful, so think about your business image before considering this.

You can also indicate that interest will be charged as a penalty for late payment (Maxwell & Black, 2009). Colleagues who have used this approach report that they have rarely been able to collect this interest, but it does serve to make clients more aware of their need to pay promptly, especially when they receive a second notice that now includes interest.

Standardized Invoices

Set up a standard template for your invoices, and number them sequentially. Your accounting package may do this automatically. Specify the project and contract number, and itemize your professional fees as outlined in your proposal. You can suggest that clients refer to your status report for more details. Separate your professional fees from your disbursements, because the tax implications may be different. If you have a tax or business number, include it on your invoice. Don't forget to say "Thank you." You are really grateful for their quick attention. (See Exhibit 12.1.)

Milestone Billing

Structure your projects so that there are regular deliverables such as monthly status reports. In this way you can ensure that you receive the cash injections you need to keep your business running smoothly. Using milestones also makes you more accountable, because knowing that you have to report on your progress at the end of the month will act as an incentive. You can't bill your client if you don't submit the status report, and you can't submit the status report if you haven't done the work. This is how you set yourself up for success.

Exhibit 12.1.   Sample Invoice

Your Letterhead	

Date   Invoice #

Your client's organization
Department specified on your contract
Address

Attn: Your client's name
Contract #
Re: Project Name

Professional Fees: **Amount**

Brief description of tasks or
reference to status report   4.75 days @ $1,000.00 $4,750.00
for specified dates (e.g., May 1-31, year)

                                                    Tax   (5%)   237.50
                            Total Professional Fees and Tax: **$4,987.50**

Disbursements:
Parking (receipts attached)   45.00
Mileage 150 km @ $0.46/km as specified in contract   69.00
                              Total Disbursements: **$114.00**
(Tax or Business Number: #)   _____
                                          Invoice Total: **$5,101.50**

Certification required by government such as:
*"I certify that I have examined the information contained in this invoice,
including the legal name, address and business number, and that it is correct
and complete, and fully discloses the identification of this Contractor."*

Thank you for your business and your prompt attention!

Your (electronic) signature

                        Your company's name, address, website and logo

Your name and title

Relationships With Clients

Your clients have to understand that, in order to make sure their projects get the attention they deserve, you need to be paid regularly. In no way am I suggesting that you should be tactless or pushy or obsessed about money; all of this financial machinery operates pretty silently behind the scenes, but there is nothing wrong with a matter-of-fact comment to your client that their fees help you keep your doors open and pay your staff. Take them to lunch to express your gratitude for their contract.

Of course, you will have already discussed money during the proposal and contract stages, but before you send your first invoice, call your client and review the details. Mention that as the end of the month is approaching, you will be sending them an invoice soon, and you want to confirm that you have the correct mailing address for the invoice and the right contact person. This may differ from the name specified in the contract. Find out if an e-mailed invoice is appropriate or if they prefer a hard copy sent through the mail.

Billing Schedules

Bill on time, because the sooner you get the invoice out, the sooner you will be paid. While this seems like a no-brainer, busy consultants have other things to do at the end of the month, like finalizing reports or preparing other deliverables. It is easy for your paperwork to slip. For your client, the 30-day clock starts to tick only when they receive the invoice and date-stamp it, so it is free money for them until you get around to asking for it.

Every extra day that you avoid sending out your invoices is a cash trap that delays your whole cash flow cycle. If you haven't been paid because you haven't sent the invoice yet, you won't have the money you need to pay your own vendors. This can become a vicious circle. If you find you are falling behind in managing your accounts, it's time to delegate this task to someone else.

Aged Accounts Receivable Reports

Your accounting software will prepare an aged accounts receivable report that lists outstanding invoices in order of due date. This makes it easy for you to keep track of what is owed so that you can follow up on accounts that are past due. Review the list at least once a week so that you can take the appropriate action.

Following Up

As soon as your aged accounts receivable report indicates that an invoice is past due, follow up with your client. There are many legitimate reasons for late payment. For example, your client might be sick or away on vacation. It could be budget time or year end, and all ongoing paperwork may be temporarily on hold. There could be a glitch in the client's accounting system. Your client may have subcontracted accounting to someone else or may have simply forgotten. Call or e-mail your client, and inquire politely about the fate of your invoice. If necessary, track the paper trail to the point where your invoice stalled. Use some creativity, and find out how to best work within your client's system.

When you have a client with a poor track record, ask for part of the contract to be prepaid. Better yet, don't take on the project at all. Follow Weiss's advice (2003, p. 90), and abandon no-growth business relationships. Pay no attention to the little voice in your head that says, "Yes, but it's such an interesting project." There are two reasons to ignore this voice: (1) If you lose money, you won't be around next year to do any projects at all, and (2) you won't have time to address those high-growth-potential, even more interesting projects that lie ahead if your energies are sapped by no-win situations.

Getting It in the Bank

Don't wait for your bookkeeper or assistant to deposit your checks for you. As soon as you receive a check, make a photocopy of it or keep the check stub, date-stamp it, and deposit it immediately. I carry a minioffice in my car with a letter opener, date stamp, and deposit book. I go directly from my postbox to the bank. Why wait? You can probably put that money to good use right away.

Direct Deposit

A few years ago, organizations discovered that by paying their bills online, they could save a lot of money in staff time, stationery, postage, and other hidden costs. Find out if your client can pay you in this way. Contact their accounts payable department, and provide the permissions they need to make this happen. Usually all that is required is a signed permission form and a cancelled check.

Ethical Practices

Billing honestly is a matter of trust. It also demonstrates that you have business systems and controls in place. Clients need to be properly informed about your fees and required payment methods before they enter into an agreement with you. These should be clear in your proposal, your contract, and your work plan, so there should be absolutely no surprises on your invoice. Your client could ask you to prove that you expended the amount of time indicated on your invoice. As you are probably tracking your time anyway, this should not be a problem. It is the client's right to know, but interestingly, they seldom ask.

Of course you must never double bill. If you work for more than one client while on a single business trip, for example, prorate your expenses by splitting the airfare and hotel costs between the two projects. While you are on site, be sure to mention to each client that you are working on the two projects and that you plan to split the expenses. They will appreciate your efficiency as well as their cost savings.

❖ ACCOUNTS PAYABLE

We never like to part with the money we have worked so hard to earn, but there are ways to beat the bill-paying blues. Here are some ways to manage your accounts payable.

Preparing Payments in Advance

Set up a system to mail your checks so that they arrive just on time. For example, we prepare a batch of checks and then attach a yellow sticky note to each envelope with the estimated mailing date. It is easy to grab one as you go out the door. You can also pay many of your bills online by setting up your vendors as payees and indicating what date the funds should be released. Taxes and payroll deductions can often be paid this way, and it saves a lot of time.

Understanding Creditors

Take a positive attitude with your creditors if you have to call with an inquiry about your bill. Understand that they are in business too and deserve to be paid. Reflect good business practice in all your dealings; you are part of the same business community.

Delayed Payments

The notion of collecting quickly and paying slowly when cash is in short supply evokes different opinions. Maxwell and Black (2009) suggest that delaying payments to your suppliers is one way to stretch tight cash. They suggest that you should try to negotiate more favorable terms, such as 45 or 60 days. However, Davidson and Dean (1992, pp. 62–63) see this as a simplistic business practice, because it neither increases revenue nor improves relationships with your creditors. Further it does nothing to eradicate the root causes of your delayed payment. The issue may have more to do with the way you manage your cash, or you may simply not have enough receivables to support your business.

❖ CASH FLOW

Cash flow is the cycle of cash that comes into and goes out of your business every month, and it can have either a positive or a negative bottom line. Your accounting package should allow you to generate current cash flow reports, so generate one every week. It is the single most important indicator of your business health, so tend it well.

Cash flow management can make scarce resources go further, particularly for start-up businesses that are cash poor. You don't want to turn away business because you can't afford to take it on. Maxwell and Black (2009) recommend a bootstrapping approach to cash management. This means that your business decisions have an impact on cash flow rather than on sales or profitability, which are more typical business indicators. Here are some bootstrapping tips.

Reducing Overhead

Having just set up your office, you are well aware of the costs involved, but you must continue to watch your overhead. Spend as little as you can, and do not take any cost as a given. Some suggestions include the following:

- Lease equipment or buy it second hand, but don't get into long-term service agreements.
- Use part-time contractors or share employees with other professionals.

- Outsource functions that aren't essential to your company, and use them only as needed.
- Turn every fixed cost into a variable cost; for example, pay staff an hourly rate as needed rather than a salary.

Managing Inventory

Be proactive about your purchasing habits, and use a just-in-time philosophy. Balance the cost of storing unused inventory against the few dollars you save by a bulk purchase. Consider storing inventory worth keeping in inexpensive storage space rather than in expensive leased office space. For example, I rent a storage locker for past project files and seven years' worth of business records. It cuts down on clutter, and the space is relatively cheap, yet I have the assurance of knowing that important files remain as a valuable archive.

Negotiating for Best Prices

Davidson and Dean (1992, pp. 61–63) suggest that you negotiate terms with suppliers. Seek favorable purchasing opportunities, and discipline yourself to be selective, to wait, or to say "no." My nephew sold stereo equipment when he was young, and he said that it was remarkable how much negotiation was possible at the end of the month when the salesman had to make his quota, and the customer was standing there with his checkbook open. So don't be afraid to bargain.

Hunt for value. Use discount plans for hotels and car rentals, seat sales for airlines, coupon books for restaurants, and reward cards for other purchases. Look for group purchasing programs or group discounts. For example, a chamber of commerce membership comes with a wide variety of vendor discounts. Professional organizations offer benefits such as group insurance. Don't be afraid to use your clients' discounts as well. For example, if you are working on a government contract, ask your client to prepare a letter confirming your engagement. Then you can ask for the much lower government rate at hotels.

Focusing on Productivity

How can you do things smarter, faster, and better? Use your research skills to analyze your timesheets and see where your time goes. When you hire staff, select them carefully, and keep them as long as possible. Staff turnover is a huge cash trap. Encourage them to share their bright ideas, and reward them for it. Many of the innovations that I still use today started with a great staff idea.

Managing Profits

Invest your extra cash, even if it is only for a week. If you can afford it, invest a proportion of every incoming check. Keep your money in safe and accessible short-term investments so that it is available when you need it. You can be sure that a rainy day will come along and your savings will come in handy.

A proactive approach to cash flow management can increase the long-term prospects of your company. Over time, your strategy will change, as costs are reduced and revenues are increased, but even when your business is more secure, the discipline that you learned through cash flow management will continue to serve you well.

❖ FINANCIAL STATEMENTS

There are two key financial reports that tell your company's financial story, the income statement and the balance sheet (Whitlock, 2003, pp. 5–8). You should look at them every month.

The Income Statement

The income statement tracks everything that happens in your business over a given period. Like a video camera that pans from month to month, it answers such questions as the following:

- Are my sales growing? (sales trends)
- Do I have the right service mix? (sales results by service)
- Has the cost of providing that service changed? (costs per service)
- What is happening to my overhead? (operating costs)
- Am I managing productivity? (personnel or subcontractor costs)
- What taxes did I pay? (tax costs)
- How well did I do? (net earnings)

The Balance Sheet

A different, but equally interesting, story is told by the balance sheet. It gets its name from the following financial equation:

$$Assets = Liabilities + Net\ Worth$$

The two sides of the equation must balance. Assets can generally be converted into cash and include your accounts receivable and your fixed assets. Liabilities are the debts your company has agreed to pay, including accounts payable, your line of credit, and any outstanding loans. Net worth is any money you have injected into the company for the long term as well as any profits that have been retained for future use. As Whitlock (2003, p. 8) explains, unlike the video of your income statement, your balance sheet is a static snapshot taken at a given point in time. It is a cumulative archive that describes the performance of your company from the time you opened your doors.

These financial statements are useful for looking at trends over time. Ask such questions as these:

- How did I do last year?
- How does this compare with five years ago? Ten years ago?
- Where am I likely to be a year from now? Two years from now?
- How have I done overall?

You can use your financial reports for your own assessment, but they can also be shared with others such as your bank manager, or, once you are incorporated, with your board of directors.

❖ GETTING A LOAN

Banks are in the business of lending money. Just as we look for good clients who will pay their invoices, banks look for good borrowers who will pay their loans. You need to understand how best to deal with the bank, because sooner or later, you will probably need to borrow money from them. There are two types of loans that entrepreneurs access frequently, the operating line of credit and the term loan.

An Operating Line of Credit

Small businesses deal with temporary cash shortages by using an operating line of credit. As funds are borrowed, the amount of credit available is reduced; as funds are repaid, the amount of credit available increases again. A line of credit allows for the steady management of your accounts payable despite the uneven inward flow of revenue into your accounts receivable. Once the credit line is established, your business can borrow the funds at any time, but it costs little or nothing to maintain when you are not using it. You have to make sure that money coming in exceeds money going out over a reasonable period of time, but this is generally an efficient way to manage cash flow variations.

Don't wait until the wolf is at the door to establish your line of credit. Do it when business is good. This will allow you to create a good credit history by repaying quickly any money that is borrowed. Banks are more likely to help you if your business does not appear to be at risk (Davidson & Dean, 1992; Whitlock, 2003).

A Term Loan

A longer-term capital loan may be required from time to time to cover one-time costs, such as purchasing equipment or renovating space. The interest rate tends to be slightly higher than for other types of loans, but the loan generally involves a fixed rate of interest for a specified period of time. Regular payments are made on a monthly basis. Typically, the bank will want collateral pledged that is equivalent to two to three times the amount of the loan.

Preparing a Loan Proposal

It takes time to obtain a term loan, and you need to prepare your proposal to the bank carefully. Your business plan will provide much of the background information. Here is a suggested outline of what your banker will want to see (Abbott, 1987).

1. Background and financial history of your business

2. Current data, including a list of aged accounts receivable and accounts payable and other upcoming, committed projects

3. Projections for your cash flow, income statement, and balance sheet and the assumptions related to these projections

4. Other information that provides a fuller picture of you and your business, such as work samples, examples, and pictures

5. Personal résumé

6. Personal financial statement

7. Your financial plan, which answers the following questions:
    a. How much money is needed?
    b. What will the money be used for?
    c. How and when will it be repaid?
    d. If something goes wrong, what is your contingency plan?

If you have already obtained a line of credit, you will have developed a relationship with your banker and may find this more formal process less stressful. You can try to negotiate a reduction in the interest rate or to whittle down other service costs by being informed about what other banks are charging.

Once the bank has agreed to lend you the money, you will receive a letter that sets out the details of your credit arrangements and identifies the security or collateral that you must provide. Failure to repay a term loan has severe consequences for your business and could result in the bank taking over your business assets, collecting your receivables, or appointing a manager of your business. You will need to sign a number of security documents and each has significant legal implications so consider having your lawyer review them.

Maxwell and Black (2009, p. 3) comment that "the raising of financing is a continuous activity for most business and it is likely that you will require multiple injections of capital, so it is best to plan for this from the start." I have had several term loans over the years and have used them to purchase computers and servers and to renovate leased office space. These loans allowed me to grow my business in ways that would never have been possible through my regular cash flow. The regular monthly payments required simply became part of the cost of doing business.

❖ GETTING IN OVER YOUR HEAD

By now it is clear that managing a consulting practice is more difficult than running many other kinds of businesses. Rather than selling a standardized product, you rely on the sale of your consulting services and on producing unique, labor-intensive reports and other deliverables. You have to provide services to your client before an invoice can be prepared, and then it generally takes between 30 and 60 days to collect the cash. Typically, when the money is received, it is used to continue supporting costs, complete the project, and generate the next project. There is a lot of room for error at each step of this cycle.

Davidson & Dean (1992, pp. 170–178) have identified eight errors made by the unseasoned or overly eager consultant that can result in cash traps:

1. Failing to closely read all parts of the Request for Proposals

2. Being unrealistic in determining your ability to perform tasks and assume risk

3. Bidding on unreliable project descriptions or on specifications that are ambiguous, confusing, or out of date

4. Bidding based on estimates instead of on actual cost data

5. Bidding under time pressure so that errors in calculation or judgment occur

6. Accepting an unrealistic time frame

7. Bidding on exploratory work when feasibility is unclear

8. Being afraid to take remedial action as soon as it is needed

Many cash traps can be avoided through a carefully prepared proposal and by setting up systematic approaches to business management such as are described in this book. However, at the end of the day, your business success depends on projects continuing to come through the door to maintain the forward momentum. This is why consultants everywhere, whether new or experienced, see marketing as their lifeblood. Profit margins tend to be low, and while successful consultants make a comfortable living, few are rich. The smart ones manage their money very, very well.

❖ USEFUL RESOURCES

- For advice on how to get paid faster, see

  http://brickyardblog.com/?tag=businessbrickyard

- For more on managing cash flow, see

  http://www.mikedubose.com/posts/managing_cash_flow_
  to_avoid_business_failure

  http://www.canadaone.com/ezine/feb11/cash_flow.html

- To find out what bankers want to know before they grant a loan, see

  http://www.questia.com/googleScholar.qst?docId=5000113849

  http://www.ehow.com/info_8044346_types-want-before
  -extending-loan.html

❖ DISCUSSION QUESTIONS AND ACTIVITIES

1. With belt tightening becoming a way of life, it is getting harder for consultants to collect payment. What do you need to understand about the payment process? What do your clients need to understand? Prepare a dialogue between yourself and one of your clients to explain why you need to get paid.

2. Review the list of monthly expenses provided in Chapter 8. How can you decrease your costs? Think of ways to stretch your cash as far as possible.

3. List five cash traps that could be a problem for you. What changes can you make to your current practice to avoid these issues and improve your business management strategies?

❖ REFERENCES

Abbott, S. G. (1987, October). *Finding money*. Paper presented at Successful Women Conference, Calgary, AB.

Davidson, J. P., & Dean, C. W. (1992). *Cash traps: Small business secrets for reducing costs and improving cash flow*. New York, NY: Wiley.

Maxwell, A., & Black, S. (2009, March 11). *Running on empty: Growing your business through bootstrapping*. Webinar presented as part of the Ready, Set, Grow webinar series of the CATA Alliance. Retrieved from http://www.innova tioncentre.ca/files/Growing_your_Busi ness_through_Bootstrapping.pdf

Toncré, E. (1986). *Maximizing cash flow: Practical financial controls for your business*. Toronto, ON: Wiley.

Weiss, A. (2003). *Million dollar consulting: The professional's guide to growing a practice.* New York, NY: McGraw-Hill.

Whitlock, M. (2003, February). *Real cash, real profit: Financial tools for success.* Workshop by Tannian Consulting, sponsored by APB Financial, Calgary, AB.

13

Ownership Structures

Highlights:

- Explore four ownership structures.

- Consider the advantages and disadvantages of each.

- Learn why independent consultants made the choice they did.

- Consider your ownership options.

Tlhere are many things to consider when thinking about an owner-ship structure for your consulting business. These include the nature and volume of your activities, your personal financial requirements, your tolerance for risk, your need for control, how long you want your firm to last, what you want to do with your profits, the nature of the legal and tax environment in which you operate, and your vision for the future of your business.

The legal and financial implications of this decision mean that you must research this topic well. There is a lot of information available online, but much of it is dry and legalistic, and if you have limited business experience, it can be hard to understand the implications for you. You will need to consult with a lawyer and an accountant before you make your selection. A lawyer will help you understand legal requirements, the registration process, required record keeping and reporting, and personal liability issues. An accountant will explain the tax implications of each option and can help you determine the most advantageous one for you.

This chapter looks at four ownership structures and the pros and cons of each. Brief vignettes of four consultants' choices are also included. There is no one-size-fits-all solution, and so you need to explore your options and then make an informed decision.

❖   SOLE PROPRIETORSHIP

A sole proprietorship is the simplest business structure, because it is owned and operated by one person. To set it up, you need to obtain only whatever local licenses are required to operate a business in your city or county and then get down to work. According to the U.S. Small Business Administration (2010), most small business owners start out this way.

Advantages of Being a Sole Proprietor

There are a number of advantages to the sole proprietorship (U.S. Small Business Administration, 2010; Gray, 2008, p. 36).

Ease of formation. Few legal restrictions and little formality are needed to establish a sole proprietorship. There are no complex forms, agreements, or contracts required between you and anyone else. In most jurisdictions, you just have to register your business and obtain the proper licenses required by different levels of government. There is nothing to stop you from starting almost immediately.

Low cost. Registering your business and obtaining required licenses involve minimal costs. There are few legal fees, because you do not need either a partnership agreement or incorporation documents. Accounting fees are low, because annual reporting is not required.

Simple requirements. The main concept to understand about a sole proprietorship is that you and your business are one and the same. Your business and personal income are taxed together. Unlike other forms of business, there is little government control, so record keeping is minimal, and few reports must be filed with government agencies and departments.

High control. As owner, you are in complete control and do not need to get approval from partners, shareholders, or a board of directors. Within the parameters of the law, you can make any decisions you see fit. Thus, you have the flexibility that a start-up company needs to respond quickly to market demands and business priorities.

Ownership of profits. You receive all of the income generated by the business, and you can keep it or reinvest it as you wish. You do not have to share your profits with anyone except the tax department, because they flow directly to your personal tax return. Losses, such as those associated with start-up, can be used to reduce your personal tax bill.

Easy termination. While you are probably not thinking about this now, the termination of a sole proprietorship is easy. Apart from any legal responsibilities you might have to employees, creditors, and clients, you can sell the business or close it and walk away.

Disadvantages of Being a Sole Proprietor

While the advantages look pretty compelling, before you decide, consider these important disadvantages.

Unlimited liability. Because you and your business are one, by far the biggest risk for the sole proprietor is your legal responsibility for all the debts and other liabilities your business may create. Your personal assets, such as your house or other property, your car, and your personal investments, as well as your business assets, can be seized to pay for outstanding debts or liabilities.

Taxation issues. A sole proprietorship has pass-through taxation. The business itself does not file a tax return. Instead the income passes through and is reported on your personal tax return. In the United States, a sole proprietor is required to pay a self-employment tax for Social Security and Medicare, and it is double the amount withheld from the paychecks of most wage earners, because it must cover both the employer's and the employee's share of the tax (Internal Revenue Service, 2010). You pay your income tax and self-employment taxes on a quarterly basis. In Canada, you must adjust your business income by the taxes paid, and you can deduct some expenses associated with the cost of doing business. You are also expected to remit on a quarterly basis (Canada Revenue Agency, 2010). Because tax laws change and loopholes come and go, it is important to consult with your accountant at least once a year. This way you can make adjustments to the taxes you have paid and determine if a sole proprietorship is still the best option for you.

Harder to borrow money. In a sole proprietorship it is more difficult to raise money. A lender wants as much security as possible, but as a sole proprietor, you have only personal collateral to offer, and this may not be attractive enough. As a result, you may have to rely on using funds from personal savings or consumer loans.

Only one decision maker. As a sole proprietor, you have lots of control, but all the decision-making responsibility falls on your shoulders. Your business could suffer due to your lack of experience. In a partnership or corporation, a broader range of skills and competencies is usually available, although still this does not ensure that the quality of decisions will be good.

Employee perceptions. A sole proprietor is generally seen as a one-man band. You may have a hard time attracting high-caliber employees or those motivated by the prospect of partnership or partial ownership, because you cannot offer them a career path.

Impact on benefits. In the United States, some benefits, such as the owner's medical insurance premiums, are not directly deductible from business income. Instead, they are only partially deductible as an adjustment to income (U.S. Small Business Administration, 2010).

Duration depends on the health of the owner. The life of your business depends on your own health. As Kubr (2002, p. 764) suggests, a disadvantage for the sole proprietor is that even with health insurance and income-loss insurance, a prolonged illness can adversely affect your business. While a firm normally ceases to exist with the death or retirement of the owner, your estate will remain liable for any outstanding debts.

One Consultant's Choice

Independent consultant Stephen Maack of REAP Change Consultants in Los Angeles chose a sole proprietorship for his business structure (S. C. Maack, personal communication, July 20, 2010). He did not want to take a lot of time, money, or effort to set up his business. He registered his firm's name as a DBA with the City of Los Angeles, deliberately choosing a name with the word "consultants" in it to give his firm added stature. He liked the idea of working on his own yet appreciated the flexibility of being able to add associates as needed. Realizing that a sole proprietorship would put his assets at risk, and needing to respond to a client's request that he have business insurance, he acquired both general and professional liability insurance.

❖ PARTNERSHIP

A partnership is an association between two or more people who combine their skills and resources to conduct a business and share their profits, losses, and liabilities. It is created by either a verbal or a written contract. The key concept is that a partnership is a relationship between individuals and is not a separate legal entity. Each partner shares the net income of the partnership, which is then taxed as personal income. Kubr (2002, p. 764) indicates that the partnership structure is common among management consultants.

There are different types of partnerships, and each has its own complexities, but for a consulting business, a general partnership is the usual choice. Partners divide responsibility for management and share the profit or loss according to their partnership agreement. Equal shares are assumed, unless there is a written agreement that states otherwise.

Because relationships are the key to any successful partnership, and because the financial rewards and liabilities can be significant, choosing a partner is a serious business. Many people think that a *gentleman's agreement* and a handshake are all you need. As Kubr comments, "Individuals who have difficulty working together, have different conceptions of professional service and ethics, or do not trust each other for any reason should avoid becoming partners" (2002, p. 764).

Kuryllowicz (2003, pp. 14–17) offers a number of tips for selecting partners:

- Don't partner with a spouse or friend—look to business acquaintances instead.
- Research your proposed partners, and check out their reputations with mutual acquaintances, suppliers, clients, and employees.
- Choose partners with skills and experiences that are complementary to your own.

- Focus on your partners' personal characteristics, including ethics, integrity, and trustworthiness.
- Make sure that your business goals and objectives are similar to those of your partners.
- Be open, flexible, and creative.
- Make sure your partners have already demonstrated success in business.
- Set boundaries between your business partners and your private life.

For your partnership to survive, you need flexibility on a day-to-day basis. Many partners develop a high degree of tolerance for different personal values and behaviors and are prepared to compromise significantly in order to support their partnership structure (Kubr, 2002, p. 764).

Once you have decided on a partnership structure, you need to devote the time and effort necessary to develop a strong and unambiguous partnership agreement. It should set out the contribution made by each partner to the business, including financial, material, and managerial support. It should define the role of each partner and how decisions will be made, profits shared, and disputes resolved. Finally, it should outline how future partners will be admitted to the partnership, how partners can be bought out, and what steps should be taken to dissolve the partnership (U.S. Small Business Administration, 2010).

Gray (2008, p. 39) suggests using a checklist to guide discussion with your prospective business partner. Then you should each consult with your own lawyer and accountant to confirm your understanding. (See Exhibit 13.1.)

Advantages of a Partnership Structure

There are a number of advantages to the partnership structure (Gray, 2008, pp. 37–38; Kubr, 2002, p. 764; U.S. Small Business Administration, 2010).

Ease of formation. Apart from the development of the partnership agreement, partnerships are relatively easy to establish, and legal formalities and expenses are few compared to incorporation.

Pride of ownership. Shared ownership and the sense of belonging to a select group of companions can generate personal motivation, especially for independent consultants who may be tired of working on their own. The profit motive can be reinforced as more people are

Exhibit 13.1   Suggested Articles in a Partnership Agreement

Use this checklist to ensure that your partnership agreement defines the roles of the partners in the business (Gray, 2008, p. 39).

- Name, purpose, and location of partnership

- Duration of agreement

- Names and character of partners (general or limited, active or silent)

- Financial contribution by partners (at inception, at later date)

- Role of individual partners in business management

- Authority (authority of partners in conduct of business)

- Nature and degree or each partner's contribution to firm's consulting services

- Business expenses (how handled)

- Separate debts

- Signing of checks

- Division of profits and losses

- Books, records, and method of accounting

- Draws or salaries

- Absence and disability

- Death of a partner (dissolution and winding up)

- Rights of continuing partner

- Employee management

- Sale of partnership interest

- Release of debts

- Settlement of disputes; arbitration

- Additions, alternations, or modifications to partnership agreement

- Noncompetition in the event of departure

SOURCE: Gray, D. (2008). *Start & run a consulting business* (8th ed.). Bellingham, WA: Self-Counsel Press.& North Vancouver, BC: Self-Counsel Press. Used with permission.

involved and have a vested interest. Internal competition may be a positive force.

Availability of more resources. A partnership can pool the funds of a number of people, while the sole proprietor has only personal resources to draw upon. The presence of more than one owner increases opportunities to raise funds, loans, or investments. Costs such as space, equipment, and administrative support can be shared.

Division of labor. A partnership optimizes partners' skills and provides an opportunity for larger and more complex assignments. The combined expertise of several partners can be more effective, especially if technical knowledge, sales ability, and financial skills are all represented. With more than one key person, the business can continue in the absence of one of the partners, providing more opportunity for vacations or professional development.

Freedom from government control. Compared to a corporation, a partnership is relatively free from legislation and bureaucratic red tape. Business decisions are limited only by the partners' ability to agree. The profits from the business flow directly through to the partners' personal tax returns.

Employee perceptions. Prospective employees may be attracted to the business due to the incentive of becoming a partner in the future. A career path is more evident than in a sole proprietorship.

Disadvantages of a Partnership Structure

Despite these attractions, there are some disadvantages to partnerships that need to be considered before making a decision.

Unlimited liability. Like the sole proprietorship, the business and its owners are seen as a single entity. Thus each partner has unlimited liability, both individually and collectively, for all the errors, obligations, debts, and liabilities of the overall partnership and for those of the various partners as they relate to the business. Each partner's personal assets can be seized if necessary to pay for outstanding business debts.

Managing conflict. Because agreement must be reached on every important decision, harmonizing partners' individual dreams, preferences, goals, and management styles can be difficult. At the outset, it may not be possible to foresee if personalities and styles will clash, but conflict is common in partnerships, and dissolution is frequent. Even if partners respect and like each other, problems can arise and destroy the partnership, causing financial and personal hardship for all concerned.

Partnership agreement problems. The larger a partnership becomes, the more complex the written agreement has to be to protect the rights and identify the responsibilities of each partner. It can be difficult to dispose of partnership interests, because, to withdraw capital from the business, approval is required from all the other partners. This takes time and involves legal and administrative expenses.

Taxation and benefit issues. The taxation issues are similar to those of a sole proprietorship with the added complication that the profits must be shared with others. In the United States, some employee benefits are not deductible from business income on tax returns (U.S. Small Business Administration, 2010).

Unstable duration. The partnership may have a limited life, because any change to the composition of the partners, such as the admission, withdrawal, or death of a partner, automatically ends the partnership. In each case, if the business is to continue, a new partnership agreement must be prepared.

One Consultant's Choice

Independent consultant Jean Haley Shumway of Hayward, Wisconsin, chose a partnership structure for her consulting firm. As she described it (Haley, 2004), her early business success and exhausting work schedule led her to look for a partner who could share the burden. She recruited someone she had worked with before who had a similar work ethic and a complementary skill set. With the help of their lawyers, they created a partnership agreement. It split project profits down the middle, but it did not reward either partner for winning a project, nor did it address the relative proportion or differing value of work contributed by each. Soon afterward, the political climate changed, business became scarce, and finances were tight. Because Jean cared so much about the firm, she could not either give up control or admit to failure. She and her partner avoided each other and did not discuss the mounting issues. Less than two years later, their partnership broke up. The dissolution process was costly and time consuming, but the emotional fallout was the most difficult part of all. Based on her experience, Jean concluded that a business structure should reflect the consultant's personality and sense of ownership as well as legal and financial requirements.

❖ CORPORATION

A corporation can be established and owned by one or more individuals. It has two fundamental characteristics. First, it is a legal entity and exists separately from its owners, meaning that it has all the legal rights and responsibilities of an individual person (Gray, 2008, p. 38).

Second, it has a life of its own and does not cease to exist when owner-ship changes or an owner withdraws from the business or dies (Kubr, 2002, p. 765; U.S. Small Business Administration, 2010). It can be taxed, it can be sued, and it can enter into contractual agreements. The own-ers are the shareholders, and they elect a board of directors to oversee major policies and decisions. Size is not an issue. It is possible to be a sole owner, sole shareholder, and sole director in a small incorporated business. Whether the corporation is large or small, owners have no personal liability for its obligations and debts.

In the United States there are several variations on the corporation that have been developed mainly for tax purposes. Their complexities are such that consulting a tax advisor is essential. They include the fol-lowing:

- A *regular C corporation* is a designation used by the U.S. Internal Revenue Service (IRS). Money left inside the corporation is taxed as profit and then is taxed again as income when an owner takes it out as dividends.

- A *subchapter S corporation* is not a separate structure but is just a tax election (U.S. Small Business Administration, 2010). While it is not recognized in all states, it is a popular structure for small businesses in the United States. You can have up to 35 shareholders and one class of stock. The shareholders can pass through earnings and profits directly to their personal tax returns, thus overcoming the double-tax problem of the regular C corporation. Further, the shareholders can offset business losses incurred by the corporation against their income (Gray, 2008, p. 43). Any shareholder who performs work for the cor-poration must be an employee, receiving wages that meet standards of "reasonable compensation." This can vary by region as well as by occupation, but the basic rule of thumb is to pay yourself whatever you would have to pay someone else to do your job (U.S. Small Business Administration, 2010). It means that you have to set up a payroll sys-tem and pay for Social Security and Medicare. If you don't do this, the IRS can reclassify all the earnings and profits of the corporation as wages, and then you are liable for all payroll taxes on the full amount. If you incorporate as an S corporation, you do not have to pay self-employment tax and can claim some earnings as a dividend (at a lower tax rate) instead of as payroll. At some point in the future, you may wish to convert an S corporation to a C corporation, and this process is quite simple, but you cannot revert back again for several years.

- A *limited liability company* or LLC is a relatively new type of hybrid business structure now permissible in most states. It is very popular for small business start-ups, because it is easy to set up and offers the pass-through tax advantages of a partnership with the liability protection of a corporation. LLCs can have more than 35 owners (called members) and can have different classes of securities. Annual fees are required, and any modification to the structure requires an additional fee. There is a time limit to the duration of an LLC, but it can be extended by a vote of the members at the time of expiration. LLCs can have foreign investors and thus can take advantage of the fast-growing international business market (Gray, 2008, p. 43). Most states allow for a single-owner LLC, but the tax implications may be the same as those for either a sole proprietor or partner. You are liable to pay a self-employment tax on the full profit of the LLC up to a certain level.

In Canada, if you decide to incorporate, you must decide between federal and provincial/ territorial incorporation, although this choice seems to relate mainly to your residency and scope of practice; you can still work anywhere in the country. There are also public, private, and nonprofit options, but tax variations like those listed above for the United States do not apply.

Whatever form of corporation you choose, you need to complete incorporation requirements prior to starting your business or, alternatively, you can determine a specific point in time to transfer from one business structure to another. There are a number of requirements you need to fulfill and, while the list may seem daunting at first, once a lawyer helps you get established, maintenance is quite straightforward. These include the following (Gray, 2008, pp. 41–42; Kubr, 2002, pp. 765–766):

- Preparing a statement of corporate purposes, a company charter, and bylaws (These can be very broad or quite restrictive, depending on where you live.)
- Identifying shareholders and preparing shareholders' agreements
- Identifying company directors
- Holding annual shareholders' and directors' meetings and recording the minutes
- Maintaining adequate accounts and records
- Maintaining a corporate bank account separate from your personal account

- Submitting payroll records
- Paying taxes and filing annual corporate reports on time
- Keeping and updating a minute book of all documents related to your corporation
- Ensuring that you have adequate capital (through either business income or financing) to meet your creditors' claims
- Being visible as a corporation with limited liability by attaching an approved designation such as "Inc." or "Ltd." to your business name
- Acting as an agent of your corporation by using your title (e.g., president) after your name when you sign official documents

Advantages of the Corporate Structure

There are some important advantages to the corporate structure (Gray, 2008, pp. 38–40).

Limited liability. The biggest advantage is that shareholders have limited liability for the company's debts. Your personal assets cannot be seized to pay for the debts incurred by the business (assuming that you have not signed any personal guarantees for the company's bank loans). There are a few exceptions to liability limitations that are mainly related to issues of fraud. The so-called *corporate veil* that protects you from your company's debts can quickly disappear if the courts determine that you have disregarded corporate requirements in some way.

Tax advantages. Regardless of what type of corporate structure you select, there are more opportunities for tax planning, and various tax advantages are available. Being able to separate the taxation of personal income (such as salary, bonuses, and dividends) from the corporation's profits may help to lower your taxes. The cost of benefits provided to employees can be deducted from corporate profits. Keeping retained earnings in the company can help to offset future losses.

Financing is more readily available. Investors and lenders find it more attractive to invest in a corporation with limited liability than to invest in a business whose unlimited liability can put their investments at risk. A corporation can also raise additional funds through the sale of stock.

Management and employee flexibility. As long as employee contracts are honored, staff in management positions can be changed as needed without invoking the stringent requirements of a partnership agreement. This flexibility allows a quicker response to changing market demands. Employees can be given stock options to share in the ownership, and this may increase their incentive to contribute their skills and expertise.

Greater credibility. The very act of incorporating is seen as an indication of greater stability and credibility than is afforded a sole proprietor. Some clients will work only with incorporated companies.

Continued life of the company. A corporation continues indefinitely as long as it is deemed a *going concern* and reports are filed annually. It is a relatively simple procedure to transfer ownership by share transfer, unless there are corporate restrictions to the contrary. Thus the number of co-owners or shareholders can change, and the company can be sold. The death of a shareholder does not affect the life of the corporation. The fact that its existence continues is an effective way to build and maintain goodwill.

Disadvantages of the Corporate Structure

Notwithstanding these strong advantages, there are some factors that can work against this option.

Taxation. They say that nothing is more certain than death and taxes, and it seems that no matter which business structure you select, taxation can be problematic. The double taxation on the C corporation's income and on dividends paid to its shareholders; the self-employment tax required of LLC owners, sole proprietors, and partners; and the payroll administration costs required of an S corporation can all be issues for the fledgling entrepreneur. In the end, it is a question of what you can tolerate the most, what your advisors recommend, and what costs the least for you.

Legal and administrative costs. Incorporation takes more time and effort to set up and maintain than other business structures. It is more expensive to hire a lawyer to work through the documents and forms required for incorporation, although you will need legal advice no matter which structure you pick. It is possible to try a do-it-yourself approach to incorporation, but unless you want to become an expert, I don't recommend taking the time to learn the ropes. Small business lawyers incorporate companies all the time and are generally up to date on new legislative requirements. Once you are incorporated and your minute book is set up, it is a simple matter to follow the regulations and file the required forms. Filing costs are minimal. Overall there is more paperwork, because you are being monitored by more government agencies, and thus administrative costs are higher.

One Consultant's Choice

Susan Wolfe of Susan Wolfe and Associates, LLC in Duncanville, Texas, chose the LLC structure for her company (Wolfe, personal communication, July 20, 2010). She wanted her venture to look official and appear larger than it was. She planned to use a network of associates, drawing on a multidisciplinary pool as needed. She also wanted the finances and obligations of the business to remain separate from those of her family so that neither could affect the other. For her, the benefits of this structure far outweighed any drawbacks.

❖ NONPROFIT CORPORATION

While the nonprofit corporation is not common, it is a business structure of interest for independent consultants with a social mission. Surplus funds are not distributed to owners or shareholders but instead are used to further the organization's goals, which may relate to promoting art, science, religion, charity, or another similar endeavor. While the corporation is not focused on profit, the employees still receive fair wages. A nonprofit corporation needs three people to set it up, and it can invite the public to subscribe for shares. There are some restrictions on the number of shareholders and shares, and some nonprofit companies are exempt from paying federal taxes.

While many nonprofit organizations are not incorporated, incorporation provides legal status and various rights and responsibilities that are similar to those of other types of corporations. For example, a nonprofit corporation can enter into contracts, buy land, borrow money, and have bank accounts in its own name. The liability of the members of the corporation is limited, and continuity can be assured regardless of membership changes.

A nonprofit corporation has to be registered with the relevant federal, state, and/or provincial agencies, and documents need to be filed on an annual basis. The objects of the corporation must be outlined in a memorandum of association, which states that no dividends or income will be paid to members and that all profits will be used to promote company objectives (Government of Alberta, 2010). A set of articles is also required to outline the rules of operation. A board of directors is established to set policies for the organization and needs to meet at least once a year. Should the corporation be sold, the proceeds must be used for public good, and neither staff nor board members may benefit from the sale. In some states the corporation cannot be sold but can be discontinued or made dormant pending later reactivation (CorporationCentre.ca, 2010).

Advantages of a Nonprofit Corporate Structure

One reason consultants select a nonprofit structure is to become eligible for government and foundation research grants that are not available to for-profit businesses. Many foundations are required to spend a certain proportion of their assets in grants each year, and these are generally awarded to nonprofit organizations. While foundations do have some contract-based funds, they are much more limited, require a different type of record keeping, and are generally used for administrative purposes only (M. Hwalek, personal communication, July 15, 2010). Thus, in this context, a nonprofit status for an applied research company has a distinct advantage.

Another key advantage is exemption from corporate and sales taxes, although the same payroll taxes, Social Security, Medicare, and unemployment deductions are required as in for-profit structures. Nonprofit corporations must file a tax form each year that outlines income and expenses, including the salaries of key staff members.

Disadvantages of a Nonprofit Corporate Structure

One of the main disadvantages is the amount of paperwork required to complete registration and obtain tax-exempt status from the IRS. Every year, the financial records must be audited. Another disadvantage reported by some nonprofits is the amount of time and effort required to manage a board of directors (M. L. Ray, personal communication, July 15, 2010).

One Consultant's Choice

Marilyn L. Ray, executive director of Finger Lakes Law & Social Policy Center, Inc. (FLC) in Ithaca, New York, worked with two other individuals to set up a nonprofit corporation, because they wanted to obtain government and foundation grants that required a nonprofit status. She explained that state laws for nonprofit corporations vary, but in New York State, she had to file a request with the Charities Bureau in the office of the state attorney general, and include a mission statement, bylaws, and information about their board of directors and the processes used to select and remove corporate officers. Once FLC was state certified, they filed with the IRS for a tax-exempt designation. If their earnings exceed expenses in a particular year, then the balance is rolled forward, but if there is a deficit, strategies such as cost cutting or obtaining a bridge loan may be required while waiting for the next grant to be received. To Ray, the main differences between this structure and a for-profit one include not being able to build up the value of the business and not being able to pay shareholders. While this nonprofit model may not be for everyone, FLC has been operating successfully since 1989 and has obtained many interesting research grants.

All of the consultants who shared their choices about ownership structure with me stressed two important points. First, the tax implications and liability issues, as well as the potential advantages and disadvantages for each structure, vary depending on where you live. Second, you need both a lawyer and an accountant to help you select the right business structure for you.

It is encouraging to note that many independent consultants are confident about the choices they have made but feel willing to revisit their decisions if circumstances change. Many start their businesses as a sole proprietorship and then move to an LLC to reduce their personal liability. Others, once incorporated, move back to a sole proprietorship as their business slows down. Depending on their relationships with colleagues, some move into partnerships, and some move out again. Others move from profit to nonprofit status as business opportunities arise. The lesson to take from this is heartening. Nothing is cast in stone, and so if you make a decision about ownership and then your circumstances change, you can change your ownership structure as well.

❖ USEFUL RESOURCES

Lots of advice on business ownership structures is available at government websites.

- In the United States

  See the U.S. Small Business Administration (SBA) Program Office at http://www.sba.gov/category/navigation-structure/starting-managing-business/starting-business/establishing-business/incorporating-registering-your-.

  To find out about tax challenges for independent workers, see http://fu-res.org/pdfs/advocacy/issue-briefs/tax-challenges .pdf.

- In Canada

  For information on incorporation, see http://www.ic.gc.ca/eic/site/cd-dgc.nsf/eng/h_cs01914.html.

  For tax implications for sole proprietorships and partnerships see: http://www.cra-arc.gc.ca/tx/bsnss/tpcs/slprtnr/menu-eng .html.

❖ DISCUSSION QUESTIONS AND ACTIVITIES

1. If you were considering establishing a consulting firm with a colleague, what key topics would you need to discuss with this potential partner? What pitfalls would you want to avoid? How would you protect this business relationship?

2. Of the four ownership structures presented in this chapter, which one seems to be the most appropriate for your business? What additional information would you need to obtain before selecting this option?

3. Interview three independent consultants in your community who have chosen different ownership structures. What were the main reasons for their choice? Would any of these considerations be important for your ownership decision? Why or why not?

❖ REFERENCES

Canada Revenue Agency. (2010). *Sole proprietorships and partnerships.* Retrieved from http://www.cra-arc.gc.ca/tx/bsnss/tpcs/slprtnr/menu-eng.html

CorporationCentre.ca. (2010, July 24). *Non-profit organizations: FAQs.* Retrieved from http://www.corporationcentre.ca/docen/home/faq.asp?id=incnp

Government of Alberta. (2010). *Non-profit companies.* Retrieved from http://www.servicealberta.ca/714.cfm

Gray, D. (2008). *Start and run a consulting business* (8th ed.). North Vancouver, BC: International Self-Counsel Press.

Haley, J. (2004, November). *Troubles in paradise: The pitfalls of partnership.* Paper presented at the meeting of the American Evaluation Association, Atlanta, GA.

Internal Revenue Service. (2010). *Self-employment tax.* Retrieved from http://www.irs.gov/businesses/small/article/0,,id=98846,00.html

Kubr, M. (2002). *Management consulting: A guide to the profession* (4th ed.). Geneva, Switzerland: International Labour Office.

Kuryllowicz, K. (2003, Winter). How to pick a partner. *SOHO Business Report.* British Columbia, CA: Dream Launchers.

U.S. Small Business Administration. (2010). *Choose a structure: Forms of ownership.* Retrieved from http://www.sba.gov/smallbusiness-planner/start/chooseastructure/START_FORMS_OWNERSHIP.html

14

Managing Risk

Highlights:

- Explore the five areas of risk that independent consultants face.

- Look at ways to assess your risk and develop a risk management plan.

- Understand the common types of insurance available.

- Learn the difference between an insurance agent and an insurance broker.

- Consider economical ways to purchase insurance.

Is your consulting business a risky business? "You bet it is!" says Susan Anastasio, author of the *Small Business Insurance & Risk Management Guide* (n.d., p. 2). Yet consultants tend to avoid thinking about threats of damage, injury, liability, loss, and catastrophe until they are forced to, and who can blame them? Insurance is a tedious and complex topic. It takes time to work through all the material available to make an informed choice. The typical scenario for an independent consultant goes something like this:

I am entering into a "quick" contracting arrangement, and the client needs me to get business insurance. I have not been required to have it before, and I have no idea what type of insurance I need. Is it really relevant for me?

Boop (2010b), a small business attorney, suggests that among business owners there are three common myths about business insurance:

• Myth #1: "Nobody will sue me, my business does not make a lot of money, and you can't squeeze blood from a turnip. My business is not collectible." False. Every business can be sued, and once a judgment is rendered, it is likely that money will be collected. Judgment liens can be renewed, wages can be garnished, equipment can be seized, bank accounts and assets can be seized. As Boop says, "Everybody is collectible at the hands of a persistent attorney."

• Myth #2: "My business is a corporation. The corporate format protects me from liability, so I don't need insurance." False. The corporate structure can protect individual investors, owners, and officers from personal liability for the actions and debts of the corporation, but the "corporate veil" can be pierced (e.g., for fraud). When that occurs, the owner may be liable personally and will have to respond to a judgment with personal assets. In Boop's view, the smaller you are, the more likely it is that this will happen.

• Myth #3: "My family and my business partners are friends. If I die or become disabled, they'll just work it out." False. Boop says that most small businesses do not survive the death or disability of a principal member. Remaining family members and business partners rarely work things out. Most businesses do not have the cash flow necessary to pay the estate of a deceased member for its interest in the business, and the business may have to be dissolved.

The odds favor a typical company incurring some type of loss at some point in time. For example, one in four CEOs will experience a disability and will be forced away from their business for weeks, if not months. How will the bills be paid then? As Davidson and Dean suggest (1992, pp. 106–107), the unforeseen, costly event has a way of rearing its ugly head when you are already down and least able to respond to it.

As they say, "You can't operate a viable business on the hope and prayer that nothing will go wrong—something will and it always has a cost."

A lack of attention to potential risks and limited knowledge about what to do prevents some independent consultants from being proactive. Like the proverbial ostrich with its head in the sand, they do not see the semi-trailer truck headed their way. They are too busy working on their latest project to worry about it. If they had anticipated potential problems, considered alternative solutions, and made some risk management decisions, they would be much less likely to encounter a problem in the first place, and when they did, they would be able to handle it more effectively. Our consultant in the above scenario will probably rush out tomorrow and buy some insurance to meet contract requirements, but she may not understand either what she is buying or if her money is well spent.

It is interesting to note that many large organizations have begun to integrate risk management into their routine strategies. They identify their significant risks and determine what tools, capabilities, strategies, and plans they need to counteract them. In Canada, for example, many government departments now publish their risk management and risk mitigation plans online. They are accountable to the public for the achievement of those plans. If the government can think about risk, so can we. This chapter provides a brief overview of the risks we face, how to identify our exposure, what types of action we should take, and, when appropriate, how to buy insurance.

❖ THE RISKS WE FACE

Before thinking about buying insurance, let's step back and look at risk. Of course there are always risks in life; you only need to turn on the TV to see what can go wrong every day. But when you look at risk a little more closely, those likely to be experienced by independent consultants fall into five categories.

Risks Associated With Running a Business

Because our business is so close to our hearts, let's explore these risks first (Gordon, 2010):

Overhead costs are unpredictable. Your budget is only a best guess. Unanticipated events can increase your costs. For example, your rent can increase without warning. Salaries or subcontractor rates can rise. Perhaps the subcontractor you wanted is unavailable, and you have to select another one at a higher rate. Specialized equipment can break down and can force your work to a standstill. How useful are you without your computer?

Revenue forecasts do not meet your target. Contracts that you are counting on may not materialize, and this will have a negative impact on your cash flow. What if you have made business decisions based on future earnings, such as taking out a loan, which you now cannot afford? What if there has been a change in the marketplace, and your service is less in demand than formerly? You will have to retool your marketing plan, but this takes time. Meanwhile, revenue is falling.

Accounts receivable cannot be collected. As we discussed in Chapter 12, you already offer credit to your clients for up to two months (one month before you send an invoice and one month while you wait for your invoice to be paid). Your accounts receivable often represents a substantial portion of the current value of your business. If a client does not pay your bill, the financial hardship for you can be significant.

Business is interrupted. While you may be insured for direct property loss (e.g., due to fire), you may not be covered for the indirect costs associated with income lost while the business is interrupted. Repairs and other business expenses, such as taxes, loan payments, salaries, interest, utilities, rent for temporary space, equipment and furniture, and overtime to catch up all need to be paid.

You use your vehicle for business purposes. The premium for your current automobile insurance policy may be based on personal use only. A problem can occur if you are involved in an accident while on the job and it is discovered that you are using your car for business purposes (Gray, 2008, p. 99).

Risks Associated With Your Property

Whether you work at home or in rented office space, your office and its contents are always at risk.

Catastrophic events are almost always unexpected. Disasters such as fires, floods, tornados, tsunamis, hurricanes, volcano eruptions, and earthquakes may be rare, but it only takes one event to close down your business permanently (RBC Royal Bank, 2009, p. 13). All of us can think of at least one catastrophe that has occurred nearby. How did it affect local business?

Vandalism, hacking, and criminal activity can inflict surprising damage. We are more likely to think of burglary or theft happening because we forgot to lock our doors or because we work in a high-risk neighborhood, but what if your computer is hacked or your laptop is stolen? What might the impact be of lost data? How might this affect your work schedule? How might your client respond? There are other, less-anticipated risks as well. If you hire staff, how much can you trust them? Employee theft, embezzlement, and forgery are more common than you think. You probably know of at least one local business that has suffered at the hands of a disgruntled staff member.

Risks Associated With Negligence of Duty

It seems like *duty* is an old fashioned word, but simply by being in business we have a number of obligations. Being unaware of these duties is not considered a legitimate excuse.

You have a duty to protect the public. A member of the general public could suffer an injury or loss as a result of negligence or fault on the part of your firm or one of your employees. For example, what if the courier slips on the ice outside your door, or a visitor trips on the carpet and suffers an injury? Whether intentionally or not, what if one of your employees damages someone else's property while working for you? You could be liable for these injuries or losses.

You have a duty to protect your employees. An employee could be injured while on the job. We often hire young workers, such as students, to collect our data for us. Sometimes we send them into situations that could be risky (e.g., interviewing high-risk clients). When we hire them, whether on a temporary or full-time basis, we are legally required to provide such minimal employee benefits as Social Security (in the United States), government pension (in Canada), and unemployment insurance. In some cases, we may also need to provide workers' compensation, although this may vary by location.

Risks Associated With the Quality of Your Work

As consultants, we are more likely aware of our professional risks than of the others we have discussed. These risks fill us with dread.

Errors can occur in our work. While this is the last thing we hope to see, human error is bound to happen sooner or later. A small mistake in a monetary calculation, for example, such as the average cost per participant per day, when multiplied by the number of participants and again by the number of days of service, could result in a large financial discrepancy and have significant repercussions for the client (M. Hwalek, personal communication, December 12, 2006).

Advice can be wrong. Hard as it is to accept, the advice that we provide our clients can have negative impacts. Like other professional advisors, such as accountants and engineers, we can be held legally responsible if our advice or recommendations cause monetary damage or loss to our client, or worse, if they cause harm to our clients' vulnerable populations (Kubr, 2002, p. 145–146).

Contract provisions can be violated. If for some reason we walk away from a contract and leave some part of it unfulfilled, or we fulfill it in a way deemed unacceptable by the client, we could be held responsible for any related losses.

Employees or subcontractors can be unqualified or irresponsible. We rely on the work of those we hire to complete contract requirements, but it is sometimes difficult to control their performance in the field. If they do the work poorly, leave it unfinished, or offend our clients in some way, we are held responsible for their poor quality work, errors, gaps, or bad judgment. It will cost us both time and money, not to mention credibility, to make things right again.

Risks Associated With Your Health

While none of us will live forever, we like to pretend that we will. The harsh reality is that our injury, illness, or death, as well as that of our partners, shareholders, and key employees, will affect our business in significant ways.

As business owners, we can suffer a serious illness, be disabled, or die. The business could close temporarily due to our illness. How will income be generated until we regain our health? How will costs be covered? Who will "mind the store"? If we should die, what happens to the business? Who inherits it? Do you have a will? If your family's savings are invested in your business, will family members manage the sale or termination of your business wisely and conserve their investment? Will they have to pay income or inheritance taxes?

The disability or death of a partner or major shareholder can bring the business to a halt. A partnership is usually dissolved when one partner dies or suffers from a disability or critical illness, but the partner's spouse and dependents may have a claim against business assets.

The duties of the surviving partners are limited to winding up the affairs of the partnership, and they will be personally liable for losses if the business cannot cover the costs. A partnership or shareholder agreement typically requires that the absent party's interest be bought out. To do this, however, the remaining players need to be able to purchase the interest without causing financial hardship to themselves, the company, or the deceased individual's heirs.

The death of a major shareholder can throw a spotlight on survivors' differences and conflicts. Typically, the shares of the major shareholder become part of his or her estate, and during the period while the estate is being settled, actions by the estate administrator could have an impact on the corporation. Examples include changing the board of directors, selling stock, or buying out heirs' holdings (Anastasio, n.d., p. 9).

The disability or death of a key employee can have a serious short-term effect. When a key employee is unable to continue, what is the impact on current projects and business operations? Loss of valuable support staff can have an effect on managing costs, productivity, and efficiency. Loss of a key researcher can affect your ability to complete project tasks, and your proposal's promise to provide this individual's expertise will be unfulfilled. How can duties be reassigned? What will it cost to recruit and train a replacement? While the business suffers from the loss of this valuable member, creditors can withdraw financing, tax liabilities can be created, and customers can go elsewhere (Anastasio, n.d., p. 10).

❖ RISK MANAGEMENT

Facing this doomsday litany of possible risks, what can we do about it? There are three steps to mitigating your risk.

Step 1: Look at Your Risk Level Broadly

Your location can affect your risk level. As Kubr (2002, pp. 146–148) points out, some societies view loss differently from others. Some feel that where there has been loss, there must be a legal remedy, while others are more fatalistic or look to less formal remedies such as mediation. It should be noted that the legal system in the United States is often described as being very litigious; lawsuits are more likely to occur there than in other countries. Even so, Kubr (2002) feels that there is a general trend toward finding liability more easily and compensating for damages more handsomely. This suggests that consultants need to consider defensive action.

Consultants who work in more than one state or province can be subject to different business laws, so legal issues can become more complex (S. C. Maack, personal communication, July 26, 2010). This is also true for consultants who work at more than one level of government or in more than one type of organization (e.g., federal, state, non-profit, private, tribal) (N. Bowman, personal communication, 2008). Further, if you operate internationally, you will be subject to the laws and legal systems of more than one government. It will be important for your contract to clarify which jurisdiction is paramount. Is it the country where the contract was signed, the home country of the consultant, the home country of the client, or the country where the work was performed? It gets very complex very quickly, and you may need to seek legal advice on potential liability issues.

The size of your firm may be a mitigating factor. Kubr (2002, pp. 146–147) suggests that if you are part of a large firm or are known to be covered by an insurance company with "deep pockets," you may be an easier target for lawsuits. On the other hand, if you are a sole practitioner or have a small firm with limited assets, it may not be economical to proceed with a lawsuit. Not everyone thinks this way. Boop (2010a) feels that any business is at risk. Clifford Carr, an independent consultant who acted as an expert witness in a consultant's lawsuit, sees insurance as a deterrent. He commented, "The other side blatantly told us, after the side I testified for won, that they never would have brought it to trial if the evaluator had had insurance. They were quite clear that the cost would have been prohibitive if an insurance company were footing the bill for the other side" (C. Carr, personal communication, 2008).

Your strong sense of professional responsibility can safeguard your legal liability. Kubr (2002, p. 149) makes a distinction between your legal liability, which is essentially a legal construct imposed by law, and your professional responsibility, a set of self-imposed values, norms, and constraints. The quality of the service you provide depends predominantly on your own judgment, and it, in turn, is guided by your sense of responsibility to the client. Legal liability will probably apply in a very small number of extreme cases where service quality has dropped to the level of malpractice and has caused damage to the client. Generally speaking it is your professional responsibility that is more likely to be breached by such issues as inadequate research, incompetent staff, hasty or superficial judgment, or failure to inform the client of relevant risks. Ultimately, individual firms or consultants are responsible for defining their professional responsibility and instilling it in their staff.

Your administrative systems and good business practice can minimize your risk. Gray (2008, pp. 105–106) mentions a number of administrative ways to avoid liabilities and losses, including the following:

- Use written contracts with clients, and draft them carefully.
- Understand the law pertaining to your specific area of work in your jurisdiction or where your contract is situated.
- Select subcontractors carefully, and make sure that your insurance covers any work performed by them.
- Keep effective systems for your files, records, billing, and office procedures.
- Remain current by developing more expertise through professional development and continuing education.
- Set up quality control systems.
- Use effective communications in all your interactions.

Step 2: Assess Your Level of Exposure

A number of checklists to assess exposure levels and insurance needs are available online. A quick checklist to assess your risk is provided in Exhibit 14.1 on page 194 (RBC Royal Bank, 2009).

Step 3: Develop a Risk Management Plan

While independent consultants are neither big business nor big government, we can learn important lessons from their management practices. For example, the state of Florida's Systems Engineering Management Plan (State of Florida Department of Transportation, 2005) defines risk management as a continuous, forward-looking process that addresses issues that could endanger the achievement of critical objectives, so that the impact of these issues can be mitigated and changes can be made, thus reducing both work disruption and costs. The plan identifies five elements in the risk management process:

1. Identify potential issues, hazards, threats, and vulnerabilities.

2. Evaluate risks with respect to probability of occurrence, severity of impact, and overall risk to the business, rating them as high, medium, or low.

3. Determine which risks are at acceptable levels and which are critical enough to warrant attention; determine a course of action for each critical risk.

4. Monitor risk mitigation efforts to determine their effectiveness.

5. Conduct periodic reassessment of risks and strategies.

Exhibit 14.1   Quick Business Risk Assessment

Key Questions	Yes	No
1. If a fire, flood, or other natural disaster forced you to shut down for a few days, would you have difficulty covering your regular expenses?		
2. Do you have specialized equipment that your business relies on to maintain operations?		
3. Would the permanent or temporary loss of a key employee (including yourself) cause financial hardship to your business?		
4. Is the amount of credit you extend to any one customer enough to cause your business financial hardship if it went unpaid?		
5. Do you own a vehicle for your business or sometimes use your vehicle for business purposes?		
6. Has it been two years or longer since you reviewed your current insurance coverage or limits?		
If your answer is yes to any of these questions, you may want to get some insurance advice to help protect your business.		

SOURCE: RBC Royal Bank, 2009, p. 15.

As researchers and evaluators, we know how to do this. We can review our business plans and identify each area that could involve risk, determine potential catastrophes, rate their criticality, and then develop strategies to prevent or limit our exposure.

For example, we could consider what contingencies can be planned for, should the unexpected occur, and what to do to ensure that funds are available to mitigate unavoidable losses. Are there alternate premises where the business can operate? Are backup files easily accessible? Is there a communication plan so that we can contact staff quickly? The risk management plan becomes an excellent way to protect your business and foster your success. It easily folds into your regular long-term planning.

❖ TYPES OF INSURANCE

Now that you have a better idea of the risks you face, it is time to look for insurance to cover the most critical ones. There are more types of insurance available than you will ever need, but the most common types are summarized by risk area in Exhibit 14.2.

Exhibit 14.2   Common Types of Insurance by Risk Area

1. Business risks:

   • *Business Interruption Insurance* replaces lost business earnings with options such as covering payroll expenses needed to retain skilled employees (RBC Royal Bank, 2009, p. 13).

   • Your *Vehicle Insurance* may need to be upgraded if you use your vehicle for work.

   • *Business Loan Insurance* is essential to cover the outstanding amount of your business loan in the event of your death.

2. Employee risks:

   • A *Group Benefits Plan* can share the financial risk of health-related expenses among a group of employees (if there are four or more).

   • *Workers' Compensation* may be required in your location.

3. Property risks:

   • *Property Insurance* generally covers fire, theft, and some weather damage, but it can cover a broader range of catastrophic and criminal events.

   • Your *Homeowner's Package* may not be sufficient for your home office to cover business equipment and assets and other business losses.

4. Negligence of duty:

   • *General Liability Insurance* covers negligence causing injury to clients, employees, and the general public. It should include

     ° money you must legally pay because of bodily injury or damage to the property of others;

     ° emergency, medical, and surgical expenses incurred from an accident; and

     ° expenses for investigation, your defense, settlements, and a trial (Gray, 2008, p. 99).

(Continued)

Exhibit 14.2   (Continued)

5. Quality of work issues:

- *Errors and Omissions (E&O) Insurance* and *Professional Liability Insurance* are interchangeable terms (Sadler & Company, Inc., 2010). E&O is different from General Liability Insurance and provides separate coverage. It protects the individual consultant or firm against litigation arising from losses incurred by clients as a result of either an error or an omission in the consultant's advice or as a result of the consultant's negligent act. This insurance is essential whether you operate independently or have others working for you. Policies vary and each must be analyzed to determine the scope of coverage. There are two types of E&O insurance (Gray, 2008, pp. 107–108):

  ○ *Claims made*: This coverage insures you only against claims occurring **during** the policy period. As the risk is reduced for the insurance company, this insurance is generally less expensive.

  ○ *Occurrence*: This coverage provides protection against claims based on the policy period **even if the claims arise long afterward**. The risk to the insurance company is considerable, as a claim can be made many years after the negligence occurred and even after your policy has expired, so premiums are higher.

6. Risks associated with illness, injury, and death:

- *Travel Insurance* is essential to cover medical bills incurred for injury or illness when you travel beyond your state, province, or country for business purposes.

- *Personal Disability Insurance* can pay a certain monthly amount if you are disabled. A broader package can include *Life, Disability, and Critical Injury* and may be appropriate for partners or major shareholders.

- *Overhead Expense Insurance* covers fixed business expenses or overhead while you are unable to earn income.

- *Partners' or Shareholders' Insurance* covers a buy-sell arrangement for a deceased partner's or shareholder's interest in the business.

- *Key Person Insurance* is life insurance that names the company as beneficiary to cover the costs of recruiting and training a replacement if a key person dies or is disabled.

- *Term Life Insurance* allows you to be insured for a specific period of time (e.g., five years) and can be purchased in the amount of your personal and financial obligations. It has no cash value but can act as collateral security for loans to your company. It is inexpensive to purchase, and if you die, the insurance company pays the full face amount to your heirs (Gray, 2008, p. 101).

❖ BUYING INSURANCE

So what advice can we give to our independent consultant? She needs to find someone to explain the options, recommend the right coverage, and help her avoid financial loss. Should she go to an insurance agent or an insurance broker? There are some important differences.

The Insurance Agent

The independent insurance agent is usually a small business owner who acts as an agent for one or more insurance companies and receives a commission for selling their products and services. The agent has been trained in risk analysis, is familiar with the coverage and financial strategies available locally, and knows the related legislation or regulations. The agent can point out what exposures our consultant may have overlooked, can suggest options, and can tailor a basic policy to her business's unique protection needs (Anastasio, n.d., p. 13).

However, as Boop (2010a) points out, insurance agents serve as an intermediary between the insurance company and the insured. Broadly speaking, their liability to their customers is administrative in nature. The agent is responsible only for the timely and accurate processing of forms, premiums, and paperwork and has no duty to conduct a thorough examination of the consultant's business or to make sure she has appropriate coverage. Instead, it is the consultant's obligation to make sure she has purchased the needed coverage. Gray (2008, p. 97) adds that individual agencies may be obliged to place a certain volume of insurance with each company they represent. Our consultant could be sold policies that do not suit her needs or are not priced competitively.

The Insurance Broker

On the other hand, Boop (2010a) describes an insurance broker as "a kind of super-independent agent" who can offer a whole variety of insurance products. A broker must have a broker's license, which generally means that this individual has more education or experience than an agent. In most states, brokers also have a higher duty to their clients, and they must analyze the client's business and secure correct and adequate coverage for it. Gray (2008, pp. 97–98) adds that brokers claim to have complete independence from any particular insurance company and thus have no vested interest in selling the policies of any one company. They will therefore attempt to get our consultant the best price and coverage to meet her needs, but this expertise comes with a higher price tag. There can be an administrative fee, or alternatively, premium payments can be higher when insurance is purchased through a broker.

Whether she selects an agent or a broker, the consultant can eliminate a large proportion of the options available by seeking an individual who is a member of a respected professional insurance organization and has five or more years of experience. It may be harder than she thinks to find either an agent or a broker because of the small size of her company. As one independent consultant commented (S. Wolfe, personal communication, August 1, 2010), "Getting insurance was really hard for me. . . . I would call potential insurers and either be told I wasn't big enough or would just be blown off and they wouldn't call me back as promised!"

A number of suggestions have been proposed about ways to purchase insurance economically (Anastasio, n.d.; Davidson & Dean, 1992; Gray, 2008):

- Decide the magnitude of loss your business can bear without financial difficulty, cover your largest exposures first, and purchase the best protection for your money.
- Arrange for insurance coverage to begin before your business opens its doors.
- Avoid duplication or overlaps in insurance.
- Use as high a deductible as you can afford.
- Negotiate for lower premiums if your loss experience is low.
- Access a package policy (i.e., bundled services) or a group purchasing plan.
- Shop around, get three competitive quotes, compare their costs relative to the risks identified, and evaluate the strengths and weaknesses of each.
- Once you find a suitable service, try to stay with that broker or agent to handle all your insurance needs. This limits complications and ensures that the individual understands your business needs.
- Don't withhold important information about your business and its exposure to loss from your insurance professional; treat him or her as another business advisor.

- Review your insurance program periodically to see if your exposure has changed or if your premiums are as low as possible, yet consistent with sound protection.
- Do everything you can to prevent losses, including those that are not insurance related, and keep unavoidable losses as low as possible.

Armed with this information, our consultant should be ready to purchase her insurance. If she is guided only by client demands, she will carry insurance to protect them from damage or loss resulting from her activities but will not necessarily protect herself. She probably needs general liability insurance and should increase her automobile insurance as well; however, if her client does not insist that she have E&O insurance, she may choose to practice without it. As Gray (2008, p. 108) comments, "If the consultant has very few personal assets and is effectively judgment proof, then personal bankruptcy may be an alternative in the most extreme circumstances if a claim is made." Even if she has an LLC, the danger lies in the fact that the client or a third party could sue her personally as well as her company, and until the trial was over, she would not know the actual amount of damages required. In addition, as Gray cautions, "It may be very difficult to project at the time you are conducting a consulting assignment what the financial damages could be if your advice is in error."

If she considers her own exposure level, she can protect her own risks. Used correctly, insurance can contribute to her business success by reducing the uncertainties under which she operates. It can improve her credit rating at the bank, make it easier to contract with clients, reduce employee turnover, and help her business continue should a catastrophic event interrupt operations. As Anastasio (n.d., p. 16) comments, "The potential benefits of good insurance management make it well worth your study and attention."

❖ USEFUL RESOURCES

- An extensive checklist for insurance needs can be found in Appendix A of the *Small Business Insurance & Risk Management Guide,* authored by Susan Anastasio and published by the U.S. Small Business Administration (n.d.), at http://www.sba.gov/tools/resourcelibrary/publications/serv_pub_mplan.html

- Group insurance plans, especially for E&O insurance, are the most economical choice. Suggested places to start your search for this coverage in the United States include

  - The nearest U.S. Small Business Administration office; see http://www.sba.gov/localresources/index.html for locations
  - A Small Business Development Center at the continuing education department of your local university
  - The nearest office of SCORE, Counselors to America's Small Business, http://www.score.org/findscore/index.html
  - Your business banker
  - Trade associations that offer group insurance programs, such as the local chamber of commerce or Better Business Bureau
  - Professional associations or societies such as the American Psychological Association, the American Educational Research Association, and the Institute of Management Consultants USA

- In Canada, suggestions include
  - Canada Business Services for Entrepreneurs at http://www.canadabusiness.ca/eng/guide/3169/;
  - The Canadian Evaluation Society
  - CMC Canada

❖ DISCUSSION QUESTIONS AND ACTIVITIES

1. What risks identified in this chapter do you currently face? If you are just considering establishing your future consulting firm, what additional risks will you face then?

2. Identify three ways that your administrative systems and business practices can help you limit potential liabilities and losses. How can you incorporate these processes into the way you do business?

3. Conduct an Internet search of business and professional organizations to determine which ones offer group rates for E&O insurance. Do a cost comparison and determine which options are the most appropriate for you. Initiate steps to obtain three competitive quotes, and evaluate the strengths and weaknesses of each.

❖ REFERENCES

Anastasio, S. (n.d.). *Small business insurance & risk management guide.* MP-28, Management Planning Series. Washington, DC: U.S. Small Business Administration.

Boop, G. (2010a). *Insurance agents vs. insurance brokers.* Retrieved from http://businessinsure.about.com/od/agentsandbrokers/a/agentnbroker.htm

Boop, G. (2010b). *Why your business needs business insurance: Three common myths about liability and understanding the value of insurance.* Retrieved from http://businessinsure.about.com/od/insuringyourbusiness/a/whybusins.htm

Davidson, J. P., & Dean, C. W. (1992). *Cash traps: Small business secrets for reducing costs & improving cash flow.* New York, NY: Wiley.

Gordon, A. (2010). *Risks that small businesses face.* Retrieved from http://ezinearticles.com/?Risks-That-Small-Businesses-Face&id=392446

Gray, D. (2008). *Start & run a consulting business* (8th ed.). North Vancouver, BC: Self-Counsel Press.

Kubr, M. (2002). *Management consulting: A guide to the profession* (4th ed.). Geneva, Switzerland: International Labour Office.

RBC Royal Bank. (2009). *Managing risk for business.* Toronto, ON: Author.

Sadler & Company, Inc. (2010). *Professional liability insurance versus errors & omissions liability insurance.* Retrieved from http://www.insurancefortechs.com/errors-and-omissions-insurance.html

State of Florida Department of Transportation. (2005). *Florida's statewide systems engineering management plan* (Deliverable 1–10: Technical Memorandum, ver. 2). Tallahassee, FL: Author.

15

Managing Contracts

Highlights:

- Understand the differences between contractors and employees.

- Learn about the potential issues associated with a verbal contract.

- See why a written contract provides a solid foundation for your project.

- Review common contract topics.

- Explore ways to manage contracts and avoid conflict.

Did you know that every time you write a proposal, you are half-way to a contract? The proposal is your offer; now the client just has to accept it, and then a contract is in effect. Unless either party has misrepresented the facts or made a serious mistake, or unless you were coerced in some way, as long as you are of legal age and are sane and sober, this implicit contract can now hold up in a court of law. Whether the agreement is verbal or written, you are on the hook to produce the work at the price and within the time frame you proposed. If you have already started working on the project, your conduct alone is an implied contract.

So if you already have a contract, why worry? You may say, "I can just assume that my client will tell me if there is anything I should know about our contract. Isn't that okay?" The answer is, "No." As long as their interests are covered, your clients will probably never even think about your side of things. If you want to protect yourself, you have to get involved in the contracting process and take the time to understand it. A little preplanning and background knowledge can help you know what to look for, what to say, and how to manage your contracts.

I have to preface this section with a caveat. I am not lawyer, and my comments cannot replace the personalized information you will get from a legal professional. It is particularly important that you do this to make sure that you are operating within the requirements of local legislation. My comments reflect my layman's perspective and the lessons I have learned from the many contracts I have signed.

❖ CONTRACTS AND CONTRACTORS

A contract describes the nature of the bargain you have made with your client. It identifies the obligations made on both sides related to a particular project (Gray, 2008; U.S. Small Business Administration, 2010). Depending on the circumstances, it may or may not be in writing, and it may or may not be signed. We all know of major business deals that have started with a scribbled cocktail napkin or a simple handshake between industry giants or IT whiz kids, but this is the stuff that myths are made of. In reality if the work is clearly defined, the parties will be better protected and the outcomes more successful.

The role of a contractor is different from that of an employee. Tax departments are always interested in this arrangement, because they want to know if it is a contract for services (independent contractor) or a contract to hire (employee). While circumstances vary, the tax implications can be significant for both you and your client. Use a four-point test to clarify your relationship (Revenue Canada, Canada Revenue Agency, 2008, pp. 4–6):

• **Who has control?** Self-employed individuals usually work independently within a defined time frame, do not have anyone overseeing their work, and are free to work when and for whom they choose. They can provide services to more than one client at a time, can market their services, and can accept or refuse work as they see fit. This project is just one of their many business activities. The working relationship they have with the client does not represent continuity, loyalty, or security.

- **Who owns the tools?** Self-employed individuals often put a significant investment into the equipment and tools they use to complete a contract (e.g., your laptop and specialized software). They are responsible for the costs of repairs, insurance, maintenance, and updates. In addition, they provide their own workspace and typically perform a substantial amount of the project work from there.

- **Who takes the financial risk?** Self-employed individuals bear the burden of financial risk and are free to make decisions that affect their profit or loss. They pay fixed monthly costs (e.g., rent, equipment leases, insurance, and staff) whether or not work is being performed for a particular client. The contractor is financially liable if he or she does not fulfill the requirements of a specific contract. This individual does not receive benefits such as health insurance from the client, as an employee does.

- **Who hires the staff?** Self-employed individuals don't have to do all the work themselves. They can hire others to do part or all of it, and the client has no say in who is hired. They are then responsible for the work done by these individuals as well as for their conduct on the job. They pay their subcontractors and staff; the client does not.

Now I have worked in situations where things are not as clear. For example, I have worked at a client's site, directed client's staff, and used a client's computer system due to project requirements, but it has always been easy to distinguish my role as that of a contractor. The issues of control and risk tend to keep things clear. I always work for more than one client at a time, maintain my own office and equipment, hire my own subcontractors, manage my own budget, and take a profit or loss with no risk to my client. If you manage your own business, pay your own taxes, and have a separate contract for each project, it is easy to confirm your independent employment status.

❖ VERBAL CONTRACTS

In the past, when a man's word was his bond, verbal agreements were used extensively. A lot of consulting still takes place on the basis of a verbal agreement, particularly for repeat business, but this arrangement is rarely satisfactory (Kubr, 2002, p. 176). You need to have the following conditions in place:

- The consultant and the client trust each other completely.
- The assignment is neither big nor complex.
- The consultant and the client are familiar with each other's billing and payment processes.
- The consultant and the client are well versed in professional practice and have demonstrated that they are ethical and reliable.[1]

While many consultants start their business with a trusting attitude, it only takes one bad experience to demonstrate the folly of relying on a verbal contract (Gray, 2008, p. 167). Problems can arise if the consultant and client disagree over their understanding of the work, its duration, its deliverables, or its price. Unless there are reliable witnesses, it may be impossible to reconstruct the original bargain. People forget, they get distracted, and they are subject to political pressures. You can end up with a "he said, she said" scenario. Worse, considering the amount of staff turnover these days, you may be the last one standing who actually remembers what you were hired to do.

If, for whatever reason, you find yourself working under a verbal agreement, consider what you can do to strengthen your position.

Follow up in writing. Once a verbal agreement is reached, follow up with a letter or e-mail to your client that confirms your understanding of key aspects of the contract. You should mention who is involved, the tasks, the fee, the time lines, and the deliverables. Ask for confirmation such as having your client sign and return your letter to demonstrate his or her understanding and agreement. Then, of course, you have a written contract after all.

Take lots of notes. Take detailed notes following each client meeting, including dates and times, attendees, and a commentary on work progress. Whenever I talk to a client on the phone or meet a client in person, I complete a Client Contact Summary (see Exhibit 15.1).

Exhibit 15.1   Client Contact Summary Form

Client:

Contact person(s):

Address/location:

Contact Details	
Meeting:	Contact date:
Phone call:	Today's date:
Conference call (list participants):	Other pertinent details:
Consultant's name:	

1. Purpose of contact:

2. Summarize the information you got (or failed to get) on each of your target questions for this contact.

3. Action steps and recommendations resulting from this contact:

4. Comments and personal observations:

   This helps me remember what happened, what was said, and what issues emerged, if any. When I prepare my monthly status report, I review my Contact Summaries to remind myself of key points. In long-term projects, these day-to-day observations allow me to recall events, see larger patterns, or remember why certain decisions were made. They can help me flesh out the description of the research process in my final report. Of course, they also document my exchanges with my client.
   Keep good records. If you keep a day book or timesheet to track your time, these records can provide the details you may need about when you worked for a specific client and how much time you expended. By knowing that you keep track of your time and can substantiate it in

this way, a client is less likely to suggest that you did not work when you said you did.

These solutions are good business practice, but as you might end up in court some day, nothing replaces the solid foundation of understanding provided by a written contract.

❖ WRITTEN CONTRACTS

Gray provides several compelling reasons for using a written contract (2008, pp. 168–170):

It clarifies your financial relationship with your client. A written contract confirms that you are not offering your services for free (as you would in a marketing or pro bono relationship) and that you expect to be paid for work performed. It specifies the terms of payment, such as monthly progress payments, and the deliverables, such as your final report. It confirms your status as an independent contractor, thus making the tax implications clear.

It enhances a positive business relationship. Clients are almost always nervous about budgets. A written contract gives them confidence that the limits of their financial obligation have been defined. It also clarifies expectations, fosters good communications, and decreases potential misunderstandings. A written contract can project a professional image. Clients with no contract experience are relieved to learn that you are comfortable with these business relationships.

It can protect you in litigation. If your contract is well drafted, it can limit your liability. If a client is untruthful or self-serving, or wishes to reconstruct events to your disadvantage, a contract can protect you. If a client claims that you acted improperly, did not complete the work, or did the work in an unsatisfactory manner, a contract can clarify the original expectations. If either you or your client should die, it could be difficult to determine the actual agreement or to find out if work was unfinished or money owed unless the contract was in writing.

It can pave the way for financial benefits. If your contract details the services you plan to perform, any required changes must be addressed in an addendum to cover the changed tasks and costs. It is much harder to do this in a verbal, undocumented context. You can also use your written contract as proof of the marketability and future value of your business when you go to a lender and request additional funds. This will allow you to expand your business and pursue other projects as well.

There are two types of written contracts: the letter of agreement and the formal contract. Over time you will acquire lots of examples of each, depending on the circumstances of each project.

The Letter of Agreement

The letter of agreement or letter of understanding is a brief contract in letter form that summarizes the agreement reached between you and your client. A letter agreement is the most common way to contract services in many countries (Kubr, 2002). In North America, more formal contracts are the norm, and a letter of agreement is typically used only when the work is straightforward, of short duration, or for a limited dollar amount. It can also be used when the consultant feels that the client would be intimidated by a formal contract as in dealing with grassroots groups. A letter of agreement should include the following (Gray, 2008, pp. 170 & 174):

- The nature of services to be performed
- The method
- The timing and amount of payment
- The start date and duration of the contract
- Resource materials provided by the client
- Personnel to be supplied by the client (if applicable)
- The names of consultant(s) who will be involved in the project.

Sometimes the client will send you a letter of agreement to confirm acceptance of the terms of your proposal. Other times, once you have reached an agreement, you can prepare the letter of agreement yourself and forward it to your client for approval and signature. Either way, as long as both parties sign the contract, it is a legal agreement.

The Formal Contract

Most public sector agencies, foundations, large nonprofits, and businesses use a formal contract for fee-for-service arrangements with contractors. These are often in the form of a standard template often called a *boilerplate* contract. These can vary from 10 to 30 pages in length and may have several appendices. While contract formats and language vary, the topics are much the same. Exhibit 15.2 provides a list of common contract topics with a brief description of each (Gray 2008; Kubr, 2002; Page, 2005).

Exhibit 15.2   Common Contract Topics

Contract Topic	Description
1. Parties	• The client and the contractor
2. Term	• Start and completion dates and schedule
3. Services	• Scope of the project 　○ Services to be performed 　○ Objectives to be achieved 　○ Description of the work 　○ Work schedule 　○ Timing and nature of deliverables 　○ Timing and nature of required meetings 　○ Travel and the nature of travel compensation 　○ Authority to use client resources, facilities, equipment, records or files, and access to client's participants 　○ Right to third party information such as participant data
4. Client participation and duties	• Any significant client input to the project in terms of managerial or technical personnel or administrative support • Any significant duties agreed to by the client to facilitate the work and provide access to required staff, records, data, or participants
5. Price and method of payment	• Payment for services 　○ Fee structure/rates 　○ Invoicing methods, records required, payment period (e.g., 30 days) 　○ Interest on overdue accounts 　○ If required, the client may hold back a portion of the fee to ensure that services are performed and delivered as agreed. • Reimbursable expenses 　○ Definition of what expenses are reimbursable 　○ Reimbursement rates (e.g., subsistence allowances, type of air tickets, mileage rates, hospitality expenses) • Responsibility for payment of any taxes, duties, or fees associated with performing the services lies with the consultant.
6. Record keeping	• The contractor will keep complete, accurate records, and accounts of all costs, expenditures, and commitments related to the contract. • The records will be kept according to generally accepted accounting principles. • The length of time the records must be maintained is specified.

(Continued)

Exhibit 15.2   (Continued)

7. Warranty and representation	• The contractor avoids providing the client with any false or inaccurate representation of the education, credentials, achievements, or skills of anyone who will be involved in conducting the work. • The services provided are at a level of competency that is generally accepted in the specific field.
8. Confidentiality	• The contractor (along with his or her subcontractors and employees) will keep all information confidential that is acquired through the contract. • This information will not be used, copied, or disclosed unless written authorization is received from the client.
9. Conflict of interest	• The contractor discloses any conflict of interest prior to entering into the contract.
10. Intellectual property	• Ownership of all materials prepared, developed, or produced as part of the contract is specified.
11. Dispute resolution	• The client and contractor will attempt to resolve any disagreement over fulfilling the obligations of the contract. • If they are unable to resolve the dispute, other means of resolution are used, including mediation, arbitration, or the courts. • During the dispute resolution process, the parties will continue to perform their respective obligations.
12. Assignment	• Only tasks that are specified in the proposal will be delegated to the contractor's subcontractors or employees. • Written approval will be obtained from the client for any replacements or changes in personnel assigned to the above tasks.

13. Other commitments or obligations	• Professional responsibilities may be specified, such as the following:
	  ° Use of a code of ethics or professional conduct
	  ° Use of an ethics review board
	  ° Use of a stakeholder steering committee
	  ° Use of specified research standards, such as informed consent

14. Notification	• The method of delivery of notices, correspondence, payment, or change of address is stated. • The time frame for notification is specified (i.e., number of business days). • The name and contact information for both contractor and client (i.e., contract manager) are specified.

Exhibit 15.2   (Continued)

15. Change request process	• A client may request additional services. • The contractor may determine that the client's request for services falls outside the current scope of the contract. • Either party may request a change in the contract (change request process is described). • Any modification to the contract is confirmed in writing and signed by both parties before additional work begins.

16. Indemnities	• The contractor is responsible for, and will protect the client from
	  ○ any claims from a third party resulting from negligence or willful acts on the part of the contractor, subcontractors or employees;
	  ○ any claims based on an infringement by the contractor, subcontractors, or employees of patent, copyright, trade secret, industrial design, trade mark, or other proprietary rights; and
	  ○ any injury or damage suffered by the contractor, subcontractors, or employees in the performance of the contract.

17. Liabilities	• The contractor's liability is limited in terms of the cost of damages, claims, costs, expenses, and losses suffered by the client that relate to a breach of contract, willful misconduct, or negligence on the part of the contractor, subcontractors, or employees.

18. Insurance	• Types of insurance are specified that the contractor should maintain at own expense, for example,
	  ○ general liability insurance,
	  ○ automobile insurance, or
	  ○ other as required (e.g., E&O insurance).
	• The contractor may be required to produce insurance certificates at required coverage levels.

19. Not an employee	• The contractor is an independent contractor and not an employee of the client. • The contractor is not eligible for any benefits or tax withholdings.
20. Termination	• The client may terminate the contract, with or without cause, within a specific time frame and with written notice to the contractor. • The contractor may withdraw from the assignment if a notice period and precise procedures are followed. • In the event of termination, the contractor will return project-related materials to the client by a certain date. • Payment should be made for work performed prior to the termination date.

(Continued)

Exhibit 15.2   (Continued)

21. Force majeure	• Neither contractor nor client is to be held liable or in breach of contract if various catastrophes occur that are beyond their control and that occur through no fault of their own and not as a result of their negligence. • A process to continue work during the disruption is described, or obligations may be suspended for the duration of the crisis. • A process for possible contract termination in the case of catastrophe is described.
22. Applicable laws	• The contractor will comply with all laws in the specified jurisdiction that apply to the performance of the required service, for example, ° freedom of information, ° protection of privacy, ° occupational health and safety, ° workers' compensation, ° workforce regulations, or ° human rights.
23. General provisions	• Examples include the following: ° The contract constitutes the entire agreement between the parties. ° Time is of the essence. ° The contract can be changed only by written agreement. ° The contract is interpreted according to the laws of the specified jurisdiction.
24. Authority	• Authorized representatives of client and contractor are named who can sign the contract and any related documentation. • A process is described to change that designation if necessary. • The contract is signed and dated by the named representatives. • Signatures may need to be witnessed.

❖ CONSIDERATIONS FOR WRITTEN CONTRACTS

Consultants may have a tendency to agree to whatever contract is offered by the client. They want to get on with the work and they may feel they have no recourse anyway. This is not the case, so consider these suggestions:

Obtain a sample contract in advance. When large organizations send out an RFP, they often include a sample contract. You should review it before you bid, so you can tailor your proposal to suit contract requirements and demonstrate your understanding of the client's perspective, time lines, and context. If you have any unanswered questions, ask your lawyer to review the sample contract to explain any potential issues. By doing this you are preparing yourself for a quick response once you win the project.

You can request changes to a boilerplate contract. These standard contracts are designed for the average contractor whose average company may be very different from yours. As a result there may be onerous or unrealistic expectations for the sole proprietor in such areas as insurance and indemnification requirements or significant gaps regarding important elements such as data access or copyright. Finally, the contract may be poorly drafted, and important general provisions, such as a change or work modification clause, may be absent altogether.

On several occasions, I have requested changes to standard form contracts, and I have never been refused. Usually, the client is surprised because no one else has ever asked, but their legal departments tend to be obliging. These added negotiations do take time, however, and may affect your project start date, unless you are willing to work in good faith while revisions are being made. I have often started work once I am assured that the contracting process is under way. It can take three or four weeks to receive a fully signed contract.

Don't sign until you are satisfied. Sometimes a contract is simply forwarded to you for your signature. Do not sign it until you have read it carefully, reviewed it with your lawyer, and requested any changes that significantly affect your interests. It is fair to take a few days to complete this review. If a client has a "take it or leave it" attitude, is unwilling to negotiate, or pressures you in some way, you have to ask yourself if you really want to work with this individual. If you sign a contract that does not protect you adequately, problems are likely to occur down the road. It is better to negotiate to remove, change, or add the clauses required so that you are satisfied with the work arrangements. If you can't do this, turn down the work. Let's be clear: I am not talking about nit-picking or word-smithing the contract; rather, any proposed changes should relate to substantive issues that could affect your ability to do your work completely, properly, and well.

Keep your own boilerplate contract on hand. Sometimes your client may not have a contract available. When this happens, you can offer one. There are many standard contracts available online. Use them as a guide to develop your preliminary draft, and then finalize it in consultation with your lawyer. Make sure that it covers all your jurisdictional and legal requirements as well as your specific consulting needs. Then you can use it with other clients who do not have their own contract precedent, and as these small projects tend to be similar, you will need to consult your lawyer again only if substantive changes are required. Having your own boilerplate available allows you to provide this service to your client but at the same provides you with comfort, because you know that your interests are well addressed.

Once you have a signed contract on hand, you need to keep it in a secure place such as a locked filing cabinet. Electronic copies should also be secured. While the contract may be out of sight, it should certainly not be out of mind, because it will continue to guide your work throughout the project.

❖ CONTRACT MANAGEMENT

Scope Creep

One of the biggest problems faced by consultants is scope creep. While change is inherent in most projects, it can become a source of financial loss if the consultant is not vigilant. These fee write-offs or cost overruns affect your bottom line and can crop up at any time. They tend to be poorly reported, because consultants feel that they reflect badly on them.

Ertel and Rudner (2000, p. 4) found that while formally tracked write-offs range between 3% and 15% of project revenues, in fact there is significantly more that remains unreported. In response to scope creep, consultants may cut corners, substitute less costly resources, or drive the project to a quick conclusion, all of which can result in lost creativity and a lower-quality product. As they comment, "In our experience, many professional service firms write off a significant percentage of their fees because they don't engage their clients in effective conversations about scope changes and appropriate fee adjustments" (p. 3).

Many issues around scope creep are related to project management. Examples include the following:

- The degree of project complexity is initially misdiagnosed.
- Project complexity grows after the contract is signed as unforeseen issues emerge.
- Project management skills and tools need to be improved.
- Fee estimates are poorly conceived.

- There are issues with quality.
- There are unexpected staff changes.

Good project management skills can often head off these problems. Success lies in strong client relationships and clear communications from the outset. Newsom-Steward (2006) believes that the core of a client–consultant relationship is found in the contract itself. However, as Ertel and Rudner (2000) comment,

The challenge is to create and maintain open and profitable relationships with your clients by developing the systems, skills, tools, and mind-set to enable you to consistently get paid for the work you do and the value you add, even when project specifics change after the original contract is negotiated. (p. 4)

They have a number of suggestions to ensure that you are fairly compensated when things change (pp. 6–7):

- Manage client expectations. If you establish a good working relationship with your client, conversations about scope change will be less adversarial. You need to incorporate a scope review mechanism at the beginning of the project to deal with the unexpected.
- Communicate openly with your own team. Make sure that problems are quickly identified and solutions found.
- Keep clients apprised of changes as they occur, using joint problem-solving techniques. It is extremely difficult to convince a client to pay more after the fact.
- Learn from each project through a postproject review. Determine what changes occurred, what happened as a result, and what lessons you can carry forward for next time.

Managing Conflict

Other contract management issues may be less easy to deal with (Ertel & Rudner, 2000, p. 3). These include the following:

- Resources clients commit to the project but fail to deliver
- Differences in expectations about what is required to solve the client's problem
- Complex dynamics between the client and other stakeholders

Challenges like these can result in tension, blaming, and avoidance. A consultant's biggest fear is to lose a client, and this fear can be a barrier to open discussion. We are not prepared for these difficult situations and often lack the conflict management, negotiation, and mediation skills we need. Yet conflict often arises, because evaluation and data collection activities can be sensitive and expensive. They appear to have limited immediate benefit (Newsom-Stewart, 2006). Your clients may feel threatened and can cover insecurity with aggression. They may feel pressured by stakeholders or external demands. A quick fix or a scapegoat may be just the solution they are looking for. A number of times I have seen bad or even irrational behavior at steering committee or board meetings, and sometimes the evaluator or researcher is at the center of the dispute. How can we sharpen our skills in conflict management? Here are a few strategies to consider.

Use interest-based negotiation techniques. Page (2005) suggests that we become familiar with negotiation techniques based on the work of Fisher and Ury (1991). They suggest the following strategies:

- Separate the people from the problem; ask, How does the world look from your client's perspective?
- Focus on interests, not positions; ask, What are your mutual interests?
- Invent options for mutual gain; ask, How can both sides win?
- Insist on using objective criteria; ask, What professional and moral values and standards define your boundaries?[2]

Use reasoning to analyze the problem. Bebeau (1995) suggests that we step back from a situation to develop a well-reasoned response. Consider the following:

- Who has a stake in possible outcomes?
- What expectations are legitimate on the part of each interested party?
- What are the consequences of alternative actions and decisions?
- What are the duties and obligations on either side?
- What is the best course of action for you?

Pursue formal dispute resolution. In times of conflict, the contract will be used to make decisions about fault, remediation, and expectations (Newsom-Stewart, 2006). Possible "last resorts" for dispute resolution include the following:

- Both parties agree to have a mediator review a contract dispute. While they are not bound by the outcome, the process may produce a resolution (U.S. Small Business Administration, 2010).
- Both parties agree to binding arbitration. A neutral party listens to the arguments from both sides and issues a decision that is binding on the parties (U.S. Small Business Administration, 2010).
- The consultant withdraws from the contract and can anticipate being sued for breach of contract.
- The consultant can consider taking legal action.

In any of these scenarios, your self-esteem, your reputation, and your pocketbook will suffer but the last two options will take the most time and money. If you are aware that the road to conflict ends here, other, more proactive ways to build client relationships and manage conflict will become very persuasive indeed.

❖ LEGAL RISKS FOR CONSULTANTS

Sadly, sometimes it is the consultant who makes significant mistakes, omissions, or errors that can result in serious legal ramifications. Here are some of the most common issues:

- **Failure to honor contractual commitments.** The most frequent source of a contractual dispute involves the failure to meet commitments in a timely manner. Others include failing to produce the required deliverables and breaching confidentiality. Gray (2008, p. 104) suggests that it is not uncommon for new consultants to miscalculate a fixed price contract, abandon the project before it is completed, and face a resulting lawsuit.

- **Misrepresentation of qualifications.** Exaggeration or misrepresentation of educational qualifications, certifications, or experience can lead to a breach of contract, and in extreme cases, to claims of fraud.

- **Demonstration of nonprofessionalism.** The demonstration of noncompliance with accepted professional standards or malpractice may lead to claims of negligence or fraud.

- **Ambiguous or unenforceable contracts.** Unclear or unrealistic contracts can result in misunderstanding and professional liability claims on the part of the client. The consultant may also need to pursue legal action due to an inability to enforce clients' promises or to collect fees.

- **Negligent advice.** Clients rely on consultants to furnish information or advice on topics that are important to them. Inaccurate advice may result in significant liabilities or business losses for the client. Sometimes it is irrelevant whether the consultant's breach was innocent, negligent, or willful (Gray, 2008). The client has to prove only that a material breach of contract occurred and that damages resulted. It is normally not a defense for the consultant to assert that he or she was merely giving advice or recommendations. As Kubr (2002) points out,

> The client has the "right" to rely on the expertise proffered by the consultant. The fact that the client was under absolutely no obligation to follow such advice or accept such recommendations counts for little . . . if it can be demonstrated that the consultant's action was patently unprofessional and did not meet the standards of the profession. (pp. 146–147)

- **Copyright infringement.** It is possible to incorporate protected work into reports and materials without obtaining permission. Remedies for copyright infringement include awarding damages to the copyright owner.

Needless to say, none of us ever wants to face any of these claims, but preventative knowledge goes a long way in protecting us from such eventualities. If we plan our projects well, establish good relationships with our clients, use written contracts, work to plan, negotiate changes, and produce excellent results, our legal risks will be minimized and our productive work life enhanced. Knowledge is power. Be sure you have it.

❖ NOTES

1. Kubr, M. E. (2002). *Management consulting: A guide to the profession* (4th ed.). Geneva, Switzerland: International Labour Office. Copyright © 2002 International Labour Organization.

2. From *Getting to Yes*, 2e, by Robert Fisher, William Ury, and Bruce Patton. Copyright © 1981, 1991 by Roger Fisher and William Ury. Reprinted

❖ USEFUL RESOURCES

- Many contract templates are available online. Check out sites for law firms, small business and employment lawyers, and government entities, but use them all with care. See http://www .independent-consulting-bootcamp.com/free-independent -contractor-agreement.html
- See what the IRS has to say about subcontractors and employees: http://www.irs.gov/businesses/small/article/0,,id=99921,00.html
- A sample consulting contract is provided on pages 181–183 of Douglas Gray's *Start & Run a Consulting Business* (8th ed., Self-Counsel Press, 2008).

❖ DISCUSSION QUESTIONS AND ACTIVITIES

1. Many consultants begin their business with a trusting attitude. What experiences might change their perspective?

2. Fee renegotiation is considered such an unpleasant task that many consultants prefer to write off cost overruns. What issues hold them back? Imagine that you are experiencing conflict with your client regarding scope creep. Prepare the dialogue you might have with your client.

3. Why might a new consultant be tempted to walk away from a project before it is completed? What legal risks might this consultant face? What advice would you provide to this individual?

❖ REFERENCES

Bebeau, M. J. (1995). Developing a well-reasoned response to a moral problem in scientific research. In M. J. Bebeau, K. D. Pimple, K. M. T. Muskavitch, S. L. Borden, & D. H. Smith (Eds.), *Moral reasoning in scientific research: Cases for teaching and assessment* (pp. 3–6). Bloomington, IN: Poynter Center.

Ertel, D., & Rudner, S. (2000). Scope change negotiations: Are write-offs inevitable? *Consulting to Management, 11*(2), 3–8.

Fisher, R., & Ury, W. L. (1991). *Getting to yes: Negotiating agreement without giving in.* New York, NY: Penguin Group.

Gray, D. (2008). *Start & run a consulting business* (8th ed.). North Vancouver, BC: Self-Counsel Press.

Kubr, M. (2002). *Management consulting: A guide to the profession* (4th ed.). Geneva, Switzerland: International Labour Office.

Newsom-Stewart, M. (2006, November). *Helping clients narrow goals during contract negotiations.* Paper presented at the annual conference of the American Evaluation Association, Portland, OR.

Page, W. J. (2005, April). *ICMCA/ CAMC legal issues and approaches 2005.* Professional development workshop conducted at the Institute of Certified Management Consultants of Alberta, Calgary, AB.

Revenue Canada, Canada Revenue Agency. (2008). *Employee or self-employed?* Ottawa, ON: Government of Canada.

U.S. Small Business Administration. (2010). Handle legal concerns: Plain English guide to contracts. *Small Business Planner.* Retrieved August 14, 2010, from http://www.sba.go v/smallbusinessplanner/manage/ handlelegalconcerns/SERV_PLAIN ENGGUIDE.html

16

Managing People

Highlights:

- Assess whether you need staff support.
- Find out whether you should hire subcontractors or staff.
- Examine the steps in the hiring process.
- Learn ways to manage new and ongoing staff.
- Understand why staff leave, and learn how to say good-bye.

One morning you will wake up and realize that you have too much work to do. It is time to think about hiring people to help you. Whether you need full-time or part-time, short-term or long-term, employee or subcontractor help, at this critical juncture you stop being an independent consultant and start to become a human resources manager as well. With this added responsibility comes a whole new set of required skills and processes.

❖ NEEDING HELP

Once you decide you need help, conduct a needs assessment to determine what essential tasks and responsibilities are covered and what gaps need to be filled. Are they administrative or project-related tasks? What competencies and skill levels are required? Who is likely to have what you need? Is it a student, a recent graduate, a young professional, or a seasoned expert?

Next, consider your current infrastructure. What can you provide in terms of office space, furniture, a computer, and a telephone? Do you have room for this person? Think about communications and file sharing. Does the individual need access to specific equipment or databases? How will you work together? Does this person have to be in the same office, same city, or same country? How essential is supervision or face-to-face contact?

Think about the time frame. You may be short on personnel for a specific project, but this does not mean you need to hire a permanent employee. Are you certain there is enough future work to guarantee employment for this individual for at least the next year? You don't want to be left with staff to pay when you have nothing for them to do. It is also not fair to hire someone unless you can provide some security for their own family and financial commitments.

Last, think about costs. No one is more aware than you are about your current and projected cash flow. What costs can safely be covered by your current contracts? Is your cash flow sustainable? Is it predictable? Even if you can't pay yourself every month, you will still need to pay your staff on time.

Questions like these will help you identify your human resource needs. Once it is clear that you need assistance, take a closer look at whether you should hire subcontractors or invest in staff.

❖ HIRING SUBCONTRACTORS

Alan Weiss, well known for his book, *Million Dollar Consulting* (2003, pp. 219–230), is strongly in favor of using subcontractors rather than full-time employees. He cites four basic reasons for this view:

- **Full-time people are full-time overhead**. You have to be able to pay them whether you have work or not.

- **Managing employees is a tremendous drain on your time.** To facilitate a successful project outcome, you need to invest time and energy managing the team, which is time away from your own research activities.
- **Your personal actions will be subject to the dynamic of an employer–employee relationship.** You become a role model when you are an employer. Your work habits, hours of work, and professional demeanor become the subject of scrutiny. Are you ready for this?
- **A relatively small number of employees will not afford you the talents required to grow your firm.** Essenmacher (2006) suggests that a small consulting business is in danger of asking employees to wear too many hats. This can set you up for failure. It may not be possible to solve all your resource needs with one or two people.

Clients hire you with the expectation that you will be personally involved in the project. They do not expect you to use a "bait and switch" approach by selling the project on the expertise of senior staff but having junior staff perform most of the work. They want to be assured that you will be in charge of the project and will perform a significant portion of it. If you need subcontractors to help you conduct more work in a short period, to provide specialized skills, or to conduct research in different geographic areas simultaneously, then prepare your client for this team approach and build subcontractors into your proposal.

Weiss (2003, pp. 138–139) suggests that you not wait until you have a specific need but rather begin to establish a pipeline of people now. Look for potential associates at professional meetings, conferences, and your local university. Look on bidders' lists. Who else has demonstrated an interest in similar work but might be interested in joining forces? Search on the Internet. Who has written about your particular topic recently? Ask clients and colleagues for recommendations.

Once you identify likely candidates, spend time with them. A lunch date is not enough. If you can, watch them in action by attending one of their presentations or workshops, or ask for work samples or articles they have written. While interpersonal relationships are important, the key is shared performance objectives and work processes.

When the time comes that you need specific individuals on your team, try to start them with fairly straightforward roles, to see how the association works. Develop a letter agreement that spells out your relationship and the services they are to perform. Everything will be subject to your approval, because, as you must not forget, you are responsible for the quality of their work. Standard clauses in their agreement will sound familiar, because these clauses are similar to many in your own client contracts. Gray (2008, p. 186) suggests that the following should be included:

1. The parties to the contract

2. The independent contractor status of the subconsultant

3. Clearly specified responsibilities or activities by task, scope, and date as laid out in your proposal or work plan

4. Term of the contract

5. Amount and method of payment for fees and expenses (a clearly defined number of days per task and agreed-upon per diem)

6. A cancellation provision in case your contract with your client is canceled

7. The method and amount of remuneration to be paid to the subconsultant up to the point of cancellation

8. A confidentiality provision stating that all client information accessed through the project is to be held in strict confidence

9. A noncompetition clause that restricts your subcontractors' access to your clients for a reasonable period following your contracts with them, to prevent them from selling their services directly to your clients

10. The return to you of all project documents by a certain date

11. Provision that the contract cannot be assigned or duties delegated to someone else without the written consent of both parties

12. Other standard provisions as recommended by your lawyer

In the same way you have made sure that you are not your client's employee, you need to be clear that your subcontractors are not yours. The same guidelines apply regarding their independence, control, and tax responsibilities.

❖ HIRING STAFF

You are taking a big step when you decide to hire staff, so invest the time needed, and pay close attention to the steps in the hiring process. You cannot afford to make many mistakes. A bad decision can be quite costly, not only financially and in terms of lost project time, but because, as Greiner and Metzger have said (1983, p. 343), "one 'bad apple' in a small firm can wreak havoc."

There are three main steps associated with the hiring process. Each of them has a number of subprocesses.

Step 1. Planning to Hire

Prepare a job description. As you have already identified your needs, you can now transform them into a number of clear requirements. A good job description forms the basis of many subsequent activities, not only in the hiring process, but also in the development of an employment contract and in the ongoing management and assessment of the individual you hire. Exhibit 16.1 provides a sample job description for a research assistant.

Determine the pay scale. Pay is dictated by two main factors: (1) market forces and (2) contract arrangements with your clients. Kubr (2002, p. 796)

Exhibit 16.1   Sample Job Description—Research Assistant

Research Assistant
This position offers you the opportunity to be part of an innovative research team working on a number of evaluation and applied research projects. Reporting to the project manager, you will act as a researcher assistant and will focus on data collection and analysis. You will ensure that our firm's outstanding customer service approach is applied to all communications with our clients and will maintain the highest professional and ethical quality in your evaluation and research activities.

Major Responsibilities

- Literature/Internet searches
- Document and file reviews
- Data collection (telephone, online, and paper surveys)
- Data entry and analysis (qualitative and quantitative)
- Preparation of graphs and tables
- Routine client contact
- Supervised report preparation
- Other research duties as required

suggests that you start with marketplace pricing. Compensation data and industry benchmarks are available online, or ask your colleagues what they pay for a similar position. Then, take a close look at your current contracts to see how much time and money have been allotted to complete the tasks you now hope to assign to someone new. If you don't know what rate to charge on upcoming projects for this position, go through a costing exercise similar to the one you did for your own rates to make sure that your overhead is covered. You will need to allot time for vacation, sick leave, and professional development, but the number of billable days for staff members will be much higher than for you. Salaries must be competitive to attract and retain competent professionals, so don't even consider hiring unless you can afford it.

Identify recruiting sources. Take some time to find appropriate recruitment sites. Newspaper want ads and equivalent online services should be used only as a last resort, because you will be inundated with inappropriate applications. Instead, start with the sources closest to you.

Universities offer multiple hiring options. For example, consider hiring short-term candidates such as those in a university co-op program where students alternate work terms and school terms. They already have work skills and usually come with basic research knowledge, reasonable writing skills, and a pragmatic attitude to life. These bright young people are eager to learn and fun to have around. Of the 14 co-op students that I hired over the years, some stayed on part time while they completed their studies, and others came back later as full-time staff.

A similar source of short-term candidates is a university internship program, which is sometimes available at the postbaccalaureate or master's level. These students are required to complete a field placement in a potential career area. While the program requirements can be demanding, and the time frame can be short, this option is an excellent way to determine if the individual will fit with your firm. You can also look farther afield for specialty programs that train applied researchers, social psychologists, and evaluators. They may also have internship programs, and sometimes graduates are willing to relocate if you can offer specialized on-the-job training postgraduation.

Local and national evaluation associations usually will advertise job openings online, and job boards are available at national conferences. Government programs sponsor recent graduates or individuals who have been in retraining programs, and sometimes financial support is provided for the first few months. Other sources such as temporary services or employment agencies can be useful to hire administrative support staff. A final source is the self-referral. Once your business becomes established, you will start to receive résumés from people who are doing their own job search. Keep these submissions on hand in case an appropriate opening arises. Be sure to respond to these job-seekers with an e-mail, letting them know that you have their applications on file. You promote your business image through these small and thoughtful gestures.

Post your job ad. Create a job posting that includes the job description and core qualifications. Indicate how applicants are to respond. Keep it short, and refer potential applicants to your website for more detailed information about your firm. Essenmacher (2006) suggests including a statement that you require preemployment background screening to deter potential applicants who have something to hide.

Step 2. The Interview Process

Screen the applicants. A close reading of the cover letter and the applicant's résumé can make short work of a daunting task. The cover letter provides an early indication of writing skills, perceptiveness, intelligence, and personality. It offers more insight into the individual than the writer ever imagined. A good letter focuses on the job as described in the ad and suggests how this position fits with the individual's career path. Once you have sorted the résumés into two piles (i.e., interesting or not interesting), create a spreadsheet based on the required qualifications and skills in the job description. Enter a brief summary of the information provided by the interesting résumés, and then sort the spreadsheet so that those individuals with the most indicators are at the top; then sort again by how well the indicators have been addressed. Plan to interview the candidates at the top of the list.

Plan your interview process. Be sure to have someone else sit in on the interviews with you to offer a second opinion. If you work alone, perhaps you can ask a colleague to assist you, and offer to do the same for her or him. Plan your strategy together. Often a two-step interview process works well. The first interview provides you with the opportunity to determine the candidate's technical skills and overall desired qualities. If you want to continue the process, invite the candidate back for a second interview to clarify any unanswered questions, provide work samples and references, and conduct a simulated task associated with the job to demonstrate skills and decision-making ability.

Prepare your interview questions. Prepare your list of questions in advance, and think about how best to elicit the information you need from candidates. You are not only looking at their academic skills, work experience, and long-term career plans; you are also assessing whether they have the social and emotional intelligence needed to handle day-to-day challenges. I have often hired young people just out of school and, as a result, have learned to assess them based on less-tangible criteria such as resilience, adaptability, self-reliance, perseverance, curiosity, willingness to learn, ethics, and objectivity. Life experience can be a good indicator of strength of character. Examples included extensive travel, volunteer work, and involvement in high-performance sports. A list of sample interview questions is provided in Appendix 8.

There are a number of questions that are unlawful to ask, so be aware of legal requirements and restrictions in your jurisdiction. Privacy and fair information principles may be complex and difficult to interpret. They have implications not only for hiring but also for what information you may use when requesting references, and returning information to those not hired (e.g., writing samples).

Conduct a second interview with the candidates who interest you the most. Essenmacher (2006) suggests testing for work-related skills such as editing a report for format or typographical errors, creating charts or tables in your word processing program, using particular software to follow a set of instructions, or completing a writing task. As I always expected my research assistants to solve problems and make good decisions in the field, I often asked candidates to respond to a scenario that required problem-solving skills. A sample scenario to test a prospective research assistant's problem-solving ability is provided in Appendix 9.

Interview the candidates. The interview has three parts. The first is to welcome candidates and try to make them feel as comfortable as possible. Provide a time frame for the interview (usually 45 minutes to one hour) and establish a pleasant rapport, but don't be overly friendly or engage in chitchat. Often candidates are very nervous at this point. Some staff members have told me later that they could not remember a single thing about this part of the process, so don't overwhelm them with information. Your job is to listen carefully and do only about 10% of the talking. Hold your phone calls, text messages, and e-mails. Watch for eye contact and body language. If you are taking notes, explain the reason (e.g., "to refresh my memory"). Reassure the individuals that everything they say will be treated in confidence.

In the second part of the interview, elicit the information you need. Ask your questions clearly and concisely, but use a conversational tone. If there are contradictions in the candidate's answers, probe for the reasons, but don't prejudge or pigeonhole the applicant. Keep your personal opinions and prejudices out of the interview. If, however, you soon feel that this candidate will not be appropriate to meet your needs, leave out the more detailed questions, and skip to generalities such as reasons for their interest in the position and questions about the job that they may currently have. At that point, treat this as an information interview, because even your unsuccessful candidates take their impressions of your firm into the broader community.

The third part of the interview is the closing. Thank the candidate for spending time with you and explain the next steps in the process, but don't make any promises. Never offer a job at this point. You and your colleague need to debrief, and you still have the rest of the candidates to interview. Only then, if you both still like a few candidates, invite them back for the second interview. However, there are still several steps to go through before you make a decision.

Step 3. Postinterview Activities

Create a short list. By now, you should have a pretty good idea of whom you want for the job. You have updated your spreadsheet based on the information gained in the interview process and are probably looking at no more than two or three candidates. By this point, chemistry is really starting to influence your decision, so be careful. There are still a few red flags to watch for. They include the following:

- Immaturity, a tendency to blame others, hypersensitivity, or overdemanding behavior
- Inappropriate dress, comments, or questions
- Overblown claims of accomplishments or aspirations beyond demonstrated ability
- Gaps in duration of jobs or schooling
- Competing life issues that can limit availability
- Frequent changes in jobs or residences
- Recent stressful life events such as change in marital status or death of a family member

Balthazard (1991) reminds us that the best predictor of future behavior is past behavior. Ask yourself, *Can I work with this person?*

Conduct reference checks. Be sure to call at least three references for each of your finalists, and try to talk to direct supervisors. Clarify their relationship to the candidate. For example, are the references provided coworkers but not supervisors, professors but not employers, family friends but not colleagues? Try to verify the information provided by the candidate, such as previous job title, salary, dates of employment, and tasks involved. Essenmacher (2006) suggests that up to 25% of applicants misrepresent their education or other credentials. It is a bad sign when a reference is not expecting your call. If the candidate has not asked permission to use the name as a reference, there is also a privacy issue. It is often surprising what these uninformed references have to say about the candidate. On the other hand, when individuals are aware of the candidate's job search, you can tell quite a lot from the warmth of their response when you ask them if they would rehire the candidate. A sample form for reference checks is provided in Appendix 10.

Conduct testing or other screening. Based on your own experience and expertise, you may require potential staff members to complete some psychological testing. In other cases, your client may require new staff to complete a security check or sign a self-disclosure form regarding any civil or criminal violations, indictments, or convictions.

Select your candidate and make an offer. Armed with all this information, it is time to make a decision. Only now can you follow your gut feeling and pick the qualified candidate you like the best. Call your chosen candidate and make the offer. Identify start date, salary, benefits, and review process (e.g., that there is a three-month probation period). Do not provide room for negotiations at this point. Indicate that you will be sending an employment contract and a confidentiality agreement for a signature and that you want them returned by a certain date. Don't make any promises that could become binding later, such as saying that there will be no overtime work or that you anticipate changes to their duties in the future. Just stick to the basic employment information, and follow up the telephone conversation with a letter stating the same points.

You can get to this very last step and still be surprised. The candidate may have taken a job with someone else or may decide that he or she does not want this job. Now what do you do? If there is a second candidate who is very close in terms of meeting your criteria, you may want to offer the job to this person. In fact, the second-place candidate may turn out to be a better choice, because there was less chemistry involved. However, don't settle for someone who does not meet your qualifications just because you feel desperate. It is better to hire temporary staff to fill the gap, and restart the search process. As Essenmacher (2006) points out, it is worth the wait for the pot of gold at the end of the hiring rainbow, because the "right" employees don't need incentives to do a good job, they will do it just because they want to.

Finally, remember to send the applicants you are not going to hire a simple rejection letter as soon as possible (Vikesland, n.d.). Don't state why they were not hired; only indicate that another applicant was more appropriate for the job. Thank them for their time, and wish them well in their job search. While these people may never work for you, they will have a good impression about your firm.

❖ MANAGING NEW STAFF

Employee contract and orientation. Similar in many ways to your other contracts, the employment contract must also address any requirements stated in the employment or labor law in your jurisdiction. Again you need to develop a template with the assistance of your lawyer, and then keep it on file to update for each employee you hire. Once you hire employees on a regular basis, you will update their contracts and will then renew these contracts annually, making changes to wages, benefits, and duties as needed based on the performance assessment. In general, the employment contract for your probationary employee should include (Barrington Research Group, Inc., 2003):

1. Job title and tasks in the job description

2. The term of employment, part- or full-time status, number of hours of work per day and week

3. Explanation of probation period, when employee will be evaluated, and consequences of that evaluation (i.e., ongoing contract or termination)

4. Description of expectations such as keeping track of time worked; working in accordance with firm philosophy; being efficient, prompt, and economical; observing all applicable laws, regulations, and standards; cooperating with other staff, etc.

5. Rate of pay and deductions

6. How to handle expenses incurred on the job

7. Termination procedures

8. Other general provisions

The orientation period, which usually lasts about two days, should be planned carefully. First of all you need to meet with new employees and go over their employment contracts and other required paperwork, such as a confidentiality agreement, payroll and tax forms, and routine firm policies. Stress your expectations for them. Then meetings should be scheduled with key staff (if any), and the newcomers should learn how to use the computer system, navigate files, and complete their timesheets. Then they need to become familiar with office culture and learn customer service policies, including how to answer the phone. Only after they have received this orientation should they be introduced to current projects. At the end of the two-day period, meet with them to answer their questions. Then it is time to get down to work.

Probation. There is usually a period of three months to confirm your hiring decisions. The terms of a probationary period usually reflect the labor laws in your jurisdiction and should be clearly set out in your employment contract. As staff members are in training, sometimes a salary raise is contingent upon a positive evaluation at the end of this period. Should a new staff member not meet your expectations, be unable to complete the tasks as outlined in the job description, or not fit with the rest of your team, you can let the person go without an extensive termination process. Sometimes a couple of days or a week is all you need to find out that the job is not for her or him. The staff member may come to the same conclusion. If the probation period is not successful for whatever reason, cut your losses and start a new search process, or hire temporary staff and reassess your needs. Never try to persuade someone to stay when the writing is on the wall.

Provide training as needed, and meet with new employees regularly to discuss their progress. Quickly move to task completion so you can begin to gauge their competency and work speed. Use a scaffolding approach so that you are building tasks in a logical manner from short, straightforward ones to ensure that the basics can be demonstrated to the more complex tasks that reflect your real resource needs. Even with experienced people, the way you do things may be quite different from they way they have done them in the past, and training may be required.

The three-month assessment. During the probation period, keep track of the tasks you have assigned to new employees, their ability to complete them, your satisfaction level, and any issues or need for improvement. This way you won't have to rely on your memory when the three months are up. When you see an employee floundering or heading down the wrong path, provide immediate feedback and guidance; don't wait for later. At the end of the period, ask new employees to complete a three-month self-evaluation survey to help them consider their own job performance. A sample survey is shown in Appendix 11.

Once the documentation is completed on both sides, meet with new employees, and go over the results carefully. Whether the feedback is positive or not, they will be grateful to receive specific guidance on how to improve. At this point you need to indicate clearly whether or not you want them to continue, and provide the reasons for this decision. Let them know the terms you are prepared to offer, and provide an updated contract for signature following the meeting. Use this opportunity to do some action planning and set some development goals. These individuals are now considered regular employees.

❖   MANAGING ONGOING STAFF

Supervision. One reason for consulting firm failure is the lack of adequate supervision and guidance for staff, poor communications, and limited opportunity for course correction. When I managed staff, I held two types of meetings every week. First, I had a meeting with each staff member I supervised to review task completion and set targets for the following week. We discussed any problems that had emerged and tried to find solutions. Second, I held a project team meeting and invited all staff and subcontractors to attend either in person or by conference call. We reviewed project goal achievement and planned upcoming strategies. We also focused on team building and an awareness of the skills that each team member contributed to build a sense of pride in the team, the project, and the firm. In this way we were able to gain significant traction on current tasks and to develop a quick response to the challenges that lay ahead.

Role modeling and coaching. When possible, I had staff members accompany me to client meetings or other related activities. This gave them a chance to gain an understanding about how to interact with clients. I provided coaching for junior consultants and tried to help them acquire appropriate problem-solving skills. As their skills improved, I would fade out coaching in that area and move to something new. Senior staff were encouraged to reflect on their own work processes, and coaching junior staff often provided them with a way to do this.

Professional development. As our field is research, we see that professional development is critical for everyone to keep current. You will need to develop some guidelines regarding which professional development activities will be supported by time off or financial support (including cost sharing). Job-related courses, conferences, workshops, and seminars may be appropriate to help employees upgrade their skills, particularly if a new project requires a new skill set or if a need is identified during their performance assessment. Be careful that staff expectations do not exceed your professional development budget. It is wise to establish an amount at the beginning of the year so that they can plan ahead.

On-going performance assessment. Kubr (2002, p. 790) suggests systematic performance assessments are more important in consulting firms than in other organizations for two reasons. The career path requires rapid development and a widening assumption of responsibilities; thus performance assessment must be frequent. Second, as the consulting environment is constantly changing, and consultants are typically involved in five or more projects in a year, ongoing professional development is imperative.

Periodic assessments can tell both the firm and the individual what development needs are required, how personnel can be better utilized, and what is needed to support an employee's motivation and job performance. If a consultant should be looking elsewhere for a career, a performance appraisal should reveal the unmet needs on both sides, and the outcome should be clear. It is not fair to prolong unrealistic expectations and delay a painful decision.

Once the probation period is over, you should hold performance reviews with staff on a semiannual basis. My staff told me that annual reviews were too infrequent for them, and they preferred to reflect on their progress twice a year so that they could set more realistic goals. As staff make performance goals based on their reviews, it is important to fold their action plans into your weekly monitoring meetings.

Retention. In the literature, the topic of retention is inextricably linked with compensation. The message is clear: Pay staff members well in order to hold onto them. But in my experience, it is the work, the team, the clients, and the colleagues that hold people, not the money. As long as they were hired using a fair market benchmark, social science researchers in an independent setting are committed to what they do. As long as they make a decent wage, additional compensation is secondary.

❖ SAYING GOOD-BYE

Eventually, people leave. Kubr (2002) suggests that management consultants tend to leave because of differing views on how to do consulting or a desire to start their own practice. More frequently, I found that working in research has an upward momentum in terms of qualifications. People leave because they want to pursue their education. Younger staff experience life changes and need more extensive benefits or higher salaries when they get married or start a family. Finally, as the consulting environment is unpredictable, stressful, and demanding, staff can tire of the work and burn out. They leave to find a more routine environment.

There are career limitations in a small firm, and sometimes, staff members see their work for you as a stepping stone. If you sense that their departure is growing close, it is better to be proactive rather than wait for their resignation. A frank discussion can lead to a mutual parting of the ways. Other times, a good opportunity may come up suddenly. It is a compliment when former staff members are hired by larger organizations. They are your "graduates" and become part of your broader network. They may well refer clients to you one day.

You can also terminate an employee for any reason, including a layoff due to insufficient work or a poor fit with the firm or projected work requirements. Very occasionally, termination is required for "cause." To protect both your firm and your employees, be sure that your termination process is clearly laid out in your employment contract. From the time employees sign their contracts, they should be aware of exit strategies. The termination process is ruled by local legislation. The amount of notice is usually related to the number of years they have been employed by your firm. You expect them to honor the commitments they made when they joined your firm; to return all company materials; to maintain confidentiality about all of your projects, clients, and firm activities now and in the future; and to not compete with you for at least a year. Whatever the reason, allow staff members to leave with dignity and grace. Wish them well and carry on.

❖ USEFUL RESOURCES

- Tips on how to hire right are provided at http://www
  .employer-employee.com/hire.html
- Check out Steingold and Delpo's *The Employer's Legal Handbook*
  (7th ed., Berkeley, CA. Nolo, 2005).
- For a classic theory of motivation, check out "One More Time:
  How Do You Motivate Employees?" by Frederick Herzberg
  (*Harvard Business Review*, 1968, Vol. 46, #1, pp. 53–56).

❖ DISCUSSION QUESTIONS AND ACTIVITIES

1. Prepare a list of potential associates whom you may contact
   should you require assistance for a consulting project. How
   would you plan to approach them to establish a potential business relationship?

2. Considering current salaries for comparable work in your
   area, determine a salary range for the research assistant position identified in the job description in Exhibit 16.1. In order to
   prepare a job ad, what other decisions would need to be made?
   Write the advertisement. Where would you post it?

3. If motivators for work performance include such factors as
   recognition for a job well done, achievement, autonomy,
   and responsibility, how can the small consulting firm ensure
   that staff are provided with the motivation they need to be
   retained?

❖ REFERENCES

Balthazard, C. (1991). Consulting talent: A guide to selecting the best. *The
CMC Journal, 2*(1), 31–34.

Barrington Research Group, Inc. (2003).
*Barrington Research Group, Inc. employee
handbook.* Calgary, AB: Author.

Essenmacher, V. (2006, November).
Hiring the right employees/sub-
contractors. In R. Hoke (Chair),

*Intermediate consulting skills: A self-
help fair.* Think tank session conducted at the Annual Meeting of the
American Evaluation Association,
Portland, OR.

Gray, D. (2008). *Start & run a consult-
ing business* (8th ed.). Bellingham,
WA, and North Vancouver, BC: Self-
Counsel Press.

Greiner, L. E., & Metzger, R. O. (1983). *Consulting to management.* Englewood Cliffs, NJ: Prentice-Hall.

Kubr, M. (2002). *Management consulting: A guide to the profession* (4th ed.). Geneva, Switzerland: International Labour Office.

Vikesland, G. (n.d.). *Hire the right employee!* Retrieved from http://www.employer-employee.com/hire.html

Weiss, A. (2003). *Million dollar consulting. The professional's guide to growing a practice* (3rd ed.). New York, NY: McGraw-Hill.

17

Managing Knowledge

Highlights:

- Learn about the benefits of knowledge management.
- Learn the five steps involved in developing a knowledge management system.
- Explore ways to translate knowledge into action.

Did you know that over 30 billion original documents are created each year in the United States alone (Microsoft Corporation, 2010), and of these, 85% are never retrieved again? Yet for every dollar a company spends creating a document, 10 dollars are spent managing it. There is something frightening about this if you consider that, for independent consultants, our greatest and sometimes only asset is our knowledge. How well are we managing it?

Clients hire us for our research and evaluation expertise, knowledge, skills, methods, and processes. The value of our firms is dependent on our ability to use our resources quickly and effectively, yet much of this treasure trove goes untapped. Here are some of the reasons for this failure:

- We work in many environments in addition to our own offices, including client locations, airports, buses, trains, lobbies, restaurants, and other public places. We are always in a hurry, and so we store our work on whatever device is convenient. It takes time and attention to integrate this fugitive information into one safe and comprehensive site.
- We work under pressure, and there is always another deadline. Managing knowledge is something that would be nice to do if only we had the time.
- Our focus is on our clients, and our work is organized around their needs and demands. We plan to get to our own needs later.
- We live to maximize our billable hours. Whatever the client is not willing to pay for has lower value in our eyes.
- Our work belongs to our clients. Why bother saving something if you can't use it again?
- We work in a competitive environment and are reluctant to share with our colleagues. We don't want them to benefit from our good ideas.

Perhaps it would help if our knowledge management were quantified. According to Skyrme (1999), a knowledge management expert, intellectual capital is worth 10 to 50 times the financial value of any company even though it is intangible. Figure it out, and see how much your knowledge is worth to you. Should you be doing something about this?

❖ THE BENEFITS OF KNOWLEDGE MANAGEMENT

The Organisation for Economic Co-operation and Development (OECD) and Statistics Canada (2003, p. 12) provides a definition of *knowledge management*, stating that it covers "any intentional and systematic process or practice of acquiring, capturing, sharing and using productive knowledge, wherever it resides, to enhance learning and performance in organisations." Here are some reasons why it should be a priority for us.

It supports efficient work processes. Kubr (2002) suggests that if appropriate solutions to urgent issues already exist, we need to use them to save time. It should be easy to search for similar proposals, projects, research tools, or background information to move our work ahead. As time is money, this will have a positive impact on our bottom line.

It improves our competitive response. Using our knowledge to develop and enhance new services, processes, and methods becomes a service differentiator (Skyrme, 1999) and a marketing tool. The details of any evaluation or research study may be unique, but the methods and processes are standard. We can get a jump on our next project if we can remind ourselves about what we did last time. If we routinely debrief and reflect on our practice, we can embed our innovations in our work. Continual improvement will give us a distinct market advantage. To do this, we need an effective knowledge management system, so we can pinpoint what we need.

It fosters knowledge creation. Converting both content knowledge and process learning into reusable services, tools, processes, and resources allows us to train our staff and subcontractors in "the way we do things here." It is also possible to share our expertise more broadly by reworking our knowledge in articles, presentations, webinars, workshops, and other knowledge translation activities.

It prevents the loss of intellectual assets. Consulting staff and subcontractors come and go. In fact, the average length of employment in consulting is considerably shorter than in other sectors (Kubr, 2002). Therefore a knowledge management system is needed to ensure that explicit knowledge generated is retained in the company when staff or subcontractors leave. Tacit or implied knowledge is even more difficult to capture. Documenting exit interviews and conducting debriefing sessions or structured dialogues with key team members can help retain some of this elusive and context-specific information.

It preserves our corporate memory. Over time, a firm becomes a repository of data, information, and knowledge. We all know how quickly study participants forget important details. Our own memory decay is no less significant, but corporate amnesia often goes unchecked. A usable archiving and retrieval system is the only way to build a memory bank.

It supports good decision making. We can create benchmarks by tracking our performance using project budgets, timesheets, and proposal success rates. This provides the evidence we need to review progress toward our goals or to make decisions going forward based on more than gut instinct. For example, is it worthwhile to prepare a particular proposal? Which professional development activity yielded the most innovations or new ideas last year? Should we hire a subcontractor or a staff member? Should we take on a volunteer role? We have the questions, and we have the answers; it is a matter of putting them together.

It provides an evidence trail. As we have seen in Chapter 15, we can reduce our exposure to liability by maintaining good records of client contact meetings and well-documented timesheets and invoices. Page (2005) stresses the importance of filing e-mails and printing copies of those with particular significance in case of future legal issues. He says, "Keep a paper trail. The guy with the better paper trail wins!"

Baastrup & Strømsnes (2003) measured knowledge management in a business context and reported that the most effective results of a knowledge management program were the following:

- Improved skills and knowledge of workers
- Increased adaptation of products or services to client requirements
- Increased knowledge sharing among team members
- New products or services

❖ DEVELOPING KNOWLEDGE MANAGEMENT SYSTEMS

Now that you see the benefits of developing a knowledge management system for your firm, here are some key processes to consider: knowledge generation, capture, retrieval, and translation.

Knowledge Generation

In the first place, you should identify key topics or areas of practice where knowledge can enrich your work. It can help you develop, improve, track, or substantiate what you do. Here are some general topics to consider:

Financial records. You need to retain accurate and thorough financial records, such as detailed tax records, payroll records, bank statements, detailed accounts payable and receivable, and year-end statements. According to Attorney General McKenna (2008), you need to keep your tax records and related documentation for at least seven years.

Administrative arrangements. There are many business agreements and documents to keep on file, such as leases and real estate information, business licenses and trade name registration, supplier agreements, insurance records, copyrights and other intellectual property, and warranties. McKenna suggests you need to keep some of these documents (e.g., warranties) only for as long as they are current. You can also shred monthly or quarterly records, such as IRA contributions, once you receive an annual statement. However, he suggests that you keep insurance records for an additional five years after the life of the policy, and real estate information (e.g., sales or improvements) for up to seven years.

Personnel files. Keep a set of individual files, one for each employee or subcontractor. The files should contain all documents and correspondence related to these individuals, from their applications for employment to their terminations or project completions, copies of their résumés, their job descriptions, their signed employment contracts and confidentiality agreements, their performance review documents, and their wage or fee histories. Scheid (2010) suggests that these files should be kept for at least seven years in case of litigation.

Activity records. Diaries, timesheets, and calendars should be retained as evidence of your project activities. As Gray comments (2008, p. 86), "If there is a legal dispute, your time record and service documentation could make the difference between winning and losing."

Client files. While the administrative files are straightforward, client files are more complex. Further, it is a pretty good guess that when you are in the middle of tool development, data collection, or report writing, your mind will not be on your filing. So here is a simple solution that has worked well in our office. Develop a client folder template, and save it on your computer. Within it keep a set of blank folders labeled as follows:

- Proposal
- Contract
- Work plan
- Background information/literature
- Correspondence and administration
- Contact summaries

- Instruments
- Data
- Status reports
- Final report

At the start of each new project, copy the template with an acronym or tag for the project name, client, and year. Now you know where to file material and where to find it again, no matter what project you are working on. You can delete file folders if they are not needed, or you can create new categories, but the template is enough to get you started. Then create a template for paper file folder labels. Add the new project tag, and print off a set of labels for your project. The folders are now ready for information as it comes in.

Process knowledge. Think about your business strategy. Identify between four and seven strategic process areas where knowledge management can improve your practice (Kubr, 2002). In these folders, file documents that you create or that cross your desk related to these topics, and begin to build your own library. Sample topics include the following:

1. Key documents from seminal projects that changed your practice in a significant way

2. Survey precedents

3. Emerging methodologies

4. Processes, methods, and templates that are easily replicated

5. Processes under review where improvements are needed

6. Knowledge related to planned conference presentations or publications

7. Innovations, creative solutions, and reflections

Knowledge Capture

Knowing now what information you want to retain, how do you implement your knowledge management system? If large organizations are challenged by this, how can a busy independent consultant with limited resources develop the daily work routines required to capture essential material? I have an image of myself standing in the middle of a field with a large butterfly net, catching knowledge as it whizzes by. If I miss it, it's gone forever. To persuade yourself that it is worth your while to stop in the middle of doing something important to file knowledge, the action has to be automatic. This requires careful planning, magical thinking, and trick psychology.

Of course, the best motivator is self-interest, so remember that you are saving yourself time, energy, thought, and money by saving your materials. Perhaps, you can use the stick and carrot method as I sometimes do. I get a trip to a glamorous and warm location as a reward for good behavior. My completely unscientific approach to motivation is also built on a stage-gate process. I have to do one particular thing before I give myself permission to do another. Thus, I have to complete a Client Contact Summary before I go to see that client again. I have to complete my project filing for the month before I write my status report. I have to submit my status report so that I can get paid, and so on. The processes are easy, because they have been set up in advance. I just have to do them.

Often, the broader knowledge transfer piece might not get done at all if it were not for the fact that I have to present a paper or workshop on one of my strategic topics in order to justify the expense of attending the next conference. By determining my topic well in advance and by maintaining a file to capture relevant materials, it is easy to collect them as they come my way.

Knowledge Retrieval

A light-bulb moment for me was discovering that filing is really not about filing, it is about retrieval. To find things again, you need to set up systems that work for you, but once they are established, there is no decision making to do, so maintenance is easy. Here are some ways to manage your retrieval process.

Centralize paper files. Keeping paper copies of essential records is still a good idea despite the promises we heard a few years ago about a paperless society. We all know stories of server crashes and other electronic catastrophes. You need two physical locations for paper files, one for short-term storage and the other for long-term. Generally it is wise to keep your project and administrative files close by for at least two years. One or two filing cabinets can usually accommodate this amount of information. Then after two years, those files that you still want to retain should be shipped off to long-term storage. This can be a location in your garage or attic, or as in my case, in an off-site storage locker. Based on my own experience, however, I don't recommend storing files in your basement. The day the sewer backed up in my house is not a pleasant memory. Pack your files in cardboard banker's boxes and label them well.

Back up electronic files. There are two basic approaches to backing up your electronic files: You can do it yourself, or you can farm it out to a virtual storage service. Security is the key consideration, but both solutions have limitations.

You may prefer to look after your own backup system and have probably already invested in a firewall and antivirus, antispyware, and malware protection. However, most of us know people who have experienced a destructive virus or had their computers hacked. The sense of invasion is even more profound than a physical breach of your office—it feels like someone has been walking around inside your head. You need to check regularly with an IT specialist to make sure that your office computer, your home computer, your laptop, and your smartphone remain protected and up-to-date. Whenever technology moves forward, new security concerns also emerge, so remain vigilant.

Establish routines to back up your files on all your computers, and consider off-site storage for backup tapes, disks, or hard drives in a safety deposit box at a nearby bank. Keep current work on flash drives and store them separately from your laptop in case it goes missing. When a project is completed, prepare a CD with all pertinent information on it as a permanent record.

The music and gaming industries and social media have pushed file sharing and web use to new heights. Some of my colleagues now store their files online. However, a word of caution is offered by Jacobi and Larkin (2006): "Servers crash and companies go out of business, both without warning. Never trust an online storage service with the only copy of your vital data." Further, they warn that, while these services take measures to lock down your data, the privacy and security of your files is ultimately up to you. As a result, you should encrypt all files holding private data. Further, you should plan for the day that your online files disappear.

As cloud computing becomes more prevalent, it will be more and more difficult to resist its advantages (Hurwitz, Bloor, Kaufman, & Halper, 2010). There is no upfront investment for a server or software licensing. You simply pay as you go. You can build or customize applications to run on your provider's infrastructure, and you may be able to access them from your mobile phone. While some corporations have adopted the cloud already, there are still some performance and availability issues. Security concerns may not yet be adequately addressed to meet both your needs and those of your clients.

Archive your files. Once a project is completed, you can cull the files and shred any nonessential material. As long as data are entered or transcribed in a usable form, the originals may no longer be needed. To confirm how long you should retain certain types of documents, check government compliance requirements in your area. Ask your clients if they have any specific regulations regarding document storage and retention. Plan for change, because whatever technology you are using now, you probably won't be using it in five years. Will your new, faster tools still be able to read your old electronic files? If you are in doubt, keep a paper copy as well.

The key to an archiving system is to develop a spreadsheet that is an archive map. The files I plan to house in long-term storage are labeled in numbered boxes, and the numbers and a summary of contents are recorded in the spreadsheet. Computer files are archived in a similar way on my server. At the end of a project, all nonessential files are culled and the appropriate versions of documents are retained within the tagged project folder template. All retired projects are filed in a main project folder called "Archived Projects."

Review your archives regularly. Over the course of a year, the file boxes start to stack up in the corner of my office. By summer, it is time to fill up my car and visit my storage locker. Before I go, I review my archive map, add the new boxes to the list, and decide which boxes have exceeded their retention limit and can be purged. So while some boxes go into the locker, others are removed. During the year you can keep a small shredder handy for your daily needs in order to protect client confidentiality and prevent identify theft, but for larger loads, like this once-a-year purge, you can subscribe to a shredding service and have the boxes carted away. These companies will provide you with a certificate of destruction.

Knowledge Translation

With knowledge at your fingertips, you can retrieve it quickly and use it well. You can convert your learning into practice improvements and innovations for your own business. You can also share it with your clients and the professional community at large.

Working with staff. With each project, your practice improves, and your skills are honed, but the real benefit starts to emerge when you critique what you have done. Turning knowledge into practice can be easy when you hold a postproject review. Make it fun by having a pizza lunch for everyone who was involved in your latest project. Use a set of structured questions to start the reflection process.

- What were some of the highlights of this project? Why did they work so well?
- What can we adopt for next time?
- What were the biggest problem areas or issues in this project? Why?
- What could we do differently next time to lessen or eliminate these problems?
- Overall, what was the best innovation or new idea that came out of this project? What are we the most proud of?
- How can we turn this idea into a new process, service, or product? What will we need to do to turn this good idea into practice?
- Who would benefit from this new knowledge? What is the best way to share it with them?

Working with clients. Reframing your work habits becomes easier over time. Your goal of becoming a learning-enhanced firm will begin to bear fruit quickly, and your reflective practice will begin to differentiate your firm from others. Clients will become aware that your practice is continually improving and that you actively look for innovations and better ways of doing things, and they will want to become part of the process, because it benefits them as well. Kubr (2002) believes that building client capacity is increasingly one of the main purposes of consulting.

Many of my clients understand the need for knowledge translation and have supported presentations to key stakeholders and conferences, staff training workshops, plain language summaries (e.g., in newsletters), and other activities that lead to policy action. What I have learned, however, is that presenting the findings is not enough. You need to be proactive and plan for knowledge translation from project inception.

Barwick (2010) has developed a Scientist Knowledge Translation Plan Template to assist scientists and other grant writers in this planning process. In her view, grant budgets should routinely contain a category for knowledge translation. She recommends that the roles of any research partners and decision makers in the research translation process be defined. The type of information to be produced from the research should be identified at the beginning of the project in order to identify target audiences. Knowledge translation outcomes need to be determined, including generating awareness, changing practice, implementing policy, imparting knowledge and tools, and informing further research. With these goals in mind, it is easier to identify appropriate knowledge translation methods and determine how they will occur. This approach makes it clear that the role of the researcher and evaluator is broader than we thought, and so we need to work with our clients and design our projects as conduits for knowledge.

Working with your professional community. Reaching out to your professional community is easier than ever. Not only do the traditional methods of conference presentations and journal articles still exist, but more time-sensitive methods such as webinars, blogs, virtual communities of practice, grey literature databases, and wikis provide expanding opportunities to share your knowledge. While some consultants may hesitate to share learning of any significance with their potential competitors, you have only to look at open source documents to understand the value of this perspective. By sharing knowledge, everyone wins.

I can offer one small example of how knowledge gets generated and shared. It relates to my own practice improvement strategy. I found that there has been a great deal of emphasis on logic models and program theory in the evaluation literature, but there were few resources available to help me with the next steps. I needed to handle my study data in a more standard way rather than relying on the personal preferences of the different researchers I hired. I started thinking about data handling processes and, throughout several evaluation projects, tried to document what we were doing. I began to capture tools and examples of data analysis with this end in mind and slowly began to develop a process I could replicate.

Then I prepared a workshop on data handling for the 2007 Canadian Evaluation Society conference, knowing that by preparing the materials for the workshop, I would also clarify the process for myself. I asked clients for permission to use examples of study materials for training purposes, and, as no findings were involved, they were agreeable. The topic was difficult to explain. The feedback I received from workshop participants was pretty mediocre. So I made a number of changes and offered the workshop several more times, revising and clarifying the materials each time based on participant feedback. Then the opportunity arose to manage an applied research study, and I used the workshop materials to train my client's staff. We were able to refine the processes further in response to the specific analysis needs of the project. Now I am revising the materials again based on that experience. While the process is far from perfect, the topic seems to resonate with people, and the knowledge is spreading. The materials have been circulated to workshop participants, and they have often asked for permission to circulate them to their coworkers. The materials are also posted on the Creative Commons on the American Evaluation Association website. One of the researchers I trained last summer is now using these methods in her doctoral research. I recently presented two more workshops on the topic, one in Atlanta, Georgia, and one in Edmonton, Alberta. You have to admit that those locations are pretty far apart. Still, I am not finished. I have another research project getting under way, and I know the material will be useful in it as well. No doubt we will refine it again. For me, this is how experience is turned into new knowledge, how best practices are built and refined, and how knowledge is translated into use.

Because you are an independent consultant, never think that you have nothing to share. By developing clear and simple knowledge management strategies and by learning how to create, retrieve, use, and translate knowledge, you are contributing not only to your own success but to that of your clients and colleagues as well. All you need is a good knowledge management system and a drive to improve what you do. Then as the ancient sage said, "Just do your work and then let go." The rest will fall into place.

❖ USEFUL RESOURCES

- For information on knowledge management, see http://www .idrc.ca/uploads/user-S/122660477011226595 6261Chapter_3% 5B1%5D.pdf
- For a primer on knowledge translation, see http://www.ncddr .org/kt/products/focus/focus18/
- For information on knowledge translation training and tools, see http://www.melaniebarwick.com/training.php

❖ DISCUSSION QUESTIONS AND ACTIVITIES

1. Over the course of a week, be aware of the information that comes your way, whether it is about your content area or about business management skills. What barriers keep you from capturing this important information? Why would retaining some of this transient knowledge be beneficial to you?

2. Barwick found that traditional methods of knowledge transfer such as academic journals and conference presentations had only mixed effects in terms of knowledge translation. Based on your own experience, why do you think that these strategies lack effectiveness? What less traditional methods could complement them and improve the impact of knowledge use?

3. Think of a time when you have translated knowledge effectively in your studies, your research, or other work. What were the conditions that made it easy to apply this knowledge? How can you continue to use this approach?

❖ REFERENCES

Baastrup, A., & Strømsnes, W. (2003). The promotion and implementation of knowledge management—a Danish contribution. In *Measuring knowledge management in the business sector: First steps* (pp. 119–142). Paris, France: Organisation for Economic Co-Operation and Development and Statistics Canada.

Barwick, M. (2010). *Knowledge translation planning template.* Retrieved from http://www.melaniebarwick .com/document/Scientist_Knowl edge_Translation_Plan_Template _June2010.pdf

Gray, D. (2008). *Start & run a consulting business* (8th ed.). North Vancouver, BC: Self-Counsel Press.

Hurwitz, J., Bloor, R., Kaufman, M., & Halper, F. (2010). *What is cloud computing?* Retrieved from http://www.dummies.com/how-to/content/what-is-cloud -computing.html

Jacobi, J. L., & Larkin, E. (2006). *Store it on the web.* Retrieved from http://www.pcworld.com/article/125729/store_it_on_the_web.html

Kubr, M. (2002). *Management consulting: A guide to the profession* (4th ed.). Geneva, Switzerland: International Labour Office.

McKenna, R. (2008). *Personal documents—keep or shred?* Retrieved from http://www.atg.wa.gov/askcolumn .aspx?id=20554

Microsoft Corporation. (2010). *The document life cycle.* Retrieved from http://technet.microsoft.com/en-ca/library/dd163515.aspx

Organisation   for   Economic Co-operation and Development & Statistics Canada. (2003). *Measuring knowledge management in the business sector: First steps.* Paris, France: Organisation   for   Economic Co-Operation   and   Development Publication Service.

Page, W. J. (2005, April). *ICMCA/ CAMC legal issues and approaches 2005.* Workshop conducted at the Institute of Certified Management Consultants of Alberta professional development workshop, Calgary, AB.

Scheid, J. (2010). *Tips on how long to keep your business documents.* Retrieved from http://www.bright hub.com/office/home/articles/144 98.aspx

Skyrme, D. (1999). *Knowledge management: The next steps.* Retrieved from http://www.skyrme.com/pubs/ kmcons.htm

Appendices

Appendix 1

A Game of Endurance

Freelance experts need more than expertise to survive. They also have to be able to take the heat and the cold shoulder. Monika Morrow puts these questions to would-be consultants (Maynard, 1992):

1. **Define the market.**
   - What skills am I selling?
   - What evidence do I have that these skills are needed in today's market?
   - Can I name five types of organizations that can use my help?
   - Can I set up information meetings with a senior person in each of these five areas to test my perceptions? What contacts and referrals can I use to set these up? My goal at this point is not to get a contract but rather to get feedback on my plans. I need to find out:

     ° Are the organizations or agencies hiring consultants in my area?
     ° What kind of background do they have?
     ° Do I fit the profile?

   - Is there a market for my skills?

2. **Identify your skill gaps.**
   - What skill areas do I have that are particularly strong?
   - What skill areas need bolstering or support?
   - What consultants do I know whose expertise complements my own?
   - How can I join forces with them on a short-term basis?
   - Can I turn my skill gaps into a full portfolio of skills to offer clients?

3. **Have enough money to get started.**
   - Can I support myself for three months while I check out the market?
   - Can I support myself for another three months to land my first contract?
   - What other financial resources can I rely on while getting up to speed? (Morrow suggests that this can take up to a year.)
   - Do I have the financial resources I need?

4. **Determine your social needs.**
   - Can I handle periods of isolation interrupted by brief spurts of client contact and data collection?
   - Do I need a colleague across the hall to commiserate with or to gain psychological support?
   - Are there other ways I can fulfill my social needs?
   - Can I work alone for long periods?

5. **Practice multi-tasking.**
   - While I am writing one client's final report, can I also work on three other projects and develop a major proposal?
   - Can I send out invoices, pay bills, and take care of office administration at the same time?
   - Am I good at multi-tasking?
   - Can I cope with competing demands on my time?

6. **Prove your resiliency.**
   - Can I respond quickly when my client or field realities change the approach I had planned?
   - Can I regroup without losing my confidence?
   - Do I brood or lose my temper when confronted with setback?
   - Am I resilient?

SOURCE: Maynard, R. (1992, October). The guru gambit. *Report on Business Magazine*, p. 68.

Appendix 2

Annual Billable Time Worksheet

Item		Weeks	Days
Total time:		*52 weeks*	*260 work days*
(less)	Annual vacation	___ weeks	___ days
	Public/statutory holidays	___ weeks	___ days
	Sick time	___ weeks	___ days
Time available:		___ weeks	___ days
(less)	Administration	___ weeks	___ days
	Professional development	___ weeks	___ days
	Research related to the business	___ weeks	___ days
	Marketing	___ weeks	___ days
Billable time:		___ weeks	___ days

SOURCE: Author

Appendix 3

Business Start-Up Costs Worksheet

Item	Needed (Yes/No)	Estimated Cost
Answering service/voice mail (deposit)		
Bank account start-up (e.g., printed checks)		
Business announcements or brochures		
Business registration, licenses, and permits (i.e., the actual cost of these business requirements)		
Equipment or equipment rentals: • Computer • Printer/scanner/fax machine • Color printer • Other		
Furniture: • Desk and chair • Filing cabinet, storage cupboard • Work table • Waste paper bin/shredder • Bookshelf • Miscellaneous furniture (e.g., guest chairs, lamps)		
Rent (first and last month or deposit as required)		
Start-up legal and/or accounting fees (i.e., professional fees associated with any registrations)		
Office supplies and stationery (including business cards)		

(Continued)

(Continued)

Item	Needed (Yes/No)	Estimated Cost
Professional and/or business memberships		
Utilities deposits and installation charges • Internet cable and/or telephone • Cell phone/Blackberry • Other		
Website development, domain name registration		
Miscellaneous or contingency		
Total		

SOURCE: Author

Appendix 4

Monthly and Annual Overhead Expenses Worksheet

Item	Needed (Yes/No)	Estimated Cost (monthly)	Estimated Cost (annual)
Accounting fees (preparation of tax return and other accounting expenses)			
Advertising, web page			
Automobile costs			
Bank charges			
Books and reference materials			
Business services			
Business taxes			
Communications: • Telephone • Fax lines • Cell phone/Blackberry • Long distance • Cable/Internet			
Conferences, courses, and professional development			
Donations			
Equipment leases or monthly purchase payments			
Interest on loans			

(Continued)

(Continued)

Item	Needed (Yes/No)	Estimated Cost (monthly)	Estimated Cost (annual)
Insurance (prorated over 12 months):			
• Health			
• Life			
• General liability			
• Theft			
• Automobile			
• Professional liability			
• Other			
Legal services (e.g., contract review)			
License renewals (prorated over 12 months)			
Loan payments			
Marketing, entertainment, and promotion			
Membership renewals			
Office rent			
Office supplies			
Printing costs			
Postage, courier, postal box rental			
Repairs and maintenance			
Retirement savings			
Subscriptions/journals			
Taxes (prorated over 12 months):			
• Business income			
• Social Security (in United States)			
• Pension plan			
• GST expense (in Canada)			
• Other			
Travel (not covered by contracts)			
Storage			
Utilities			
Salaries, wages, and benefits (not yours)			
Miscellaneous/contingency			
Total			

SOURCE: Author

Appendix 5

Daily and Hourly Fee Calculation Worksheet

Step	Calculation	Estimated Amount
Step 1	Desired salary	$ ____(a)____
Step 2	Overhead costs (from Appendix #4)	$____(b)____
Step 3	Total costs	(a) + (b) = $___(c)___/year
Step 4	Total costs/___billable days (from Appendix #2)	(c) /___billable days = $___(d)___ base daily rate
Step 5	Profit @ 10%	(d) x 0.10 = $___(e)___
Step 6	Final daily rate	(d) + (e) = $___(f)___ Round it up if needed: $___(f)____
Step 7	Hourly rate	(f)/8 hours = $_____/hr

SOURCE: Author

Appendix 6

Marketing Contact Summary

Potential Client:
Contact Person:

Contact Type	Key Dates
Meeting:	Contact date:
Phone call in:	Today's date:
Phone call out:	Action to be done by:

1. Purpose of Contact:

2. Summary of Contact:

3. Comments and Personal Observations:

4. Action Steps Resulting from this Contact:

SOURCE: Author

Appendix 7

Sample Letter Proposal

Your Letterhead

Date

Your client's name and title,

Department,

Agency,

Address

Re: Evaluation of Child and Family Obesity Network

Dear [insert client's name]:

Thank you for this opportunity to submit this brief proposal to provide senior evaluation support for the Child and Family Obesity Network. With over 10 years of experience, [insert your firm's name] is recognized as a leading evaluation and applied research firm whose mission is to [insert mission statement]. We are known for our [insert your competitive advantage]. We have conducted many community-based evaluations, most recently working with [name recent clients and projects].

We understand that as part of the funding you received from [name of government agency] you are required to conduct an evaluation of the Network to determine [insert evaluation requirements as provided in funding documents; an example follows] if *children and their families have had their service gaps addressed, if communication among stakeholders has improved, if community capacity has been enhanced, and if efficiencies have been gained.*

Following our recent meeting on [insert date], and based on the information you provided at that time, [insert your firm's name] has prepared this brief task analysis:

Task	Description	Schedule

Task 1: Develop Evaluation Plan	• Develop evaluation plan.
	  ◦ Review background documents.
	  ◦ Meet staff and kick off project.
	  ◦ Develop logic model.
	  ◦ Develop data collection framework.
	• Develop and/or select tools.
	  ◦ Search for/review proposed tools.
	  ◦ Develop additional tools as needed.
	  ◦ Develop data entry template.
	• Finalize evaluation plan.
		January–March/ year

Task 2: Validate Plan With Stakeholders	• Validate plan with stakeholders.
	  ◦ Meet with project manager to plan team meetings.
	  ◦ Meet with community teams, obtain feedback, discuss data collection issues and strategies, revise plan.
	  ◦ Validate the evaluation plan with the evaluation steering committee; revise as needed.
		January–March/ year

Task 3: Collect and Analyze Data	• Collect data, working with community teams to ensure that access to study subjects is enhanced. • Enter data. • Analyze data according to the evaluation plan.	April/year– March/2nd year
Task 4: Project Administration	• Meet with project manager for regular updates. • Prepare monthly status report (attached to invoice). • Report to the steering committee on evaluation progress.	Monthly Monthly Quarterly

(Continued)

Task	Description	Schedule
Task 5: Report Preparation	• Prepare final evaluation report (draft). • Disseminate report-to-community teams for discussion and feedback. • Revise report and submit to steering committee. • Meet with steering committee to receive feedback. • Revise report as needed and appropriate. • Submit final evaluation report.	April/year–June/year

Three staff members will conduct these activities, including myself, a senior researcher, and a research assistant. We will be supported by our administrative assistant. Résumés for research staff are attached.

This total price of $75,000.00 is exclusive of tax. A brief budget based on the task analysis is attached. Monthly invoicing will be provided, and each invoice will be accompanied by a status report to apprise you of project progress.

Thank you for asking us to prepare this proposal. I look forward to the opportunity to provide you with evaluation support for this important project. Please feel free to contact me at [insert phone number] or [insert e-mail address] for more information about this proposal or to make suggestions for its revision.

Yours sincerely

Your (electronic) signature

Mary Smith, PhD

President

SOURCE: Author

Attachment to Letter Proposal: Budget

Personnel		Rate/Day	Task 1 Develop Eval Plan	Task 2 Validate Plan	Task 3 Collect & Analze Data	Task 4 Project Admin	Task 5 Report Prep	Total Days	Total Cost
Personnel		**Rate/Day**	**Days**						
Project Director	PD	$1,000	8.00	9.00	3.00	7.50	10.00	37.50	$37,500.00
Senior Researcher	SR	$700	4.00	-	12.00	-	12.00	28.00	$19,600.00
Research Assistant	RA	$400	4.00	4.50	20.00	2.00	6.00	36.50	$14,600.00
Administrative Support	AS	$300	1.00	1.00	1.00	1.00	2.00	6.00	$1,800.00
Total Staff Time			**17.00**	**14.50**	**36.00**	**10.50**	**30.00**	**108.00**	**$73,500.00**
Disbursements									
Travel			-	475.00	-	50.00	475.00		$1,000.00
Long Distance			-	-	-	-	-		$0.00
Postage/Courier/Shipping			-	-	-	-	-		$0.00
Supplies/Materials			500.00	-	-	-	-		$500.00
Translation			-	-	-	-	-		$0.00
Total Disbursements			**$500.00**	**$475.00**	**$0.00**	**$50.00**	**$475.00**		**$1,500.00**
Grand Total			$13,200.00	$11,575.00	$19,700.00	$8,650.00	$21,875.00		**$75,000.00**

SOURCE: Author.

Appendix 8

Sample Interview Questions for Hiring a Research Assistant

Prepare a work sheet with the following questions. Conduct the interview with another interviewer. Compare notes afterwards.

1. Job history/experience

2. University experience, research courses, academic quality

3. Quantitative and qualitative research experience (software programs used, experience with content analysis)

4. Writing skills

5. Formatting skills (e.g., charts, graphs, and tables)

6. Interviewing skills (in person, telephone)

7. Survey development (including online)

8. Literature reviews, familiarity with Internet for research, processes to organize material

9. Data entry experience

10. Familiarity with databases, Excel, SPSS, PowerPoint

11. Career or long-term goals, or "Where do you see yourself in three years?"

12. Reason for interest in this position

13. Examples of work skills in each of the following areas:

a. Database knowledge

b. Organizational skills

c. Telephone skills

d. Attention to detail

e. Team work

f. Stress management

g. Ability to multitask

h. Working with people in different age groups, socio-economic groups, and ethnic/racial/linguistic groups

14. Recent biggest challenge (in work or life)

15. Questions for us

16. Rapport

17. Availability

18. References

19. Security check

SOURCE: Author

Appendix 9

Sample Scenario to Test Problem-Solving Ability—Research Assistant

Provide key candidates with the following scenario, and ask them to describe how they would respond to the situation. Give them a computer, a quiet room, and an hour to complete the task.

The scenario:

A small agency provides outreach services to senior citizens in the city's inner core. Our firm has been hired to do an evaluation of their government-funded program. A survey is required that involves 1,000 seniors living in four high-rise apartment buildings. In-person interviews will also be conducted with approximately 100 recipients of the agency's outreach services.

The seniors live in secured buildings that have on-site managers. Outreach workers have entrance keys to three of the buildings but must be "buzzed" into the fourth building. The agency will give you access to a list of client names by apartment building, but the seniors' phone numbers and addresses are confidential.

Your job:

Consider the following questions:

- What do you need to think about when designing this survey?

- What planning do you need to do before you conduct the survey?

- How will you encourage the seniors to complete the survey?

- How will the surveys be returned?

- How will you arrange the interview process?

- Whose cooperation do you need to make this study a success? How would you make this happen?

- How will you get invited into the homes of those you want to interview?

- How can you encourage their participation and frank responses?

- What security issues do you need to consider?

- How can you minimize research costs?

SOURCE: Author

Appendix 10

Sample Reference Check

Applicant:	Position:	Date:
Person contacted:	Position and organization:	Relationship to applicant:
Reference's phone #:	Reference's e-mail:	

1. What were the applicant's responsibilities in your organization?

2. What is your general evaluation of his/her work?

3. What is your understanding of his/her educational qualifications/training/relevant courses?

4. Can you please comment on the applicant's following attributes:

   a. Strengths
   b. Weaknesses/areas needing development
   c. Technical competence and skills
   d. Cooperation with staff and supervisors
   e. Work habits
   f. Absentee record

5. Why did the applicant leave your organization?

6. Would you rehire this person? Why or why not?

7. Do you have any other comments that might help me in making my hiring decision?

Thank you very much!

SOURCE: Author

Appendix 11

New Employee Self-Evaluation Survey—
Three-Month Review

[Provide a satisfaction scale as appropriate and space for comments for each of the questions below.]

Reflect on your accomplishments over the last three months, and rate your skills on the scale provided:

1. How satisfied are you with your communications skills with staff?

2. How satisfied are you with your interpersonal skills (tact, ability to explain, ability to persuade others in a nonconfrontational style, ability to see the other person's point of view, keeping other staff informed, listening well, etc.)?

3. How satisfied are you with your contribution to your key functional areas?

[List functional areas from the job description and add new areas as required.]

4. Have you learned what you expected to learn? List five key things you learned.

5. Have you used skills that you already knew? List the five skills you used the most.

6. Are there skills that you hoped to learn but didn't get around to? (What are they? What prevented you from learning them?)

7. How satisfied are you with your ability to get things done? Has anything kept you from achieving what you wanted to? If so, what barriers did you encounter?

8. How satisfied are you with your ability to cooperate and be a team player in your project team? In the firm overall?

9. How satisfied are you with your supervision? Has help and support been available when you needed it? If not, what needs did you have that went unmet?

10. Overall, how satisfied are you with your performance during this period?

11. Is there anything else that the firm could have done to help you achieve your goals during this period?

12. What goals do you have for the next three months? How do you plan to achieve them? How can the firm assist you?

SOURCE: Author

Glossary

Accounts payable: a list of money owed by your company to others

Accounts receivable: a list of money owed to your company

Arbitration: a form of dispute resolution outside of the courts, where the parties to a dispute are referred to one or more third parties by whose decision they agree to be bound

Asset: something of monetary value that is owned by a firm or an individual

Balance sheet: a business financial statement that lists the assets, debts, and owners' investment as of a specific date

Billable time: the amount of work time available in a year for which you can charge fees for client work. It is calculated by deducting nonbillable time from the total number of work days in a calendar year.

Boilerplate contract: a standardized contract

Bootstrapping: ways of helping yourself through improvised means

Cash flow: the difference between cash coming into your company and cash going out over a given period of time

Cause: a reason at law to justify termination of a contract

Cloud computing: on-demand, pay-as-you-go Internet-based computing resources, software, and information provided by a third party

Confidentiality: a situation in which important information must be kept secret

Confidentiality agreement: an agreement whereby an individual promises to not divulge information about the activities of an organization to anyone else

Contingency fee: a financial arrangement with a client that is based on the achievement of agreed-upon results

Contract: a spoken or written agreement that is enforceable by law

Contractor: an individual who contracts to supply services to an organization at a particular price

Copyright: a legal right to control dissemination of your work

Corporation: a business that is legally completely separate from its owners

Credit: an arrangement whereby payment is deferred

Creditor: a person or organization to whom money is owed

Daily rate: the fee you can charge your client for one day's worth of work. It is based on a calculation that includes your desired salary and overhead divided by the number of billable days in a year. A profit margin can also be added.

Direct deposit: electronic transfer of a payment directly from the account of the payer to the individual being paid

Dispute resolution: a process for resolving disputes between parties

Employee: an individual who gets paid regularly to work for an organization for a wage or salary

Financial statement: a consolidated statement of a company's financial health

Financial year: a 12-month period as defined for tax purposes

Fixed assets: tangible property used by a business and not for resale, such as furniture, fixtures, and equipment

Fixed fee: a flat rate charged to complete a project regardless of how many hours are expended by the consultant

Force majeure: a natural and unavoidable catastrophe that interrupts work

Fraud: producing false documents or false information or pretending to be something that you are not

Hourly rate: your daily rate divided by eight hours or the typical number of work hours in a day

Income statement: a business financial statement that lists revenues, expenses, and net income throughout a given period

Indemnity: a legal exemption from liability

Insurance: a contract between a client and an insurance company to guard against property loss or damage, whereby the client makes regular payments, called premiums, to the insurance company, and the insurance company pays an agreed-upon sum in the event of loss or damage to a client

Insurance agent: an insurance company representative and advisor who sells insurance policies

Insurance broker: a person who, independent of any insurance company, represents the interests of the buyer in searching for insurance coverage to ensure that the buyer receives the highest benefit at the lowest cost possible

Intellectual assets: an employee's knowledge, experience, and skills that can be used for the benefit of an organization

Intellectual property: something someone has created that no one else can legally copy or sell

Invoice: a bill stating the details of services that you have provided and expenses that you have incurred on behalf of a client

Job description: a description of the responsibilities associated with a given job

Knowledge management: any intentional and systematic process or practice of acquiring, capturing, sharing, and using productive knowledge, wherever it resides, to enhance learning and performance in organizations

Knowledge translation: application of new knowledge for the benefit of society

Liability(1): a financial obligation or cash outlay that must be made to someone else

Liability(2): a legal responsibility

Line of credit: an amount of money available for you to borrow as needed up to a specified maximum

Litigation: the process of taking legal action

Mediation: a form of dispute resolution involving the two parties and a mediator to assist in the negotiation of a settlement

Milestone billing: billing a client at agreed-upon intervals as each specified segment of contracted work is completed

Monthly expenses: the ongoing operating costs paid every month to keep your business running. Most expenses are paid on a monthly basis, but some expenses are paid quarterly or annually. These can be prorated by month to give a more accurate picture of monthly expenses. This is also called *overhead.*

Negligence: failure to give care or attention in such a way that harm or damage could result

Negotiation: a dialogue between two or more parties to reach an understanding or resolve a point of difference

Net worth: an individual's or company's assets minus liabilities

Nonbillable time: the amount of work time in a year not directly attributable to client work, including annual vacation, statutory holidays, sick time, and business maintenance activities such as administration, marketing, networking, research, and professional development

Orientation: an introductory period in which a new employee is indoctrinated to the organization

Overdraft: the amount of money you have spent that exceeds the amount you have in your bank account

Partnership: shared ownership among two or more individuals who agree on the distribution of profits and losses and the extent to which each will share the liabilities

Probation: a specific period of time during which new employees are observed to see if they can do the job well enough to be retained

Pro bono: work provided for free to an organization the provider wishes to support

Profit: amount of money left in your business at the end of the year after your salary and all monthly and prorated expenses are paid out

Recovery rate: the measure of billable time available compared to total possible working days in a year

Reference check: a background check to evaluate an individual's appropriateness for a position

Request for proposals (RFP): a document that tells vendors and service providers what type of service or products a client is attempting to purchase and solicits potential contractors to submit their bids in a competitive process. The process is similar to the tendering process and has rigid requirements, processes, and deadlines.

Retainer: an agreed-upon monthly fixed fee for a consultant's services. The consultant receives this fee whether she or he provides any services in a given month or not.

Revenue: income generated by your company

Risk: the chance of injury or loss

Risk management: a method of assessing, minimizing, and preventing loss through the use of safety measures and insurance

Salary: personal income paid to you out of the revenues of your business

Scope creep: uncontrolled changes in a project's scope

Service charges: an additional fee charged for a service in addition to the original total

Short list: a list of finalists or applicants who are suitable for a job and from which the successful individual will be selected

Sole proprietorship: a business owned by a single individual who has unlimited liability for its debts and obligations

Standing offer: an arrangement with a potential client whereby you submit your qualifications, and if you are selected, you agree to provide your services at a set rate over a specified period of time

Start-up costs: expenses related to setting up your business. Most of these are one-time costs.

Status report: a monthly report to a client that outlines activities conducted during that period and identifies progress made toward project goals

Subcontractor: an individual who takes a portion of a contract from the principal contractor

Tender: formal offer or bid stating the terms of a contract at a certain price

Term loan: a loan that is repaid in regular payments over a period of years

Termination: the end of a contract or agreement to conduct a job

Vendor: a person or organization that sells something to your company

Warranty: a written guarantee issued to a purchaser by a manufacturer promising to repair or replace a defective article within a specified period and under certain conditions

Index

Abbott, S.G., 162
Accounts payable, 157–158
Accounts receivable:
  business risks, 188
  financial management, 152–157
Action plan, 119–120
Adaptability, 21
Adult Learning (Commission of the
  European Communities), 32
African Americans:
  evaluation consultants, 11
  management consultant
    business, 10
Aged accounts receivable report, 155–156
Age demographics:
  evaluation consultants, 10
  management consultant business, 10
Alaskan Natives, 10
Allen, C., 51, 52, 57
American Association of Colleges of
  Nursing, 18
American Evaluation Association (AEA):
  blog, 55
  cultural competence, 33
  ethical guidelines, 27
  knowledge translation, 249
  professional involvement, 55
  professional network, 121
  professional organizations, 7
  Topical Interest Group for Independent
    Consulting, 10–11, 122
American Indians, 10
Anastasio, S., 185, 199
Annual expenses worksheet, 259–260
Appendices, 81–82, 84–85
Applied research:
  growth drivers, 9–10

industry profile, 6
science hierarchy, 49
Arbitration, 210 (exhibit)
Arthur Anderson, 27
Artist's Way, The (Cameron), 57
Artist's Way at Work, The (Bryan,
  Cameron, and Allen), 57
Asian Americans, 10
Assets:
  balance sheet, 161
  corporations, 178, 186
  sole proprietorship, 171
Association of Fundraising
  Professionals, 121
Audits, 115, 181
Authenticity, 30–31
Automobile insurance, 188, 195 (exhibit)

Bait-and-switch approach, 223
Balance sheet, 161
Bank accounts:
  credit information, 151
  financial management, 151
  monthly statement, 151
  online banking, 151
  Operation of Account
    Agreement, 151
  overdraft protection, 151
  printed checks, 151
  service charges, 151
  Verification Agreement, 151
Bank deposits, 156
Bank loans. *See* Loans
Barrington Research Group, Inc., 281
Bebeau, M. J., 216,
Benefits:
  consultant profile, 10

About the Author

Dr. Gail Vallance Barrington is a well-known Canadian program evaluator who has made significant contributions to the profession through her evaluation practice, writing, teaching, training, mentoring, and service to the field of evaluation. She founded her consulting firm, Barrington Research Group, Inc. in Calgary, Alberta, in 1985 and has conducted more than 125 program evaluation and applied research studies at the federal, provincial, and grassroots levels. Her studies range from health promotion and health services to education and training, research, and knowledge exchange. Her recent work on evidence-based evaluation has led to the development of more rigorous evaluation designs, and she is currently advising a number of organizations about the adoption of this approach.

She is a graduate of McGill, Carleton, and the University of Alberta and holds a doctorate in educational administration. She is a Credentialed Evaluator and a Certified Management Consultant as well as a certified teacher. She instructs a Master's level course on the evaluation of health services and systems for the Centre for Health Studies at Athabasca University. For many years, Dr. Barrington has conducted workshops on evaluation topics, most recently at the Claremont Graduate University Summer Professional Development series in Claremont, California; at the Summer Institute in Atlanta, Georgia, jointly sponsored by the Centres for Disease Control and the American Evaluation Association (AEA); and at the national conference of the Canadian Evaluation Society (CES).

She has been an active member of AEA and CES since 1985, has served on a number of their committees, and was a member of the AEA Board of Directors from 2006 to 2008. She is also a member of the newly instituted Canadian Evaluation Society Credentialing Board and is an

Emeritus Board Member of the Canadian Evaluation Society Education Fund. She is a member of the editorial board for New Directions in Evaluation and co-edited Issue #111 (2006) on Independent Evaluation Consulting. In 2008 she received the Canadian Evaluation Society award for her contribution to evaluation in Canada.

SAGE Research Methods Online
The essential tool for researchers

Printed in the United States
By Bookmasters